The New Apologetics

The New Apologetics

Defending the Faith in a Post-Christian Era

Edited by
Matthew Nelson

WORD on FIRE.
— INSTITUTE —

Published by the Word on Fire Institute, an imprint of
Word on Fire, Park Ridge, IL 60068
© 2022 by Word on Fire Catholic Ministries
Printed in the United States of America
All rights reserved

Cover design, typesetting, and interior art direction by Nicolas Fredrickson, Cassie Bielak, Clark Kenyon, and Rozann Lee.

Excerpts from the English translation of the *Catechism of the Catholic Church* for use in the United States of America Copyright © 1994, United States Catholic Conference, Inc.— Libreria Editrice Vaticana. Used by permission. English translation of the *Catechism of the Catholic Church*: Modifications from the Editio Typica copyright © 1997, United States Conference of Catholic Bishops—Libreria Editrice Vaticana.

25 24 23 22   1 2 3 4

ISBN: 978-1-685780-04-3

Library of Congress Control Number: 2021922718

CONTENTS

PART IV – NEW ISSUES

FOREWORD

"Always be ready to make your defense to anyone who demands from you an accounting for the hope that is in you; yet do it with gentleness and reverence" (1 Pet. 3:15–16). This is the charter of Christian apologetics: we must be ready, and can be ready, to offer a rational accounting for our Christian life and faith, and for the hope that impels us. Our life in Christ is reasonable and not the result of mere subjective emotional enthusiasm, which comes and goes like the clouds in the sky.

Rational explanation, of course, has never been sufficient. The even more ancient classical wisdom of the art of persuasion reminds us that if we are effectively to give an account for the hope that is in us, we must first establish the bond of trust and touch the heart, thus disposing the hearer to be attentive to the reasons we offer. In an age in which scandals have shattered trust and people's hearts are lured away by the emotionally potent distractions of our secular world, they will not pay attention to words and reasons alone.

The early Dominicans built trust through austere, sacrificial lives that were radically different from those of the corrupt clergy of their day, and through a life of prayer and simple piety they touched the hearts of those who had deserted the Church. Then they were able to offer clear reasons for Christian hope, refuting the false ideas of their time. The stern St. Charles Borromeo and the charming St. Francis de Sales won the trust, and won the hearts, of their heretical contemporaries because of the gentleness and reverence of their saintly lives. Then their clear teaching could have an impact.

But if reason is not sufficient in itself, it is nonetheless the essential foundation of apologetics. So many people are being led away from life in Christ by specious reasoning. And our secular society is caught up in all kinds of irrational delusions about the nature of the human person and the purpose of life; these have quickly hardened into an anti-Christian orthodoxy that it is perilous to oppose.

The New Apologetics is a fountain of life-giving clarity in a sterile secular desert, offering priceless assistance to us so that we can give a reason for the hope we have. Truth is simple, but error is complex, and the many short chapters address the complex challenges to Christian faith in these days, which require fresh thinking from the Christian apologist.

God placed our heads in such a prominent place on our bodies that surely he wants us to use them. A dumbed-down and mindlessly subjective faith is useless; we can rejoice in the fruitful insights offered by each of the many authors in this book, each examining one of the many facets of the modern apologetical enterprise. And each offering is blessedly brief, a lesson for us all in how to communicate, especially in a modern society of restricted attention spans. Each brief but insightful chapter invites the reader to go beyond what is offered to the feast of faith and reason to which it leads.

Cardinal Thomas Collins, Archbishop of Toronto

ACKNOWLEDGMENTS
Matthew Nelson

From start to finish, editing this book has been a labor of love. First, thank you to the contributors of this volume. I was asked to put together my all-star team of philosophers, theologians, apologists, and evangelists for this book. Recruiting so many first-rate contributors for a single volume seemed in the beginning like a far-fetched dream. But given what a book like this could do for the Church, it was worth a shot. So, I went for it; and by God's grace, you all said yes. Thank you—not only for your contributions to this book, but for what you continue to do in your own apostolates and professions for the greater glory of Jesus Christ and his Church.

Equally, thank you to the master apologists who first showed me the incredible power of apologetics done well: Patrick Madrid, Scott Hahn, Tim Staples, Jimmy Akin, Peter Kreeft, Mark Brumley, Trent Horn, Stephanie Gray Connors, Steve Ray, Edward Feser, N.T. Wright, William Lane Craig, John Lennox, and Bishop Robert Barron. I am especially grateful to Karlo Broussard for his friendship and encouragement. You are one of the best, brother.

I owe an immeasurable amount of gratitude to my friends in the Word on Fire publishing department: Brandon Vogt, Matt Becklo, Dan Seseske, Jason Paone, Edyta McNichol, and James O'Neil. Thank you for all of your hard labor and intellectual rigor that you have quietly invested into making this book into something special. I constantly marvel at your ability to make good writing great.

Additionally, thank you to Rozann Lee, Cassie Bielak, and the design team for making this book look and feel like gold. You have proven once again that alchemy is real.

Finally, I would like to extend my thanks to Oxford University Press for permission to reprint a revised version of "The Mirror of Evil," from *God and the Philosophers: The Reconciliation of Faith and Reason.*

INTRODUCTION
Matthew Nelson

In my early twenties, I ditched Catholicism for the world. It did not take long for my religious convictions to become doubts. A few years later, after a reluctant but providential visit to the confessional, I returned home to the Catholic Church. This spiritual reversion was marked by an immediate and profound "conversion of heart." But my "conversion of intellect" was not so immediate. Despite my existing belief in Christ, which was basic but deep, I still harbored questions, hesitations, and criticisms, all of which remained in me like mental cobwebs.

Those cobwebs were eventually cleared away—but not without a process. I was introduced to the writings of C.S. Lewis, Frank Sheed, G.K. Chesterton, Pope John Paul II, and Pope Benedict XVI, all of whom taught me indispensable truths of the faith, while pointing me back to more ancient teachers like Aquinas, Bonaventure, Anselm, and Augustine.

Maybe most impactful on my intellect was the discovery of the books, talks, lectures, and debates of contemporary "ace" apologists like Patrick Madrid, Scott Hahn, Peter Kreeft, Steve Ray, Tim Staples, N.T. Wright, William Lane Craig, and Bishop Robert Barron. Their subtle mix of charity, creativity, intelligence, and tact exemplified for me then—and continue to exemplify now—how apologetics should be done.

With a new sense of where we are and where we are going as a culture, this book is meant to contribute to and carry forward the evangelical task embraced by those apologists. The cultural moment we now find ourselves in demands, possibly more than any other time in history, a potent and spirited renewal of apologetics in the Catholic Church.

The Duty of Apologetics

In more recent times, apologetics has gotten a bad rap, being falsely conflated with "arguing about religion," in the worst sense of the phrase. But for Christians, apologetics, or giving a reasoned explanation or defense of the faith, is a necessity and duty; and it has been since St. Peter declared in his first epistle, "Always be ready to make your defense [*apologia*] to anyone who demands from you an accounting for the hope that is in you" (1 Pet. 3:15).

During his apostolic journey to the United States in 2008, Pope Benedict XVI fervently echoed St. Peter's summons. To the American bishops, he insisted that "the Church needs to promote at every level of her teaching—in catechesis, preaching, and seminary and university instruction—an apologetics aimed at affirming the truth of Christian revelation, the harmony of faith and reason, and a sound understanding of freedom."[1]

Notice the grand scope of Pope Benedict XVI's vision, with training in apologetics being promoted *at every level of Church life*—in the home, parish, seminary, and university. Given the unique and compounding intricacies of the modern world, there is an urgency to respond to this papal summons.

What Is the New Apologetics?

First, here is what the New Apologetics is *not*. It is not a rejection of arguments and methodologies from the past. Rather, it is a necessary refinement of these arguments and methodologies according to new cultural trends and the circumstances of our times. Indeed, there is a sense in which every major cultural shift demands a "new" apologetics. Thus, the New Apologetics is a recalibration of sorts, a reconsideration and adjustment of arguments, methods, and expressions according to the specific requirements of what is now a post-Christian, post-religious, post–new atheist, relativistic, scientistic, ideology-ridden society. It is in the spirit of and in conformity with Pope St.

---

1. Pope Benedict XVI, "Responses of His Holiness Benedict XVI to the Questions Posed by the US Bishops," April 16, 2008, Vatican.va.

John Paul II's "New Evangelization," and he has sketched a framework for how we ought to proceed.

The New Apologetics must be sophisticated, smart, and joyful. It should be outward-facing, both online and on the ground, to reach a more expansive public audience. More specifically, the New Apologetics must pay special attention to the questions asked by young people. It must reflect the Catholic Church's reverence for the physical sciences and be devoted to the affirmation and clarification of the relationship between science and religion. It must seek to know the enemies of Christianity better than they know themselves and understand the history of religious skepticism—including the polemics of figures like Sartre, Nietzsche, and Marx—and how much of contemporary atheism is rooted in it.

The New Apologetics must be engaged with the robust intellectual tradition of the Church. Apologists must be steeped in (to borrow a phrase from Matthew Arnold) "the best which has been thought and said"[2] in the Christian tradition, drawing especially from the wisdom of the Doctors of the Church; and while doing so, it must simultaneously maintain a spirit of creativity by which it will integrate new and inventive arguments and methods.

Furthermore, the New Apologetics must be imaginative, fixing beauty as its arrowhead and never forgetting its evangelical potency. In Bishop Barron's words:

> Balthasar intuited something in the middle of the twentieth century, just as the postmodern critique was getting underway—namely, that initiating the theological project with truth or goodness tends to be a nonstarter, since relativism and skepticism in regard to those transcendentals were powerful indeed. If such subjectivism and relativism were strong in the fifties of the last century, they have become overwhelming at the beginning of the twenty-first century; Ratzinger's "dictatorship of relativism" is now taken for granted. Any claim to know objective truth or any attempt to propose

---

2. Matthew Arnold, *Culture and Anarchy* and *Friendship's Garland* (New York: Macmillan, 1924), xi.

objective goodness tend to be met now with incredulity at best and fierce defensiveness at worst: "Who are you to tell me how to think or how to behave?" But there is something less threatening, more winsome, about the beautiful.[3]

Our presentation of the Catholic faith must appeal to the heart as much as it does to the head. As Msgr. Ronald Knox once wrote, we must combine "the lucidity of St. Thomas with the unction of Pascal."[4] The New Apologetics must therefore be *person-centered*. While applauding recent renewals in apologetics, Avery Cardinal Dulles nonetheless insisted that a proper incorporation of the personalism advocated by Pope John Paul II has been lacking. Dulles highlights the potential efficacy of testimony, for instance, which can "attune us to biblical thinking and especially to the Gospels as documents of faith."[5] Person-to-person apologetics must not become excessively abstract, as though we were merely "thinking things"—that is to say, minds lacking bodies, senses, moods, appetites, and the like. And just as the Church must tailor its apologetics to the unique needs of a given era or culture, the evangelizing Christian must also attune his methods and arguments to the needs of every individual to whom he preaches Christ. For every single person comes with his own distinctive abilities, assumptions, attitudes, dispositions, experiences, and influences.

Finally, the supreme requirement of the New Apologetics—without which the entire project is doomed to fail—is that it be *driven by the Holy Spirit*. The indwelling of the Holy Spirit is absolutely primary. Prayer and the sacramental life animate the life of the apologist and make it possible for his efforts to be supernatural in effect. To be grounded in the Spirit, we must be open to it. We do that by making prayer and sacrament our nonnegotiable

---

3. Robert Barron, *Renewing Our Hope* (Washington, DC: The Catholic University of America Press, 2020), 23.

4. Ronald Knox, *Proving God: A New Apologetic* (London: The Month, 1959), 43.

5. Avery Dulles, "The Rebirth of Apologetics," *First Things*, May 2004, https://www.firstthings.com/article/2004/05/the-rebirth-of-apologetics.

first priority. Indeed, the interior life is, in Jean-Baptiste Chautard's words, the "soul of the apostolate."

What Lies Ahead

This book is intended to make the New Apologetics a manifest reality. It is a manifesto of sorts, a starting point—a public declaration of what we must do if we are going to "become all things to all people," as St. Paul did, that we might save some (1 Cor. 9:22).

The New Apologetics is not essentially a compendium of arguments, though it contains many within its pages. It offers something more fundamental: a necessary prelude to systematic argumentation. Arguments are no good if they are not heard. It is neither being learned, nor being eloquent, nor being witty, that is the vital outcome for the apologist; it is *being heard*, for "faith comes by hearing" (Rom. 10:17). Thus, *The New Apologetics* is a kind of intellectual and tactical map for the apologist who wants to be heard in today's world.

Part I acquaints apologists with the people they will meet—the "New Audiences" of our times. In the twentieth century, it was primarily Protestants who occupied the attention of Catholic apologists. In the early 2000s, it was the "new atheists" who were of principal concern. Though both Protestantism and atheism remain important interests for Catholic apologists, today's spiritual landscape is now riddled with dogmatic relativism, religious disaffiliation, spiritual indifference, and anti-religious sentiment. This first section of the book focuses especially on these cultural demographics.

Part II zeroes in on "New Approaches." These chapters consider the various trends and nuances of contemporary culture and offer practical insights and methods for engagement of nonbelievers, given who they are, what they are, where they are, and how they are most likely to be reached.

Part III of this book offers "New Models" for apologists. This section highlights some of the people in Church history, ancient and modern,

Catholic and not, who have best exemplified what it means to "destroy arguments and every proud obstacle raised up against the knowledge of God, and . . . take every thought captive to obey Christ" (2 Cor. 10:4–5). All of the models in these chapters were, in their time, formidable in the rational defense of the truth—and all were models of steadfastness in "gentleness and reverence" toward critics (1 Pet. 3:15).

Part IV is the largest section of this book and is dedicated to the "New Issues" of our times. Although many of the topics discussed in this section are not unique to today (indeed some, like the problems of evil and divine hiddenness, are perennial), the treatment of these issues is truly new and cutting edge. The theologians, philosophers, and scientists who authored these chapters look at the big questions and assumptions of our time and offer profound insights into how we might convince people to see the world as the Catholic Church sees it.

At the turn of the millennium, Pope John Paul II provided a cultural diagnosis that is as accurate today as it was then. "Today we face a religious situation which is extremely varied and changing," he observed. "Peoples are on the move; social and religious realities which were once clear and well defined are today increasingly complex."[6] Given this complexity, and the ever more prominent post-religious nature of society, the time has come once again for a new resurgence in apologetics—a New Apologetics for our time. It is my prayer that this book might serve as a powerful impetus for this necessary and urgent missionary undertaking.

---

6. Pope John Paul II, *Redemptoris Missio* 32, encyclical letter, Vatican.va.

PART I

NEW AUDIENCES

1

Nones Are Not "Nothings"

Stephen Bullivant

"None." "Nonreligious." "Nothing in particular." "Unaffiliated." Despite often being described as America's fastest growing religious affiliation, such terms can feel a little awkward as personal labels. Some scholars have argued that "none" and its compatriots aren't genuine identities at all. They're just the artificial by-product of tick-box surveys. To suppose one can speak of "nones" as a genuine group, this line of argument goes, is as silly as thinking that "Other (please specify)" is a real occupation.

There's some truth to this, to be sure. The nones *are* a very large, broad, and diffuse category. They have to be. They currently make up about a quarter of US adults (and a third of young adults), and over half of British adults (and two-thirds of young adults): it's hard to fit that many people into a single "type." And they are, to a certain extent, a statistical convenience. Many of those who end up counted within the "X% of nones" on handy infographics may not instinctively describe themselves in that way. But the same is true of other familiar abstractions like "liberals," "Hispanics," "mainline Protestants," or "LGBTQ." These are all accepted as being useful and meaningful short-hands, precisely *because* they bring together a diverse collection of much more specific identity groups.

That said, supposedly empty categories like "none," "nothing," or "non-religious" very often *can* be personally owned. And this is frequently true for those brought up and/or still living in deeply religious contexts—something true of a high proportion of America's nones. Prior to the pandemic, my team and I had the great pleasure of traveling around the US—not *quite* "from California to the New York island, from the redwood forest to the Gulf Stream waters," sadly, but not all that far off—interviewing dozens upon dozens of different nones. Those living in the southern states, or those who were raised in highly religious families, often genuinely owned the identity of being *non*religious.

Even for those preferring a more specific identity—"atheist" or "agnostic," say—adopting a generic label can often be useful. "Oh, I'm nonreligious," "I'm not really very religious," or "I guess I'm one of those 'nones' you keep reading about" feel like more socially acceptable replies when the subject comes up (as it inevitably does) at parties, in the workplace, or on dates.

For each of these nones, though the precise meaning and personal salience of such a broad label clearly varies, it's far from just a statistician's fiction. (Note, too, that the meaning and salience of broad labels like "Christian" or "Jewish" or "Buddhist" differ greatly among self-ascribers.) As the British sociologist Lois Lee puts it, "Generic non-religious identifications are not merely imposed on people by social researchers but can be made and performed by them in their everyday lives. . . . It is wrong to assume that the 'nones' are always nothings."[1]

In America, this is likely becoming more the case simply because being a "none" has become a definite *thing* in the past decade or so, helped greatly by the term gaining common currency through media reports. Not incidentally, this is similar to how "Evangelical" and "Born-Again Christian" suddenly became widely understood and embraced identities in the 1970s. It's not that such people didn't exist before, but now they had both a "brand" and the self-confidence that comes from headlines inducting them into a millions-strong movement.[2] People like to belong. This is true even among self-conscious nonconformists: the goths, emo kids, and AV clubbers are as

---

1. Lois Lee, *Recognizing the Non-Religious: Reimagining the Secular* (Oxford: Oxford University Press, 2015), 132, 153.

2. Robert Wuthnow, *Inventing American Religion: Polls, Surveys, and the Tenuous Quest for a Nation's Faith* (Oxford: Oxford University Press, 2015), chap. 5.

much high school "tribes" as are the jocks and cheerleaders (if not more so). And for Americans turned off by religion to varying degrees, "a quarter of the US population and growing" is a serious tribe to feel part of, even for those with little desire to seek and hang out with the others.

There's a lot that can be said about "the nones" as a socio-demographic group—that is to say, about *who* they are in terms of sex, age, ethnicity, geographical distribution, political convictions, religious/spiritual beliefs, and all the rest of it. That's important and interesting work, but all it can show us is various *average tendencies* within what is, after all, a very large and growing chunk of the population. *As a group*, nones have a distinctive profile: in the United States, they tend to be, say, a little bit younger, maler, and more politically liberal than the general population. But—and this is very important to realize here—one never, ever meets nones *as a group*. Likewise, it's perfectly possible to construct a picture of the "typical none," based on the midpoint of various statistical distributions. But then this really *is* a statistical fiction. The vast, vast, vast majority of real nones certainly won't conform perfectly to the image of the "typical none." And indeed, a very large proportion of them won't even come close to it.

A couple of years ago, for fun, I ran the numbers from the highly respected General Social Survey to come up with America's "average weekly Mass-going Catholic." For the record, it was *a forty-eight-year-old white woman, with no college degree, who lives somewhere toward the eastern side of the Midwest, and who quite likes reggae, hates rap, and has mixed feelings about opera.* Now this is, as the young folks say these days, a "true fact," and I have the stats to prove it. And, to a very limited extent, it might tell us *something* about the makeup of churchgoing Catholics. But it obviously doesn't tell us very much about them. It certainly wouldn't be a sound strategy for, say, a business targeting the Catholic market, to tailor its whole product range to just this person. Likewise, Church leaders definitely should not start basing their entire pastoral strategy around catering to this hypothetical person's needs and whims.

5

Something very similar, of course, is true of "reaching the nones." Just think, for example, of all the people you know who would, or might (since you're unlikely to know for sure), regard themselves as having no religion, or being religiously unaffiliated. Even in your own families and friendship groups I imagine that the nones will add up to a very diverse bunch of people indeed. And this will be true, even if, as with "nones in general," the group "skews" in particular ways.

Furthermore, just as each is different in all manner of outward and obvious ways, they will also be different in their inner moral, religious, and/or more broadly spiritual lives too. Crucially this is true not only of the present—America's nones include out-and-proud atheists, New Agey "spiritual" types, doubting churchgoers and synagogue-goers, and all points in between—but of the past also. In the United States, as indeed in many other countries, a large proportion of nones will likely have been brought up in a religion, at least to some extent. Roughly 70 percent of American nones, for example, say they were raised religiously. Incidentally, this group includes 16 million ex-Catholics, 7.5 million ex-Baptists, 2 million ex-Methodists, 2 million ex-Lutherans, and 1 million each of ex-Episcopalians and ex-Presbyterians.

For all these reasons, anyone hoping to engage with "the none" needs, first of all, to stop thinking in terms of *the nones*, and instead start thinking in terms of this or that individual and unique friend, family member, co-worker, social media sparring partner, or what-have-you. Fortunately, finding out more about Chad, or Juanita, or Zeke, or Cindy-Lou, or Chip, or Shawn, or Taylor, or Bud, or Darleen doesn't require learning a lot about statistics. All you have to do is ask them.[3]

---

3. Parts of this essay have been adapted from the Word on Fire Institute course "Understanding the 'Nones' and How to Reach Them" and from Stephen Bullivant, *Nonverts: The Making of Ex-Christian America(ns)* (Oxford: Oxford University Press, 2022).

2

Awakening the Indifferent
Bobby Angel

We're living in what I like to call a "Culture of Meh."

Having taught for almost nine years at an all-boys Catholic high school, I am well acquainted with the apathetic shoulder shrug of the modern young man who simply "can't be bothered" about matters of morality, Scripture, or even the question of God himself.

This inability of modern men and women to muster the slightest energy to care about a philosophical idea or issue of moral depth elicits, in even shorter phraseology, the pithy response "I can't even."

People are indifferent. And such people simply can't be bothered with the big questions of life.

But all human beings, including the religiously indifferent, share certain irrevocable cravings.

We—being the humans we are—*do* crave meaning, purpose, and depth, and we all have the need to belong and to be understood. We do want someone to call greatness out of us (look no further than the "Jordan Peterson effect" upon young men for evidence of this ache). Passion *does* exist in the heart of modern men and women, although it's often directed toward greater societal justice (if we could agree on a definition of justice), environmental stewardship, or the grievous flaws in the latest comic-book movie. Simply put, our passionate energies get directed toward politics or entertainment. But when it comes to questions of higher purpose, the origins of morality, and the nature of God, our generation tends to, as Bishop Barron often states, drop these questions *just* when they become truly interesting!

Morally speaking, our generation is in a relativistic stupor. Good and evil are considered antiquated concepts that our enlightened society should cast aside in favor of universal, bland tolerance. As Christina Hoff Sommers, a resident scholar at the American Enterprise Institute, writes, "When tolerance is the sole virtue, students' capacity for moral indignation, so important for moral development, is severely inhibited. The result is moral passivity and confusion and a shift of moral focus from the individual to society."[1] When everything is mere preference, opinions, and value clarification, nothing is worth even getting that upset about. An abortion elicits the same moral response as an ice cream preference: "Meh."

Furthermore, with the conveniences of modern technology, it's all too easy to live as practical atheists, as though God didn't exist at all. *If* God exists, he's just a nice uncle in the sky who wants us to be decent people, have fun, and not kill anyone. Otherwise, we're free to live in our air-conditioned bubbles, have products shipped directly to our door, and post online for a reward of dopamine while simultaneously signaling how virtuous we are. The sociologist Christian Smith calls this conceptualization of a disinterested deity who simply wants our unrestricted happiness "Moralistic Therapeutic Deism," a vision Smith outlines in his book *Soul Searching: The Religious and Spiritual Lives of American Teenagers*. Matters of sin, repentance, prayer, and holiness are outmoded; my subjective happiness reigns supreme.[2] Only when personal or global tragedies occur do a few individuals bother to angrily assert, "Where *was* God?" as if we were promised to never suffer at all; as though we are entitled to know the mind of the divine.

How, then, do we reach the indifferent?

A sailor can always work when the wind is blowing, even if the wind is

---

1. Christina Hoff Sommers, "Ethics Without Virtue: Moral Education in America," *The American Scholar* 53, no. 3 (September 1984): 381–389, at 386.

2. Christian Smith and Melinda Lundquist Denton, *Soul Searching: The Religious and Spiritual Lives of American Teenagers* (Oxford: Oxford University Press, 2005), 162–164.

blowing violently. It's arguably easier to dialogue with a passionate atheist who has a visible zeal for life, than it is to attempt a conversation with someone who is apathetic and indifferent (I know from experience). When there's no wind to be had, little sailing can be done.

As an evangelistic strategy, I propose a few angles.

First, we need patience. To return to the ocean metaphor, surfers, sailors, and fishermen alike know that one must be patient for the catch. We cannot manipulate a person into desiring the things of God; we must wait, shoring ourselves up for the propitious moment. Christ taught about the efficacy of prayer and fasting (Mark 9:29) and so we should approach every person not as a project but as a beloved creature of God, interceding for them by prayer and fasting. If there will be any softening of the heart and conviction of the will, that work shall be done by the Holy Spirit and not by us. So, fish with patience and watch the horizon for the beginnings of the wave.

Second, show interest in the areas a person *does* care about. We so often want the student, friend, coworker, or family member before us to know the love of the Lord and experience his mercy as we've encountered it, but starting off on that foot can be perceived as pushy, preachy, or overwhelming because they simply aren't ready yet. It may cause you frustration that this individual doesn't care deeply about what *you* care about, but zero in on areas they have a passion for and meet them in that space. It might be a love of skateboarding, movies, computers, dieting, or music. "Oh, you like the music of ___? Tell me about that." Once common ground is discovered and goodwill displayed, then follow-up questions might be, "Why do you find that beautiful? What do you think makes something beautiful? Where does beauty come from?"

One student I taught missed just about every Sunday Mass because he was frequently traveling for baseball tournaments. I would try to teach this freshman with conviction about the God who revealed himself through the Old Testament and in the person of Jesus Christ, the evidence for God's existence from Aquinas and modern authors, and the life-giving vision of John

Paul II's theology of the body. Meh. He wasn't having it. It wasn't until I visited him in the dugout of the baseball field one day after school and displayed an interest in how his pitching had improved and listened to his rant on the upcoming Anaheim Angels' prospects that something deeper inside him clicked: *This teacher actually cares about me; he cares enough to listen and try to know me.* From then on, this young man made a better attempt at making Mass, even while traveling, and started to pay attention in class. As young men are often reluctant to give heartfelt affirmation of any kind, I would only find out years later of the deeper impact I had on this young man when his mother told me that something clearly happened to her son through this theology class because he took his Bible to every game he ever traveled to since. All glory to God.

Third, be ready for the long game, and be ready for the interruption. We are all sowers of the Word that has been sown in us. Some people till the soil, some sow the seed, some provide water and nutrients, others prune, and finally there are those who are privileged enough to witness the final form burst forth from the ground. We may be serving in any one of those stages, and we are not entitled to see the fruit of our work. To be sure, God graciously gives us moments where we do see and witness the transformation that the Holy Spirit has worked through us, but we need to realize that we are not owed that privilege.

The Gospels often record how Jesus was interrupted while en route from one place to another. This is when the pivotal moment of grace offered and received is materialized. The request to assist at the wedding feast of Cana (John 2:1–12), the hemorrhaging woman grasping at Jesus' garment (Luke 8:43–47), and the blind Bartimaeus crying out on the side of the road (Mark 10:46–52), among many others, illustrate how Jesus was "on the way" when the providential, life-changing moment occurred. It might not be the time for the indifferent individuals around us to have that moment of encounter; in fact, it might not be for many more years. But when it happens and we find ourselves at that privileged point of intersection, we must be willing to be personally interrupted so that we might incarnate that merciful love of Christ. Welcome that interruption, as others were likely interrupted for your sake.

Jesus also loved people enough to respect their free will, knowing that all he could do was offer the opportunity for conversion; individuals were, and still are, free to reject that gift. In the end, we can never force anyone to respond to the offer of Christ to receive life in abundance (John 10:10). All we can do is pave the way and work to make the Gospel as attractive an option as possible.

We are surrounded by people self-identifying as "nones" and seemingly indifferent to the deepest questions of humanity that have been pondered throughout the centuries. I contend, however, that men and women are hungrier than ever to have meaning in their lives and to belong to a community where they are known—and, in turn, to be increasingly open to the strange and stubbornly historical person of Christ.

Be patient, find common ground, and lean into relationships with joy and zeal. As Pope St. John Paul II, the model of a patient and joyful evangelist, affirmed to the young people of World Youth Day in Rome in 2000: "It is Jesus who stirs in you the desire to do something great with your lives, the will to follow an ideal, the refusal to allow yourselves to be ground down by mediocrity, the courage to commit yourselves humbly and patiently to improving yourselves and society, making the world more human and more fraternal."[3]

---

3. John Paul II, "15th World Youth Day Address of the Holy Father John Paul II: Vigil of Prayer," Tor Vergata, August 19, 2000, Vatican.va.

3

Why Catholics Fall Away:
A Priest's Perspective

Fr. Blake Britton

In his opening speech at the convocation of Vatican II, Pope St. John XXIII highlighted a passage from the Gospel of Luke that has since become a foundational principle of the New Evangelization: "Read the signs of the times" (Luke 12:54–56). The Council Fathers echoed these words in *Gaudium et Spes*, reaffirming the Church's responsibility of "scrutinizing the signs of the times and of interpreting them in the light of the Gospel" so as to carry out her task of sanctifying the modern world.[1] The Church is not a spectator of history. By her very nature as a sacrament, she is intrinsically bound to the world and its ultimate end.

This requires Catholics—especially apologists—who are keenly aware of the various movements and trends in the culture, while simultaneously recognizing the desires that give birth to these tendencies in the first place. It is not enough to simply affirm or deny society's impulses; we have to understand them at their root and wrestle with them in the depths of our being.

There are few people who appreciate this better than priests. More than anyone else, our vocation—if it is lived genuinely—requires us to dive into the remotest recesses of souls and regularly navigate the drama of life. We cannot afford to see things superficially or at face value. Every day that we wake up, the Lord entrusts us with the most precious gift of creation, the

---

1. Vatican Council II, *Gaudium et Spes* 4, *The Word on Fire Vatican II Collection*, ed. Matthew Levering (Park Ridge, IL: Word on Fire Institute, 2021), 217.

12

human soul; each syllable we utter and every action we take directly influences people's eternal destiny.

This affords priests a unique and indispensable perspective in regard to apologetics. Whereas a typical apologist might promote or defend the faith in response to a set of proposed ideologies, the priest must "see into the heart" (see 1 Sam. 16:7) and approach the same set of questions from a pastoral perspective. This is colloquially termed, "meeting people where they're at." And that is precisely the purpose of this essay, to help the reader better appreciate the state of average Catholics in our parish pews—to see where they are at. The Lord provides a wonderful and clear explanation in the Gospels.

Let us consider this familiar scene from the Sacred Scriptures:

That same day Jesus went out of the house and sat beside the sea. Such great crowds gathered around him that he got into a boat and sat there, while the whole crowd stood on the beach. And he told them many things in parables, saying: "Listen! A sower went out to sow. And as he sowed, some seeds fell on the path, and the birds came and ate them up. Other seeds fell on rocky ground, where they did not have much soil, and they sprang up quickly, since they had no depth of soil. But when the sun rose, they were scorched; and since they had no root, they withered away. Other seeds fell among thorns, and the thorns grew up and choked them. Other seeds fell on good soil and brought forth grain, some a hundredfold, some sixty, some thirty. Let anyone with ears listen!"

"Hear then the parable of the sower. When anyone hears the word of the kingdom and does not understand it, the evil one comes and snatches away what is sown in the heart; this is what was sown on the path. As for what was sown on rocky ground, this is the one who hears the word and immediately receives it with joy; yet such a person has no root, but endures only for a while, and when trouble or persecution arises on account of the word, that person immediately falls away. As for what was sown among thorns, this is the one who hears the word, but the cares of the world and the lure of wealth choke the word, and it yields nothing. But as for what was sown on good soil, this is the one who hears the word and understands it, who indeed bears fruit and yields, in one case a hundredfold, in another sixty, and in another thirty."

Matthew 13:1–9, 18–23 is one of the few occasions in which Jesus clearly expounds a parable word for word. The Lord notes four different types of tendencies or attitudes that develop in the human heart: those who hear and do not understand, those who hear and fall away, those who hear and become worldly, and finally, those who hear and bear fruit. It is helpful to interpret the first three analogies as states of the soul that eventually lead to a life of sin. For the purposes of this essay, we will not spend much time reflecting on the good seed, as its meaning is self-explanatory. Rather, since this book is intended for apologists, I think it better to provide an exposition on the three analogies of the seeds that do not bear fruit, since this will help apologists better know the heart of their listener, especially one that is struggling with or outright rejecting the faith.

State 1—Those Who Hear and Do Not Understand

It was Plato who said that only the ignorant can refuse the good. Created in God's image and likeness (Gen. 1:26), humanity is innately drawn to what is comely and wholesome. Whatever smacks of truth stirs our innermost being. Nothing is truer than Catholicism. Willingly rejecting the Church, therefore, can only be the result of a failure to see her beauty and appreciate her wisdom. This is most certainly the case for millions of Catholics who have left the faith in the past sixty years.

Sadly, the majority of Catholics who stop practicing their faith—especially those who leave the Church and return later in life—do so out of ignorance. "Father, if I only knew what the Church actually believed"—I hear that phrase far too often in the confessional or in counseling. However, it is hard to know what is not taught. Even more, it is difficult to believe what is taught if the teacher lacks conviction or proper knowledge. As Pope St. Paul VI said so aptly, "Modern man listens more willingly to witnesses than to teachers, and if he does listen to teachers, it is because they are witnesses."[2]

I find in my pastoral ministry that many Catholics in the pew suffer from an ignorance of the faith. Not just its basic teachings, but its ethos as a whole. These are the Catholics most likely to become "nones" or "unaffiliated." The Evil One takes them because they do not have a good synthesis of the faith—which is to say, an authentic and comprehensive understanding of its nature. The uniqueness and profundity of Christianity is lost on them. With such a lack of knowledge, it is only a matter of time before something has to fill the void. As C.S. Lewis keenly observes, if we starve the spiritual sensibilities of the people, it makes them "easier prey to the propagandist when he comes. For famished nature will be avenged."[3] And it has been avenged viciously. The restless heart of humanity is desperately searching for fulfillment. Netflix binges, porn addictions, Amazon Prime shopping sprees, career ladder-climbing, social media trending, political activism, pop-star adulation, socialist movements . . . the list goes on and on. Every sinful tendency manifested in the culture is nothing more than humanity's attempt to fill the existential void only faith can fill.

This is especially true for Millennials and members of Gen Z. We are among the first generations raised by a secular, practically atheistic culture. Society tells us God is dead and the world can make us happy in his stead. So, we abandon our souls to materialism, running from pleasure to pleasure, confusing stimulation for satisfaction. Of course, these things leave us empty, and we become desperate. Every day is a concerted effort to escape, medicate, or in some way fill the hole in our hearts. But no matter how successful we are or how much we achieve, that nagging thought gnaws at the back of our mind, telling us there has to be something more to life. Eventually, the seed

---

2. Paul VI, *Evangelii Nuntiandi* 41, Vatican.va.
3. C.S. Lewis, *The Abolition of Man* (New York: HarperOne, 1944), 14.

of faith is trampled by jadedness and depression as we suffer from the human need for transcendence while constantly striving to suppress it. The existential tension is too much. The voice of the enemy is welcome relief. The seed is ready to be stolen.

State 2—Those Who Hear and Fall Away

"Unless you change and become like children, you will never enter the kingdom of heaven" (Matt. 18:3). Why? What unique characteristic does a child possess? There are multiple answers: innocence, enthusiasm, confidence, trust, etc. But there is one specific attribute that stands out among the rest: wonder. Children are wonder-*full*. Everything around them is an adventure. Life is never tiresome or humdrum. All is gift. Yet somewhere along the way, the world starts to beat that wonder out of us, to mock and deride it as an infantile fantasy. We become boring and stifled by a hyperactive self-awareness that is more concerned about perception than reality. Slowly, we lose sight of what is most valuable and waste our energies on things that ultimately mean nothing. The same is true in our faith.

Following our First Holy Communion, it is tragic how quickly we tend to forget it. The jubilant expectation of that day fades away within the year and the poison of complacency set in. The rocky ground of passing concerns stunt the roots of faith, keeping us superficial. We remain Catholic, but as a spectator. We start going through the motions of faith. We do not necessarily live horribly sinful lives or leave the Church, but at the same time, we are not actively striving for holiness.

The Church Fathers refer to this vice as *the demon of acedia*. This demon specializes in mediocrity and comfort. His goal is to make sure we never progress in the spiritual life. To put it another way, *acedia* is the demon that whispers in our ear, "That's too hard," or "Someone like you could never be holy." Only Christians striving to improve, learn, and change are dangerous to the reign of evil. The best way to combat the demon of *acedia* is to avoid putting our faith on autopilot. We need to actively engage in the practices of our Catholic faith and constantly seek to grow. Only then can we become what the demon fears most: a saint.

State 3—Those Who Hear and Are Choked

We live in a materialistic society. This is a direct result of secularism. If there is nothing beyond the material, then we had better get as much as we can while we can. Jesus employs a powerful image when describing this mentality: choking. There are few sensations more infuriating. To desperately gasp for life and powerlessly fear death.

The worldly forces vying for our freedom are countless: politics, health, career, finances, social media, technology. In addition to these external influences, we have internal struggles, such as personal trauma, spiritual or family wounds, vices, and addictive habits. Without being rooted in Christ, these things can easily strangle us. Intimacy with the Lord allows us to see reality with proper perspective, whereas distance from God skews our perception. The further we are from Christ, the more intimidating or important worldly things become. Darkness grows as light diminishes. That is why we either succumb to the anxiety of these forces or sell our soul for a false sense of control over them.

Every Catholic sitting in the pew has a story. There are countless sentiments and apprehensions that ebb and flow throughout their daily lives. Part of being a good apologist is speaking directly to these concerns by reconciling the truth of faith with the reality of an individual's unique experience of the world. Christ does not exist in abstraction, but in the drama and rawness of being. That is what makes Christianity more beautiful than any other religion. We believe in a God of flesh, an "Emmanuel," a "God-who-is-with-us." Catholic apologetics does not start with convincing someone that we are right, but rather with convincing them that there is something more. It is not in conveying the wrongness of someone's action, but the ability to recognize the goodness they long for and how it can only be fulfilled in Jesus. This style of apologetics is not primarily rooted in words or ideas but in our own innate joy and enthusiasm for Catholicism, the unmitigated fact that we have met someone and that someone has changed our lives by removing the weeds of worldliness and allowing us to live "in the freedom of the children of God" (Rom. 8:21).

Signs of Hope

When seeking to explain and defend the faith, it is vital to know the heart of the listener. In particular, when trying to evangelize fallen-away Catholics, we have to appreciate the struggles they are experiencing. In my pastoral ministry as a parish priest, I find the Lord's words in Matthew 13 quite insightful. Average Catholics in the pew want to believe. Their hearts desire Christ and the fullness of truth. But ignorance of the faith leads to lukewarmness and complacency. This in turn makes the heart hungry for sustenance. That is when the world comes in and tries to fill the void, leading Catholics astray. That being said, I join St. John Paul II in calling myself a "witness to hope." My parishes have seen a recent uptick in the number of Millennials coming back to the Church, particularly through the sacrament of Reconciliation. Love for the sacred liturgy and the tradition of the Church is also on the rise among youth. They are realizing quickly that the world cannot satisfy them. Now, we just need to show them the splendor of our faith.

4

The Reason and the Remedy:
Bringing the Lapsed Christian Home
Tod Worner

Gulags and gas chambers, show trials and Stasi,[1] barbed wire and the Berlin Wall—when one surveys the ideological bloodbath that was the twentieth century, it is nearly impossible to find anything encouraging. After all, story after brutal story catalogs the lengths to which people would go to fill a certain inner emptiness with a grander meaning. And even when, in the bright light of history, the manipulation and lies, intimidation and exclusion, torture and mechanized murder are on full and shameful display, some among the intellectual best and brightest have offered an unsettling justification for such horrors.

In 1994, in the wake of the Soviet Union's collapse, Michael Ignatieff interviewed revered British Marxist historian Eric Hobsbawm, asking him, "In 1934, millions of people are dying in the Soviet experiment. If you had known that, would it have made a difference to you at the time? To your commitment? To being a Communist?" Hobsbawm sniffed, "Probably not." Ignatieff pressed further: "What it comes down to is saying that had the radiant tomorrow actually been created, the loss of fifteen, twenty million people might have been justified?" "Yes," Hobsbawm admitted.[2]

---

1. The official name of the secret police agency of the communist German Democratic Republic (East Germany).

2. Richard Aldous, "'Eric Hobsbawm: A Life in History' Review: The Outsider as Insider," *Wall Street Journal*, May 3, 2019, https://www.wsj.com/articles/eric-hobsbawm-a-life-in-history-review-the-outsider-as-insider-11556898407.

To call this chilling would be an understatement. And with a classically Orwellian headshake, one might agree that some ideas are so absurd that only an intellectual could believe them. But there is something deeply instructive about our inexorable draw to modern, horrific ideologies promising an earthly paradise. There is a seduction found in "immanentizing the eschaton." But why?

This is the spark of encouragement that comes out of the ashes of the twentieth century. The hunger we have for deeper meaning, fulfilling purpose, and enduring truth (though often misdirected) says something extraordinary about humankind. It reveals the presence of our inner, God-shaped hole. As St. Augustine described in his own wayward journey to God, "You have made us for yourself, and our hearts are restless until they rest in you."[3]

Many in the twentieth (and, now, twenty-first) century who found their way to the intoxication of ideology were once Christians. They would now be considered "lapsed" Christians, derived from the Latin *lapsi*, which means "fallen." The *lapsi* were those who abandoned their faith under periods of persecution (first named during the wicked reigns of the early Roman emperors). They either fled the faith to save their life or raced to the new ideology in pursuit of new comfort. Today, more often than not, to be a lapsed Christian is not to have been driven from faith. It is not even that dramatic. Today, to be a lapsed Christian is to have simply and unceremoniously walked away.

But why would a Christian leave? What would make someone forswear their allegiance to a faith and culture? The answer, of course, is legion, but let me offer the following as the most common reasons.

Boredom. Lapsed Christians often leave the faith without ever having tried it. They are simply bored by it. Their faith was a commitment of culture more than conviction—a faith of Easter brunches and Christmas parties, periodic Masses and oft-forgotten prayers. Unexplored, it remains a coloring-book image of old, dust-coated men in cloaks and sandals—quaint, curious, and

---

3. Augustine, *Confessions* 1.1.1.

hopelessly irrelevant. In *The Diary of a Country Priest*, Georges Bernanos describes the deadliness of boredom to the life of faith. Boredom, Bernanos' priest observes, is like fine, imperceptible dust—ash even.

> To shake off the drizzle of ashes, you must forever be on the go. And so people are always "on the go." . . . I wonder if man has ever before experienced this contagion, this leprosy of boredom: an aborted despair, a shameful form of despair in some way like the fermentation of Christianity in decay.[4]

Boredom not only reveals a lack of effort but, even more, a fundamental lack of interest. To paraphrase G.K. Chesterton, "[Christianity] has not been tried and found wanting; it has been found difficult and left untried."[5]

Distraction. Lapsed Christians often leave due to inattention. In a world worshiping at the altar of efficiency, achieving more and more in less and less time is deemed worthy of a badge of honor. We are told to juggle, balance, and multitask. Being is eclipsed by forever becoming. Pope Benedict XVI once observed, "We are no longer able to hear God. . . . There are too many frequencies filling our ears."[6] A faith deeply rooted in prayer and worship, patience and formation runs counter to the frenetic and distracting demands of each day.

Anger. Lapsed Christians frequently leave because they are angry. To be sure, there is no shortage of human fallibility on display in the operations or membership of the Church. Hilaire Belloc, in one of his more prickly moments, insisted that "the Catholic Church is an institution I am bound to hold divine—but for unbelievers a proof of its divinity might be found in the fact that no merely human institution conducted with such knavish imbecility

---

4. Georges Bernanos, *The Diary of a Country Priest* (New York: Carroll & Graf, 2002), 3.
5. G.K. Chesterton, *What's Wrong with the World* (New York: Dodd & Mead, 1910), 48.
6. Benedict XVI, "Homily of the Holy Father," September 10, 2006, Vatican.va.

would have lasted a fortnight."[7] And G.K. Chesterton mused, "Suppose the village atheist had a sudden and splendid impulse to rush into the village church and denounce everybody there as miserable offenders. He might break in at the exact moment when they were saying the same thing themselves."[8] To be sure, anger about sin within a divine institution is proper. But to leave the truth of Christ over the brokenness of his followers is to imperil the soul in pursuit of a counterfeit.

Anxiety. Lapsed Christians leave because they are worried. Everyone wants relief from their fears . . . and we all want it *now*. Surely this ideology, this distraction, this experience, this drug will give me what I want—control— over what seems to be uncontrollable. To cultivate an interior life, to engage in prayer, to wait, to suffer a bit seems intolerable to those who want relief *now* and in the way of their choosing. Hans Urs von Balthasar, considering how much Christianity wrestles with anxiety, came to this heartening conclusion: "When one surveys even from a distance how often and how openly Sacred Scripture speaks of fear and anxiety, an initial conclusion presents itself: the Word of God is not afraid of fear or anxiety."[9]

When Christians lapse, they leave Something for something else. One never lives for nothing. If it isn't for God, then it will be for wealth or honor or pleasure or power. Criticized by a fashionable *literatus* for being a "dogmatic" Catholic (and, thus, forever a second-rate writer), Chesterton laughed, "In truth there are only two kinds of people, those who accept dogma and know it, and those who accept dogma and don't know it."[10] Everyone, to be sure, has a dogma. Lapsed Christians are no exception.

So, what are we to do? How are we to bring the lapsed Christian back into the loving arms of Christ and his Church?

---

7. Robert Speaight, *The Life of Hilaire Belloc* (New York: Farrar, Straus, and Cudahy, 1957), 383.

8. G.K. Chesterton, *The Collected Works of G.K. Chesterton,* vol. 27 (San Francisco: Ignatius Press, 1986), 576.

9. Hans Urs von Balthasar, *The Christian and Anxiety,* trans. Dennis D. Martin and Michael J. Miller (San Francisco: Ignatius Press, 2000), 39.

10. G.K. Chesterton, *Fancies Versus Fads* (London: Methuen, 1923), 86.

"To convert somebody," it has been said, "you take them by the hand, and guide them." When the famed physician William Osler happened upon an incredible medical finding, he shouted exultingly to his medical residents, "Hoity-toity, boys! Look at this!" Our role is to show lapsed Christians the faith anew ("Look at this!"), so they can see what they are missing. The faith lies dormant within them; let us embark on its awakening.

And what shall we tell the lapsed Christian?

The Catholic faith is true. Chesterton offered:

> There is no other case of one continuous intelligent institution that has been thinking about thinking for two thousand years. Its experience naturally covers nearly all experiences; and especially nearly all errors. The result is a map in which all the blind alleys and bad roads are clearly marked, all the ways that have been shown to be worthless by the best of all evidence: the evidence of those who have gone down them.[11]

But even the intellectual brilliance of St. Thomas Aquinas was dwarfed by his encounter with a moment of God's revelation. "All I have written," he uttered, "now seems to me like so much straw compared with what I have seen and with what has been revealed to me."[12] The truth of faith touches everything. It begins with questions, and it ends with a silence bathed in peace and wholeness.

The Catholic faith is beautiful. To be sure, Catholicism can boast the works of Mozart and Caravaggio, Dante and Flannery O'Connor, but its true sublimity is barely touched upon in our worldly state. In beholding the beatific vision in the final canto of the *Divine Comedy*, Dante stammered,

---

11. G.K. Chesterton, *The Collected Works of G.K. Chesterton*, vol. 3 (San Francisco: Ignatius Press, 1986), 129.
12. Quoted in James William McClendon and James William McClendon Jr., *Ethics: Systematic Theology*, vol. 1 (Nashville: Abingdon, 2002), 64.

> In its profundity I saw—ingathered
> and bound by love into one single volume—
> what, in the universe, seems separate, scattered:
> substances, accidents, and dispositions
> as if conjoined—in such a way that what
> I tell is only rudimentary.[13]

God reveals himself in glorious, exquisite fragments, but beckons us to return to ultimate wholeness. He only asks for us to open our eyes.

The Catholic faith is good. To understand faith's goodness means we must engage with Jesus Christ, the embodiment of the good. In his justice and mercy, in his strength and humility, in his sheer presence and limitless love for us, we encounter Someone (unlike anyone else) unfailingly invested in our well-being. This is the otherworldly goodness that our heart so deeply craves.

The lapsed Christian has walked away from truth and has embraced (consciously or unconsciously) something infinitely less. Man-made ideology is no substitute and, in fact, risks making people into, as Georges Bernanos would observe, "horrible unformed monsters—stumps of men."[14] Evelyn Waugh once wrote, "The human mind is inspired enough when it comes to inventing horrors; it is when it tries to invent a Heaven that it shows itself cloddish."[15] If as Christians we truly believe what we think we believe, let us tell the lapsed Christian the story anew. And let us tell it with faith and vigor. Let us lead him by the hand and exult in its wonder. Let us love as Christ loves and share as Christ shares so that we may be the agent of grace who leads, at last, to the proper filling of the God-shaped hole.

---

13. Dante Alighieri, *The Divine Comedy: The Inferno* (New York: Random House, 2016), canto 33, 85–90, Google Books.

14. Bernanos, *Diary of a Country Priest*, 109.

15. Evelyn Waugh, *Put Out More Flags* (New York: Little & Brown, 2002), 71.

5

Moral Relativism:
Arguments For and Against
Francis J. Beckwith

Here are some moral rules:

- Love your neighbor as yourself
- Thou shalt not commit adultery
- Do not intentionally kill the innocent
- Do not take what is not yours without permission
- Parents ought to care for their infant children
- Shun ignorance and try to live at peace with your neighbors
- One ought not to rape anyone

If you believe that these moral rules—and perhaps others not mentioned—ought to be obeyed by everyone regardless of time, place, or culture, then you are a moral objectivist. You believe that morality is real and that it can be known by everyone—that is to say, that morality is more like mathematics than it is like the rules of etiquette. On the other hand, if you believe that morality depends exclusively on one's time, place, or culture—that there is no universal objective morality that transcends society and circumstance—then you are a moral relativist. You do not deny that there are moral rules, but what you do believe is that these rules are nothing more than your own society's ethical code, which may be different, but no better or worse, than the ethical code of another society. So, you believe that morality is more like the rules of etiquette than it is like mathematics.

Because the Catholic Church teaches that morality is objective,[1] a person who believes in moral relativism may hesitate to consider the Catholic faith. For this reason, in what follows, we will take a careful look at some of the reasons people give for why they are moral relativists and how a Catholic might address those reasons.

Why are some people moral relativists? In my experience, I have found two main reasons for belief in moral relativism: (1) There is just too much diversity on moral issues both in and across cultures, and (2) it is intolerant to believe that one's moral view is universally true and that the moral views of others are wrong. We will call the first, *the Argument from Disagreement*, and the second, *the Argument from Tolerance*.

1. The Argument from Disagreement

Disagreement on moral issues is everywhere. In the United States alone, there are an array of questions over which sincere citizens hold contrary views. We can almost recite them by heart: abortion, marriage, critical race theory, physician-assisted suicide, religious liberty, and animal rights. Internationally, it's no different. While some cultures practice polygamy and prohibit the killing and eating of cattle, to cite but two examples, other cultures practice monogamy and open up steak joints. But not only is there disagreement in the present across space, there is also disagreement across time. Think of all the civilizations throughout history that thought it was perfectly permissible to enslave fellow human beings, torture heretics, or rape and pillage conquered nations.

Given the wide diversity of moral opinions and practices across space and time, it is easy to see why someone would be a moral relativist. It should not surprise us then that two of the most widely read academic defenses of moral

---

1. See *Catechism of the Catholic Church* 1956.

relativism—by social scientists Ruth Benedict (1887–1948) and William Graham Sumner (1840–1910)[2]—appeal to this diversity in making their cases. They essentially argue that because there is wide disagreement on moral beliefs and practices, there is no universal objective morality, and thus moral relativism is true.

Although the argument from disagreement may seem impressive at first, since it appears to be based on an undeniable fact (moral disagreement), it is remarkably weak once one begins to critically examine it.

First, as a matter of simple logic, the fact of moral disagreement does not *entail* moral relativism, just as the fact of disagreement over the shape of the Earth does not *entail* that the Earth has no shape. Perhaps some cultures and individuals have gotten morality wrong, which is something we all already believe deep down. Who, for example, would say that what the Nazis did to the Jews was morally permissible because their culture said it was right, or that racial segregation as once practiced in the United States was not immoral because the society at the time believed it was okay?

Second, in order for the argument from disagreement to work, the moral relativist must assume this proposition: Whenever there is disagreement on any issue (e.g., the correct moral position on X), there is no universal objective truth on the matter. Now, suppose we say in response, "I disagree with the proposition 'Whenever there is disagreement on any issue, there is no universal objective truth on the matter?'" But this means that we can reject the proposition on its own grounds![3] It is what philosophers call a self-refuting claim, much like the claim made by the person who says to you, "Don't believe anything I say," or "I can't speak a word in English."

Third, disagreement is overrated. Take, for example, the issue of abortion. Although it is true that pro-lifers and pro-choicers disagree on its morality,

<hr>

2. Ruth Benedict, "Anthropology and the Abnormal," in *Moral Relativism: A Reader*, ed. Paul K. Moser and Thomas L. Carson (New York: Oxford University Press, 2001), 80–89 (excerpted from Benedict's "Anthropology and the Abnormal," *Journal of General Psychology* 10 [1934]: 59–82); and William Graham Sumner, "Folkways," in *Moral Relativism*, 69–79 (excerpted from Sumner's *Folkways: A Study of the Sociological Importance of Usages, Manners, Customs, Mores, and Morals* [Boston: Ginn, 1906]).

3. See Hadley Arkes, *First Things: An Inquiry Into the First Principles of Morals and Justice* (Princeton, NJ: Princeton University Press, 1986), 132.

they do not disagree on the moral principle that it is wrong to intentionally kill innocent persons. What they disagree on is what counts as a person or how we should understand the meaning of innocence. Defenders of abortion-choice typically argue either that the fetus, though genetically a human being, is not morally a person during most if not all of its gestation,[4] or that the fetus, though morally a person, is not technically innocent if it is trespassing in the mother's body without her explicit consent.[5] Although as Catholics we think both types of abortion-choice arguments are mistaken,[6] we should recognize that each is employed by its advocates precisely because they already agree with us that it is morally wrong to intentionally kill innocent persons.

This kind of reasoning can be applied to other issues as well. If you think of the debates over marriage, physician-assisted suicide, and critical race theory, the differing factions appeal to the *exact same* moral goods and principles to justify their positions: fairness, justice, relief of suffering, love, and protection of the vulnerable. Where they disagree is over the proper application of those goods and principles and the right way to answer questions about the nature of the reality to which they are being applied (e.g., What *is* marriage? Is systemic racism *really* everywhere?). This is why the Catholic Church teaches that even though objective morality is known by all, it is "not perceived by everyone clearly and immediately. In the present situation sinful man needs grace and revelation so moral and religious truths may be known 'by everyone with facility, with firm certainty and with no admixture of error.'"[7]

Fourth, the argument from disagreement leads to absurd consequences. If moral relativism is correct (that there is no universal objective morality),

---

4. See Francis J. Beckwith, *Defending Life: A Moral and Legal Case Against Abortion Choice* (New York: Cambridge University Press, 2007); Christopher Kaczor, *The Ethics of Abortion: Women's Rights, Human Life, and the Question of Justice*, 2nd ed. (New York: Routledge, 2015).

5. See Mary Anne Warren, "On the Moral and Legal Status of Abortion Rights," *The Monist* 57 (1973): 43–61.

6. See David Boonin, *Beyond Roe: Why Abortion Should Be Legal—Even if the Fetus Is a Person* (New York: Oxford University Press, 2019).

7. *Catechism of the Catholic Church* 1960, quoting from Pius XII, *Humani Generis* (August 12, 1950), 3.

then it is not wrong everywhere and always to rape another person, intentionally kill the innocent, torture children for fun, judge Mother Teresa as no better than Adolf Hitler, and abandon one's infant offspring to the elements if one finds them inconvenient. It also means that there can be neither moral progress (such as the eradication of chattel slavery) nor moral reformers (such as Martin Luther King Jr.), for progress or reformation presuppose a universal objective morality that societies and individuals may be moving toward and by which we can make judgments about ourselves as well as those outside our culture or society.

2. The Argument from Tolerance

Some people argue that because it is intolerant to believe that one's moral views are right and the moral views of others are wrong, it follows that moral relativism—the view that there is no one universal objective morality—best establishes tolerance. (This was the thinking behind the once popular primary and secondary teaching technique called *values clarification*.[8]) There are several reasons to reject this argument.

First, the moral relativist seems to be affirming at least one absolute moral principle: tolerance. But in that case, she is no longer a relativist. Second, moral relativism need not lead to tolerance. After all, someone could say, "Although I believe all morality is culturally relative, I prefer my culture's morality to all others, and thus I want my nation to ban all immigrants from other cultures including yours." Third, the practice of tolerance seems valuable because it establishes certain goods, such as living at peace with others and better understanding those with whom one disagrees. But these goods seem to be functioning as if they were part of some universal objective morality, which is inconsistent with moral relativism.

---

8. Richard A. Baer, Jr., "Teaching Values in the Classroom: Education or Indoctrination?," *Principal* 61, no. 3 (January 1982): 17–21, at 36.

Conclusion

Moral relativists typically have their hearts in the right place. They rightly recognize differences of moral beliefs and practices between individuals and across cultures, while at the same time wanting to advance the cause of tolerance and understanding. But, as we have seen, despite their good motives, the view they hold, moral relativism, has many significant weaknesses.

6

Countering Scientific Materialism

Stephen Barr

One of the main contemporary challenges to the Catholic faith is a rationalistic, reductionist, and anti-religious ideology sometimes called "scientific materialism" or "scientism." It is materialist in asserting that all of reality is reducible to matter and that its behavior can be accounted for by the laws of physics and chance. It is "scientistic" in claiming that the only justified beliefs are those that can be established by the methods of the natural sciences.

This ideology makes three main claims against religion:

(1) Religion has historically been at war with science (e.g., the Galileo affair and fundamentalist Christian opposition to evolution) and an impediment to its progress.

(2) The outlooks of science and religion are inherently and fundamentally opposed, because science is based on reason and evidence, whereas religion is contrary to reason and is based on belief in entities (e.g., God, the soul, angels, etc.) for which there is no evidence. Science is based on natural explanations and natural laws, whereas religion is based on the supernatural and miraculous.

(3) The discoveries of science since Copernicus have revealed a world that ever more diverges from "religion's" picture of it. Copernicus has shown that humanity is not the center of the universe. Newtonian

physics has shown that Nature has no purposes or goals but is purely mechanical and governed by blind and impersonal forces. Modern astronomy has shown how small and insignificant we are compared to the cosmos as a whole. Darwin has shown that human life is an accident and that human beings differ only in degree from lower animals. Advances in neuroscience and artificial intelligence have demonstrated that the supposed "soul" is nothing but the workings of the brain, a complex biochemical computer. And modern cosmology has shown either that the universe had no beginning, or that physics can explain the beginning as a quantum fluctuation.

To meet the challenge of this ideology, all three claims must be countered.

Claim (1), the so-called "warfare thesis" or "conflict thesis," while very widely believed by non-experts, is unanimously rejected as a myth by contemporary historians of science, who trace its origin to late-nineteenth-century anti-religious and anti-clerical propaganda. The following easily documented and communicated facts are effective in debunking it: (a) The way was prepared for the Scientific Revolution of the sixteenth and seventeenth centuries by the invention of the university in the Middle Ages. The medieval universities—Catholic institutions—were the places where the study of science first received a stable institutional basis. (b) Virtually all the great figures of the Scientific Revolution were devout Christians (e.g., Copernicus, Kepler, Galileo, Descartes, Pascal, Boyle, and Newton). Most scientists were religious believers well into the nineteenth century (including the greatest physicists of the nineteenth century, Faraday and Maxwell). And there have been great scientists who are religious down to our own day (e.g., Juan Martin Maldacena and Francis S. Collins). (c) Several branches of science were founded by Catholic priests, including Georges Lemaître (Big Bang cosmology), Gregor Mendel (genetics), Bl. Nicolas Steno (geology), and Marin Mersenne (acoustics). Members of the Jesuit order have made great contributions, especially to astronomy and to seismology—seismology has even been called the "Jesuit science." (d) The Galileo affair was an aberration: no comparable incident occurred in the eight-hundred-year relationship between the Catholic Church and science.

Claim (2)—that religion is opposed to reason and to natural explanations of the world—is based on fundamental misunderstandings of both history and Christian theology. The following points are key to correcting these: (a) Christianity radically distinguished the Creator from the created world and taught that God is not a part of the world but the Author of it, who lies beyond it. The world was therefore no longer seen as the abode of capricious deities but as the creation of Reason (Logos), who imposed upon it some intelligible order. In this way, Christianity stripped the universe itself of divinity and contributed to its being seen as a natural world. (b) A central argument for the existence of a Creator, made by many of the Church Fathers and theologians since, is that the orderliness of nature points to a "giver of order" (to use a phrase of St. Irenaeus). (c) The very concept of "laws of nature," conceived of as mathematical rules, was first explicitly proposed in the seventeenth century by Descartes and Newton, who based it on the Christian idea that God is the Lawgiver to the cosmos, an idea found in Scripture itself. While scientific materialists claim that the laws of nature are the ultimate ground of all explanation, they have no explanation of why there *are* laws of nature, and no awareness of the religious roots of that concept. (d) A central mistake of scientific materialists is to think that God and natural explanations are in competition, so that one must choose between them. The antidote to this error is the traditional Catholic distinction between the "primary causality" of the Creator and the "secondary causality" of created things. This can be explained simply and effectively by the analogy of a novel, in which the events within the novel's plot have causes within the plot, but equally (and noncompetitively) are caused by the author, who conceives of the entire novel and all of its plot in his creative mind.

Claim (3) fails to take into account scientific developments since the nineteenth century. A number of discoveries up to that time were widely seen as moving the scientific conception of the world further and further from that of Christianity. But there were several "twists in the plot" of the story of science in the twentieth century—scientific developments that moved in the other direction, bringing the scientific and religious pictures closer together. Here are five important ones:

(a) Whereas science had once seemed to be moving toward the conclusion that the universe is infinitely old, and the idea of a cosmic temporal beginning was coming to seem like a relic of religious mythologies, in the early twentieth century Einstein's theory of gravity, the discovery of cosmic expansion by astronomers, and Georges Lemaître's "primeval atom" theory—now called the Big Bang theory—showed that the universe could have a beginning. The weight of scientific evidence and theory now very strongly points toward a cosmic beginning.

(b) It was a staple of atheist arguments that the progress of science increasingly showed that human beings arose by accident in a purposeless universe. But since the 1970s, it has become increasingly clear that many features of the fundamental laws of physics as we currently know them are peculiarly conducive to the possibility of life's emergence. These features are sometimes referred to as "anthropic coincidences." A very important example is that the "inhumanly" vast age and size of the universe are preconditions for the emergence of life in it, given the laws that it has.

(c) Another standard atheist argument is that the orderly structures found in nature (the solar system, living things, etc.) are the consequences of the laws of nature, rather than of a "designing hand." But the extreme mathematical richness and subtlety that twentieth-century physics has discovered at the deepest levels of the laws of nature gives new strength to the argument that the universe is the product of a mind.

(d) From the time of Newton until the 1920s, evidence increasingly suggested that the laws of physics rigidly determine how events unfold in time ("physical determinism"), allowing no room for human free will. But the discovery of the probabilistic nature of quantum mechanics overthrew physical determinism.

(e) In the standard formulation of quantum mechanics, the makers of measurements or observations ("observers") play a role that arguably requires them to possess minds not entirely reducible to physical mechanism. This has led a number of great physicists (e.g., von Neumann, Wigner, Peierls) to argue that quantum mechanics is not consistent with materialism.

To sum up, the ideology of scientific materialism is based on discredited history, philosophical false dichotomies, and a view of the physical world that is outdated by more than a century. A final point: the goal of apologetics in this area should not be to "prove" religion from science, but to remove obstacles to belief that are connected in some way to science. It is to open minds by showing people facts, ways of looking at things, and questions that they had not known or considered. If they come away with more respect and understanding for Christianity and the Church, even if they do not come to faith, that is an important achievement.

PART II

NEW APPROACHES

7

Digital Apologetics: Defending the Faith Online

Brandon Vogt

I remember sitting in front of my computer in 2008, swiveling my head every few minutes to make sure nobody was watching. After all, I was a Protestant college student looking at a Catholic website. It was the homepage of Catholic Answers, the leading Catholic apologetics ministry. What would my Protestant friends think if they caught me? What would my pastor think?

Thankfully, nobody discovered my secret reading. Yet over the ensuing months, what I found on that website dismantled many of my issues with the Catholic Church, and on Easter Sunday 2008, I formally entered the Church. I read several books during my conversion process, but the internet—and that site in particular—played an indispensable role.

Little did I know that my conversion took place during a renaissance in Catholic apologetics. The 1980s and 1990s witnessed an explosion of books, magazines, and audio tapes defending the Catholic faith. However, around the turn of the millennium, much of that energy shifted from print media to the internet. A second renaissance gave rise to new apologetics websites, blogs, podcasts, YouTube channels, Facebook groups, and apps.

How New Media Changed Apologetics

Though many of the arguments remained the same, the internet dramatically shaped Catholic apologetics in four major ways.

First, digital repository sites made it quicker and easier than ever to find apologetical answers. The Vatican became one of the first institutions to enter the world wide web by launching its website in 1995. It began as a text-heavy database of Church documents (and unfortunately hasn't evolved much since then), soon adding the full text of the *Catechism of the Catholic Church*. With all these documents, digitized and searchable, the Vatican made it easy for curious people to determine what the Church actually, officially teaches.

But the biggest advance came with the launch of Catholic.com, the website I surreptitiously browsed as a Protestant. The online home of the Catholic Answers apostolate, it quickly became the go-to source for anyone with questions about the Catholic faith. The site boasts thousands of articles and videos, covering every major apologetical topic, and its search bar makes it easy to filter and find exactly what you need. There's no more valuable tool for today's Catholic apologist.

Other repository sites followed. Two that I oversee are StrangeNotions.com and ChurchFathers.org. The former site was created to bring Catholics and atheists into dialogue around thoughtful content, and it features some of the brightest Catholic minds engaging top atheist arguments. The latter site pulls together quotes from early Christians on topics such as the Eucharist, papal authority, Baptism, and Mary, making it a one-stop shop to understanding what the early Church believed, and how those beliefs align with Catholicism.

These repository sites are a boon for apologetics. They provide easy-to-find and easy-to-share answers for Catholics who want to defend the faith, and they give seekers a reliable source to discover what the Catholic Church actually believes and why.

A second shift with new media apologetics involves the rise of video debates. In-person, formal debates are hard to pull off. An organization has to find two speakers, settle on the topic, fly them into town, book a large hall or auditorium, set up the audio/video technology, promote the event over several months, register people, and hope an adequate crowd shows up. It's a lot of work. But thanks to digital tools such as Skype, Zoom, and YouTube, online debates can be organized in a matter of days. The two debaters have to travel no further than their own living room or office. Thousands of viewers can tune in live, and thousands more can view the replay at their convenience. Other than a camera and, maybe, a couple lights, the production costs are minimal. All this has led to a proliferation of online debates.

Several Catholic apologists have mastered this format. Matt Fradd's *Pints with Aquinas* show regularly hosts debates on topics such as God's existence or the papacy. The *Reason and Theology* YouTube channel presents lively roundtable discussions with thinkers who hold conflicting views about the Catholic faith. John DeRosa's *Classical Theism* podcast unpacks many of these video debates through debriefing episodes, often with the debaters themselves.

Many Protestants have jumped on this bandwagon too, and Catholics can learn from their success. Two examples are Cameron Bertuzzi (*Capturing Christianity*) and Justin Brierly (*Unbelievable?*). Both hosts regularly welcome guests onto their shows, usually a believer and a skeptic, and they have mastered the online debate format.

Debates are valuable because they tend to attract more attention than books do. The average person might not be interested in reading a three-hundred-page exposition on apologetics, but he will gladly watch two smart opponents debate on video, disagreeing vigorously about a topic for a couple of hours.

Debates are also helpful because they allow apologetical arguments to be tested and gauged in the real world. It's certainly valuable for Catholics to read an apologetics book by another Catholic, but that can fuel confirmation bias. It's often more valuable to see those same arguments used and challenged in real-world debates, among people who disagree.

A third exciting online trend is what I call accidental apologetics. This is the phenomenon of non-Catholics unwittingly stumbling across apologetical content online. In past decades, it would have been extremely rare for a non-Catholic to suddenly encounter a Catholic apologetics book. Someone typically would have to be hunting for such a volume to find it. But that's not the case online. Thanks to algorithms on every major social platform, it's common for apologetics content to be recommended to viewers who aren't necessarily looking for it. For example, someone casually watching a Jordan Peterson video on YouTube might see a suggestion to watch a related Bishop Robert Barron YouTube video discussing the meaning of faith. This happens regularly.

I've heard from atheists who stumbled, unwittingly, across one of my YouTube apologetics videos, and from Protestants who came across my podcast only because their podcasting app suggested it. But my favorite example involves an email we received at Word on Fire, written to Bishop Barron. A woman explained:

> You won't believe how I found your videos. It started when I was poking around online, looking for news about Charlie Sheen. On Sheen's Wikipedia page, I learned his father was the famous actor Martin Sheen, who played the President on *The West Wing*. I started reading about Martin Sheen, and learned, from his Wikipedia page, that "Martin Sheen" wasn't his birth name. It was actually a stage name borrowed from Fulton Sheen, the Catholic televangelist from the 1950s. Curious, I Googled him, too, and one of the results pointed me to an article where someone described you, Bishop Robert Barron, as "today's successor to Fulton Sheen." So, with more curiosity, I clicked on your name, read about you, watched some of your videos, and from there I was hooked. I'm writing now to tell you not only have I binge-watched much of your content, but I was just recently confirmed in the Catholic Church, thanks to your arguments and videos.

After reading that email, I remember thinking, "Wow! Well, there it is, the power of the internet. What other tool can bring someone from Charlie Sheen all the way to the Eucharist?" That's the strength of accidental apologetics. When Catholic apologists post a vast amount of content online, across several platforms, they increase the odds that people will stumble upon it.

A fourth and final trend is the ability to enter into apologetical conversations with seekers whom we would never otherwise engage. This might be the most exciting feature for apologists and evangelists. Even just twenty years ago, it was difficult for Catholic apologists to connect with people who had questions about or objections to the Catholic faith. How can we find them? Where can we engage them? Yet the internet has made that easy today. Catholics can log in to Reddit, a massive discussion website, and immediately begin interacting with atheists and skeptics. They can hop over to a Protestant Facebook page and engage people who are posing questions about Catholicism. It's not hard to open these types of conversations.

St. Peter tells Christians to "always be ready to make your defense to anyone who demands from you an accounting for the hope that is in you" (1 Pet. 3:15). But, of course, a seeker cannot make such a demand without being in contact with you. That's the necessary first step—connection—and the internet facilitates it.

What's Next for Digital Apologetics?

I suspect all four of these trends will continue to deepen and flourish. However, what other developments can we expect over the next decade or two? In my view, three seem especially likely.

First, a larger space will open for introverted apologists. Traditionally, Catholic apologists have been charismatic speakers with strong rhetorical gifts. They're confident on stage and comfortable talking face-to-face with strangers. But in the digital age, many top apologists are more reserved and introverted. Although smart and savvy, they prefer working behind the scenes, off camera, building websites and apps, running big Instagram accounts, creating motion-graphic videos, writing blog posts, or recording podcasts. They recognize that while they might not be charismatic or smooth-speaking, that's okay. The internet still allows them to flourish. As a result, I expect we'll see even more prominent, impactful, yet behind-the-scenes Catholic apologists.

Second, online apologetics will become hyper-niched. Apostolates such as Catholic Answers and Word on Fire have created resources answering most of the basic apologetical questions. For instance, it's easy to find Catholic videos outlining the history of Eucharistic doctrine or explaining where Purgatory is found in the Bible. So, rather than repeating these same general defenses, many apologists have sensibly niched down, focusing their efforts on more discrete topics, arguments, and objections.

I expect this to escalate. We'll see entire websites devoted to one particular argument, such as the *kalam* argument for God's existence, taking a deep dive and meticulously engaging all the relevant points and counterpoints. We'll see podcasts focusing not just on general Catholic apologetics but on very specific sub-issues, such as the historicity of the Resurrection, Thomistic metaphysics, or the philosophy of mind.

A third development I expect is that the Catholic-atheist front will become far more significant online than Catholic-Protestant apologetics. Atheists are disproportionately active on the internet, as any visit to the YouTube comment boxes will confirm. They tend to be more pervasive and aggressive online. Because of this, Catholics of the digital age will have to spend more apologetical energy engaging atheists than engaging Protestants or people of other religions. As apologetical discussions have shifted from print to the internet, so the focus must shift from Protestants to atheists.

Apologists are still getting used to the many new tools now available to them thanks to the internet. Of course, these tools can be and have been abused. But on the whole, apologists should welcome them as gifts from God in service of the great task of defending and explaining the faith.

8

New Epiphanies of Beauty
Michael Stevens

*Late have I loved Thee, O Beauty so ancient and so new; late have I loved Thee!
For behold Thou wert within me, and I outside; and I sought Thee outside and
in my unloveliness fell upon those lovely things that Thou hast made. Thou wert
with me and I was not with Thee. I was kept from Thee by those things, yet had
they not been in Thee, they would not have been at all. Thou didst call and cry
to me and break open my deafness: and Thou didst send forth Thy beams and
shine upon me and chase away my blindness.*[1]
—*St. Augustine,* Confessions

As an artist striving to evangelize through beauty, this famous passage from
St. Augustine's *Confessions* has always struck me as especially relevant to my
daily work. Not only is it one of the most moving reflections on beauty ever
penned, but it also shows how central a role beauty can play within the context of conversion. In these words, St. Augustine masterfully captures how the
wonders of the created world have a charged, directional momentum—they
lead us *toward,* leaving us wanting more, and still more. They provoke in the
human heart a thirst for beauty that will remain unquenched until it possess-
es Beauty itself, the very source from which all lesser beauties flow.

This restless, inescapable hunger for *more* drove not only Augustine to
Christ, but many other great lovers of beauty as well. For the elderly

---

1. Augustine, *Confessions* 10.27, trans. F.J. Sheed, ed. Michael P. Foley (Park Ridge, IL: Word on Fire Classics, 2017), 258.

Michelangelo, this hunger was expressed in his poetry, as he realized that neither painting nor sculpting could ultimately calm his yearning for God. For C.S. Lewis, it was his agonizing quest for what he called "Joy"—a homesick longing for the vast, ancient landscapes of Norse mythology, for which he had no satisfying explanation until after his conversion. Through such testimonies, St. Augustine's witness to beauty's attractive power continues to resonate through time.

Appreciating how the pang of the beautiful can prod the soul so powerfully, many Catholics today have taken a renewed interest in the role aesthetic experience can play in evangelization and apologetics. A new phrase has even emerged to characterize this evangelical approach: "Leading with beauty." The revival of this strategy at this moment in history is no coincidence: beauty responds uniquely to the challenges of our divided and hyper-secularized world. Unlike rational argument, which is often met with either knee-jerk defensiveness or relativistic apathy in today's ideological arena, the beautiful is less confrontational in its persuasive power. However, once it has taken hold in an alert mind, the beautiful can begin to raise questions of a distinctly religio-philosophical kind—questions that the Church's intellectual and spiritual tradition are ideally equipped to answer.

It is important to note that within this beauty-led framework, apologetics, philosophy, and theology still play as strong a role as ever. The difference is that in this model, they lend their resources to a process already set in motion. What results is a truly comprehensive evangelical effort: one where devout painters, composers, graphic designers, poets, and architects stand shoulder-to-shoulder with clergy and lay apologists. To use an idiom borrowed from liturgical music, leading with beauty "pulls out all the stops," drawing from the full wealth of the Church's offerings. It presents a view of the faith that captures its panoramic and kaleidoscopic riches.

Because my work as a graphic designer and artist is so fundamentally oriented toward the beautiful, I have been excited to see this rekindled appreciation for its power. At the same time, this renewed emphasis on leading with beauty implies that we must acknowledge that a certain amount of ugliness has accrued in the meantime. What springs to mind, in particular, is the sappy, sentimentalized religious art that seems to be so common in our devotional spaces, more incidentally than deliberately. The accumulation of such mediocrity can disastrously undermine the Church's efforts to lead with beauty. In the first half of the twentieth century, it took the form of cheaply produced holy cards with soft, rosy-cheeked illustrations of Christ. In the second half, it became crafty felt banners adorned with Picasso-styled grapes and chalices, and generic, quasi-modernist sheaves of wheat set in stained glass. While they were intended to reach a wide audience, today they seem to reach no one, possessing neither a connectedness to the tradition, nor a relevant modernity. Furthermore, their bland sentimentality simply fails to do justice to the solemn mysteries of our faith.

As a solution to the problem of sentimental devotional art, the first impulse might be to focus our efforts exclusively on re-presenting the art of previous centuries. As someone who *lives* for the Church's great tradition of sacred art, I understand the temptation to focus all of our attention on the great things we have already made. Whether in the quiet mysticism of a Rublev icon or the grand scale of a Michelangelo fresco, the art of the past often seems to possess a quality and depth that much recently made religious art lacks. But to *exclusively* revive, restore, and refurbish ignores the fact that the Church has always had a special interest in commissioning *new* art. Relying completely on our past output in every situation would also seem to deny artists today their God-given instinct to, as Pope St. John Paul II put in his Letter to Artists, "search for new epiphanies of beauty."[2] Old things are beautiful, to be sure, but so are new things. Both the broad, knotted oak and the fragile, dew-dropped sprout inspire their own sense of delight and awe. The best art is able to capture both of these conditions together—existing in a realm of aesthetic evergreen. I believe this is what St. Augustine meant when he described God's beauty as "so ancient and so new."

---

2. John Paul II, "Letter of His Holiness Pope John Paul II to Artists," 1999, Vatican.va.

If the task of leading with beauty in the future will involve the integration of both art and apologetics, the ancient *and* the new, how might we all support the effort? In particular, how might we do our part to foster the creation of new works of beauty? Below are a few suggested starting points for any Catholic.

Explore the Church's Vast Creative Output Across the Centuries

As a foundation for understanding the many different ways beauty can be a part of the Church's life, I would recommend beginning by exploring the sacred art of the past. Tremendous resources and tools are available to this end. Check out a book from your local library on the art of the Italian Renaissance or the Gothic cathedrals of Europe. Take a family field trip to the medieval wing of a nearby art museum. Visit a beautiful church in your area and spend a half-hour taking in the architecture in silence. As you explore, remember one thing: these treasures were never intended to be viewed as museum artifacts. They were made expressly to aid in the liturgical and devotional life of the Church—both for the people who lived at the time of their creation, and for you and me *here and now*.

Venture into the Modern Galleries of the Art Museum

Modern and contemporary art has a reputation for being shocking and bizarre, and many Catholics (and Christians in general) seem to simply avoid it altogether. While I understand how problematic some contemporary art can be, there is a surprisingly wide variety of art being made now, and much of it is fascinating and beautiful. I would especially urge my fellow practicing artists and designers to spend a lot of time with modern and contemporary art. If we are to make beautiful art here and now that engages our broader culture, then we must understand the art it already values and its stylistic underpinnings.

Support Catholic Artists and Graphic Designers, and Seek Their Expertise

Lastly, I would urge everyone reading this to support sacred artists and Catholic graphic designers as they live their vocation of bringing beauty to the Church and the world. This could be as simple as following a handful of Catholic artists and designers on Instagram and showing your support in the comments, or as involved as commissioning a custom piece of artwork. If you are creating a book, website, or any other form of media for public consumption, collaborate with a graphic designer. This will help to ensure that the beautiful content of the faith is given appropriate visual form.

It's exciting to imagine how the Church's tradition of beauty in the visual arts might develop in the coming decades and centuries. My great hope is that by incorporating beauty as a central feature of our evangelical efforts, a new alliance between art and apologetics will be formed, and many souls will be led to Christ. Even now, he cries out to break through the deafness of the world and to chase away its blindness with his rays of divine light.

9

Sowing "Seeds of the Word"

Andrew Petiprin

In Bishop Robert Barron's preface to his essay collection *Seeds of the Word: Finding God in the Culture*, he recounts a conversation with his mentor Msgr. Robert Sokolowski, who explained that "the integrated icon of Christian doctrine . . . exploded at the time of the Reformation and the Enlightenment."[1] The modern evangelist is therefore always on the hunt "to find bits and pieces of it everywhere."[2] Mainstream culture, mostly detached from the Church, has been a ground littered with artifacts that are useful for sharing the Gospel, precisely because the Gospel is in them, perhaps unbeknownst to the person who put them there.

But less than a decade after Bishop Barron published his collection of cultural commentaries and reviews—the sort of thing that brought people like me into his orbit via YouTube—things have drastically changed. With the explosion of social media and streaming, the amount of ground which the evangelist must cover has grown exponentially. We are still thinking in terms of "culture" instead of "cultures," and we therefore fail to spread out wide enough or dive deep enough to speak to people's priorities and interests. A new understanding and a new strategy are called for.

Modernity created real problems for religious unity, but World War II provided a glorious last gasp in which religious participation was at an all-time high, and culture-friendly religion was given a place of honor within the

---

1. Robert Barron, *Seeds of the Word: Finding God in the Culture* (Des Plaines, IL: Word on Fire, 2017), x.
2. Barron, x.

culture itself. Billy Graham and Fulton Sheen were household names, along-side Frank Sinatra and Doris Day. Whereas there were once many "folk cultures"—which gave way in the nineteenth century to "mass culture," primarily associated with the lower classes—the twentieth century saw the rise and fall of a "media culture," a truly "popular culture" that cut across almost all socioeconomic lines. This new kind of culture placed the television at the center, and "pop" culture became its abbreviated name with the onset of "pop" music in the 1950s. Still, the Christian evangelist had a place in the entertainment lineup; and there was strong social pressure on respectable people to conform to superficial religious norms as a defense against the godless Communists behind the Iron Curtain. Ross Douthat calls this era "a kind of Indian summer of orthodox belief," now gone.[3] For a few decades, "spectacle and piety went hand in hand in postwar Hollywood."[4]

In this rare climate in the United States, both the opportunity and the challenge described by the ancient Christian apologist Justin Martyr were apparent. Justin said of people in his own second-century context, "So it seems that there were indeed seeds of truth in all men, but they are proved not to have understood them properly since they contradict each other."[5] For a long time in modern America, we took for granted that we would have relatively full churches and that people would pay respectful attention to a duly appointed religious leader sharing basic Christian teachings in a public forum. But the internal contradictions about which Justin worried, as well as a tidal wave of decadence made possible by continual leaps in technological innovation and changing mores, made a "seeds of the Word" strategy for winning souls far more difficult. Today, not only are our churches not full, but no one watches the same shows or movies or is held captive to Christian preaching or any other morally edifying content on a limited number of television channels. There are as many entertainment options as there are

---

3. Ross Douthat, *Bad Religion: How We Became a Nation of Heretics* (New York: Free Press, 2012), 21.

4. Douthat, 22.

5. Justin Martyr, *First Apology* 44, ed. and trans. Edward Rochie Hardy, in *Early Christian Fathers*, ed. Cyril Richardson (New York: Touchstone, 1996), 270.

individuals to consume them. Just compare a sample of a few finales of popular television shows.

In 1983, *M*A*S*H* went off the air with 125 million Americans, or 53.5% of the population, watching. In 1998, *Seinfeld* signed off forever with 76.3 million people watching, or 27.7% of the American people.[6] The audience across all platforms for the finale of HBO's *Game of Thrones* in 2019 was 19.3 million,[7] a jump up from the finale of *The Sopranos,* which had 11.9 million viewers on the threshold of the streaming era in 2007.[8] The big picture is that even the most wildly popular things today are far less popular than the most-watched media offerings of an earlier age. The few extremely popular things that appeal to most demographics today—like the films of the Marvel Cinematic Universe—may still be useful conduits to aspects of the Gospel, but their application may be limited. We can only make the Superhero-Christ analogy so many times.

In a way, we find ourselves now in a position more like where we were a hundred years ago, before mass media. The consensus shared by the Greatest Generation and their supposedly rebellious successors, the Baby Boomers, has disappeared, even though the latter group still make up the lion's share of churchgoers and clergy. We have suddenly rediscovered the abyss of secular atomization that has been beneath our feet for some time, and the tightrope we must use to walk across it appears impossibly thin. And yet, the Great Commission has not been rescinded, nor has Christ broken his promise that the gates of hell will not prevail against the Church. As T.S. Eliot said in a prescient way in March 1939, *before* the post–World War II mass media consensus emerged, "The fact that a problem will certainly take a long time to

---

6. M. Carter, "10 Highest Rated Series Finales of All Time," *ScreenRant*, December 10, 2015, https://screenrant.com/highest-rated-series-finales-all-time-tv/.

7. Toni Fitzgerald, "'Game of Thrones' Finale by the Numbers: All the Show's Ratings Records," *Forbes*, May 20, 2019, https://www.forbes.com/sites/tonifitzgerald/2019/05/20/game-of-thrones-finale-by-the-numbers-all-the-shows-ratings-records/.

8. "'The Sopranos' Ratings: Only 11.9 Million?," The Vulture, *New York*, June 12, 2007, https://www.vulture.com/2007/06/the_sopranos_ratings_only_119.html.

solve, and that it will demand the attention of many minds for several generations, is no justification for postponing the study."[9]

So, how do we proceed?

We must finally move completely out of the shadow of our preoccupation with the twentieth century's cultural cohesion, and the evangelistic strategy that accompanies it. Even if, following Eliot, we imagine a singular Christian culture in the distant future, our lived reality is that there are now many cultures, all of which need a Christian presence within them for the sake of transformation for the life of the world. In 2013, the Canadian Catholic novelist Randy Boyagoda threw down the gauntlet with his seminal essay "Faith in Fiction," in which he argued that Catholic thinkers are too wedded to the likes of Flannery O'Connor and J.R.R. Tolkien:

> These writers brilliantly and movingly attest to literature's place in modern life, as godless modernity's last best crucible for sustaining an appreciation of human life's value and purpose that corresponds to our inherent longing for the good, the true, and the beautiful. But what else do they have in common? They're all dead.[10]

We do not give up our old favorites, but we must also read, watch, listen to, and ultimately appreciate and promote more artists and works, both old and new. And we need not worry that fewer people will receive the seeds of the Word we discover in less obvious places. In a sense, we can divide and conquer, filling the myriad small spaces that do exist rather than pretending we can re-create the large ones of the past. We must face the fact that if the secular world uses terms like "communities" and "cultures" (e.g., cycling community or coffee-roasting culture), we need to take these self-definitions seriously. We might even think of these groups as a return to a "folk culture" diaspora, but in a postmodern idiom. Whereas these groups may embrace a

---

9. T.S. Eliot, *Christianity and Culture* (New York: Harcourt, 1968), 5.

10. Randy Boyagoda, "Faith in Fiction," *First Things*, August 2013, https://www.firstthings.com/article/2013/08/faith-in-fiction.

"Live and let live" and "You do you" philosophy, we mean to proclaim the Lordship of Christ amid the infinite expanse of preferences, drawing boundaries only around morally impossible circumstances like sexual immorality or extreme violence. Our work is to build up substantial, enduring things around the void, rather than bothering to knock down the many weak and temporary ones already in place. To break my own rule and borrow yet again from a twentieth-century master, C.S. Lewis' challenge to educators is even more pertinent for today's evangelists: our task is "not to cut down jungles but to irrigate deserts."[11]

Finally, we must take seriously the call to reform and beautify our own Christian culture(s) to offer a refuge from exhausted cultural seekers and to infect and transform the other cultures, which we have taken pains to know and love first.

The marketing labels "Christian" or "Catholic" simply will not cut it. Nor should we imagine that a throwback or pastiche of an older aesthetic will be appealing, although re-invigorating traditional forms may be essential. A small number of faithful, creative thinkers may be enough to get the ball rolling, since the cultures around us—although wrongheaded and fragmented—maintain an innate longing for truth and unity. As R.R. Reno concludes in his own updated variation on T.S. Eliot's theme, "America is full of people who sense the poverty of our postmodern paganism"; therefore, "a relatively small number of Christians can inspire and reinvigorate the public imaginations of the disoriented majority."[12]

Although we must think of our problems and opportunities differently than in previous generations, the same underlying reality obtains. There are seeds of the Word out there. The hunt continues until the Lord returns.

---

11. C.S. Lewis, *The Abolition of Man* (New York: HarperOne, 1944), 13–14.
12. R.R. Reno, *Resurrecting the Idea of a Christian Society* (Washington, DC: Regnery Faith, 2016), 7.

10

The Heart of Affirmative Orthodoxy
John L. Allen Jr.

When Cardinal Joseph Ratzinger was elected as the new leader of the Catholic Church in April 2005 following the death of St. John Paul II, taking the name "Pope Benedict XVI," he was hardly an unknown. For almost a quarter century he'd been the Vatican's doctrinal czar, right in the middle of every major Catholic controversy of the time—from birth control and women's ordination to liberation theology and religious pluralism—and usually it was his job to draw lines in the sand. A bit like a Dean of Men at a boys' high school, only on a much bigger scale, it's not really a prescription for popularity. Thus, in the popular mind, Ratzinger was the great "Doctor No" of the Catholic Church, the draconian authority figure who meted out punishment on those who crossed lines.

To switch terms of comparison from James Bond to Star Wars, Ratzinger was like Darth Vader in a cassock, and you could almost hear the "Imperial Death March" echoing in people's heads when Ratzinger walked into a room.

Imagine the tremors set off around the world, then, when word began to make the rounds in 2005 that this new pope, in his first encyclical letter, planned to treat—of all topics—sex. Many people anticipated an angry screed, along with threats of hellfire unless people changed their ways. Yet what we got instead was *Deus Caritas Est*, dated Christmas Day 2005, which turned out to be a soaring, almost poetic papal tribute to love, including styling human erotic love as an icon of the love among the persons of the divine Trinity.

It was positive, uplifting, encouraging, and anything but an exercise in papal finger-wagging. Asked later to explain the approach in a 2006 interview with the German section of Vatican Radio, Benedict laid out the essence of what's come to be called "affirmative orthodoxy":

> Christianity, Catholicism, isn't a collection of prohibitions. It's a positive option. It's very important that we look at it again, because this idea has almost completely disappeared today. We've heard so much about what is not allowed that now it's time to say: We have a positive idea to offer. . . . [Everything] is clearer if you say it first in a positive way.[1]

To put the point differently, the heart of affirmative orthodoxy is to place the focus not on that to which the Church says no, but rather on the much deeper and more satisfying yes to full human flourishing that underlies those specific nos.

In describing affirmative orthodoxy, it's important to give equal weight to both terms. It's "orthodox" in the sense that it implies a full-bodied commitment to traditional Catholic identity, expressed in doctrine, worship, and practice. It's not a watered-down, fudged, or compromised version of Catholicism, but the real deal.

Yet it's also "affirmative," in that the idea is not to be constantly condemning anything less than that full-bodied Catholic lifestyle, always on the prowl for enemies of the faith from within and without. It's not naïve about the manifold challenges in today's world, but it understands that judgment and excoriation are rarely persuasive evangelical tools. It begins with the premise that if someone sees the beauty and the passion of Christian living, only then will the rules of the game, so to speak, make sense.

Benedict led a teaching pontificate, fitting for one of the finest theological minds in twentieth-century Catholicism, and one could argue that affirmative orthodoxy was the heart of his message. It represents a sort of potential

---

1. John L. Allen Jr., "The Real Ratzinger Revealed," *The Tablet: The International Catholic News Weekly* 14 (April 2007), 6–7.

Copernican Revolution, if not in the content of the Christian message, at least in how it's presented to the world.

Alas, Benedict was not always well served by the administrative and bureaucratic apparatus around him, which repeatedly generated scandals, embarrassments, and meltdowns which obscured, and often overshadowed, what Benedict was trying to get across.

But if we step back from such passing episodes and try to put things in historical context, affirmative orthodoxy appears as the maturation of an impulse in Catholic life that might best be described as a reaction to secularism. When pillars of traditional Catholic identity—for example, participation in the Church's worship, the prestige of vocations to the priesthood and religious life, or adherence to basic Catholic norms on marriage—are no longer encouraged and reinforced by the surrounding culture, but in some ways actively discouraged, the Church needs some strategy to shore up those pillars in another way.

The Second Vatican Council in the mid-1960s was, in a sense, the last great crescendo of a reasonably intact Catholic culture, one in which most of the bishops and theologians who shaped the council were products of such a culture at its best—confident, optimistic, eager to open up to the world, taking the fundamentals of Catholic identity for granted as a point of departure.

The election of St. John Paul II in 1978 marked the beginning of a new realization that such an assumption was no longer warranted, and that in a postmodern secular milieu, the Church had to be intentional about defending its identity. For much of the late 1970s, 80s, and 90s, that defense was often expressed in a series of historic nos: to rethinking St. Paul VI's ban on contraception, to women priests, to unlimited theological dissent, to politicizing the faith in liberation struggles, to relativizing the salvation won by Christ in a bid to reach détente with other religions.

However necessary, those episodes forged an impression that Catholicism is primarily about saying no, and few people realized that better than

Cardinal Joseph Ratzinger, the future Pope Benedict XVI and the intellectual architect of the defense of Catholic identity under John Paul.

Thus, the election of Benedict XVI in 2005 marked the ratification and consolidation of the "orthodox" element of the formula, but also the great shift to the "affirmative." Much of Benedict's teaching over the next eight years—including his remarkable triptych of speeches on the relationships among faith, reason, and secularity at the Collège des Bernardins in Paris in 2008, Westminster Hall in London in 2010, and the Bundestag in Germany in 2011—would be about laying the foundations for an affirmative thrust in presenting and defending orthodoxy.

With the transition to Pope Francis in 2013, other issues and challenges emerged, and the Church once again appears to be passing through a period in which some aspects of Catholic identity are being reexamined and, to an extent, renegotiated.

Yet no matter where Catholicism stands when the dust settles, its perennial task of offering the good news of the Gospel will remain. Part of that effort implies marking boundaries between choices and beliefs that are genuinely Christian and those that aren't. The question is where one begins and puts the accent, and the heart of affirmative orthodoxy is to choose the positive, on the conviction that the world will never understand, let alone accept, the Church's nos if it doesn't first hear its far more sweeping yes.

Perhaps the zone of Catholic life where all this will be worked out first is by, and among, the Church's evangelists, because that may well be where the need for affirmative orthodoxy is most pressing.

In his book *Civilization on Trial*, famed historian Arnold J. Toynbee wrote:

> The things that make good headlines attract our attention because they are on the surface of the stream of life, and they distract our attention from the slower, impalpable, imponderable movements that work below the surface and penetrate to the depths. But of course it is really these deeper, slower movements that, in the end, make history, and it is they that stand out huge

in retrospect, when the sensational passing events have dwindled, in perspective, to their true proportions.[2]

Affirmative orthodoxy seems a good candidate to be one of those "deeper, slower movements," a thrust that endures well after the specific circumstances that gave rise to it fade away. And, if that is the case, Catholicism will probably have its evangelists to thank.

---

2. Arnold J. Toynbee, *Civilization on Trial* (London: Oxford University Press, 1946), 213.

11

Truth, Meaning, and the Christian Imagination

Holly Ordway

The idea of an *imaginative* approach to apologetics can seem counterintuitive. But just as "apologetics" does not mean "apologizing for" the faith (quite the opposite), "imaginative apologetics" does not mean basing our Christian witness on things that are imaginary. What, then, does it mean?

Let us start by consulting the *Oxford English Dictionary* (always a worthwhile endeavor). Here we find that "imaginary" and "imaginative"—though often conflated in common usage—have different etymologies. *Imaginary* comes from the Latin *imāginārius*: "a mere semblance, unreal, pretended." *Imaginative* derives from the Latin verb *imāgināre*: "to form a mental image of something."[1] Here we see an essential distinction. To *imagine* something is to conceive in one's mind a mental image of it. The image may be of something real, or something unreal (imaginary); in either case, it is the work of the imagination to form that image in the mind. The stronger the imagination is, and the more material that it has to work with, the more vivid the resulting image will be.

The work of *imaginative apologetics*, then, can be described as helping people to form meaningful and correct images in their minds of the truths of the Christian faith. As such, it supports the use of rational arguments and the work of catechesis, because people will be much more interested in

---

1. "Imaginary," adj. and n., last modified September 2021, and "Imaginative," adj. and n., last modified June 2021, *The Oxford English Dictionary*, oed.com.

understanding whether something is true, or why it matters in their life, if they have a robustly meaningful image of that concept. Indeed, without an imaginative grasp of these ideas, it is unlikely that a person will be interested in, let alone convinced by, even the best rational arguments for the truth of the faith.

What makes imaginative apologetics *new* is the extent to which it is needed, and the basic quality of the concepts that require an imaginative presentation. With the steep decline in both general religious literacy and practice in the West, it has become increasingly the case that we cannot take for granted a common basis of meaning for Christian concepts. Even visual literacy has declined precipitously; stained glass windows, statues, and paintings that for centuries served as a visual catechism for the illiterate are now incomprehensible to people with far more education than the original audience.

Evangelists and apologists today cannot count on people having already formed robust or even minimally accurate images related to what we believe. The result is what I have called the "meaning gap."[2] When we evangelize, terms that *we* use such as "salvation," "grace," "sin," and so on are often mere jargon-words for our interlocutors.

When a word is empty of meaning for someone, it is seldom the case that nothing whatsoever comes to mind related to that word. Rather, the concept is vague, abstract, unrelated to anything else; it lacks significance and certainly does not impel the person to investigation or action. We must find a concept meaningful before we will care whether or not it is true.

The function of the imagination is to produce meaningful images; it does this work by assembling a picture from a combination of sensory data, abstract information, memories, and associations. The depth of meaning of the image depends both on the strength of the imagination as a faculty, and the amount and quality of the materials supplied to it. In this way, the imagination could produce a strong mental image of things that are *imaginary* (that is, unreal), or, conversely, produce a weak mental image of real things. For

---

2. See Holly Ordway, *Apologetics and the Christian Imagination: An Integrated Approach to Defending the Faith* (Steubenville, OH: Emmaus Road, 2017).

instance, I have a vivid mental image of a pegasus, because my imagination can draw on images of horses and eagles from personal experience, as well as images of winged horses from books and art. In fact, my idea of a pegasus is considerably more robust than, say, my idea of an aardvark. I know intellectually that an aardvark is a real creature, but insofar as I have a mental image of it, it's a confused mix of anteaters and armadillos.

The more meaningful an image is, the more it is able to involve the emotions, engage the intellect, and stir up the will. My image of a pegasus is associated with stories of high adventure and excitement; if I see a mention of it, it will catch my interest. In contrast, my image of an aardvark is thin and weak, with correspondingly little impact on my will. If I were visiting the zoo and saw the sign "Aardvark exhibit this way," I might look at it on the way to another exhibit I was interested in (such as the tigers) but I wouldn't make a special point to visit it. In this way, the strength or weakness of meaning for an idea affects our will: it provides more, or less, motivation to act in certain ways.

I have deliberately used nonreligious examples thus far in order to make two points. First, the imagination's work of meaning-making is always operating, whatever the concept may be and whether or not it has adequate or inadequate materials upon which to work. Second, we are often not consciously aware of this process, and therefore make judgments about ideas being true or false, important or irrelevant, with only a weak or flawed sense of the meaning of the idea. Such is the condition of many Christians and most "nones" and fallen-away believers in the present culture with regard to the content of the Christian faith.

Consider the word "sin": in general usage, it has become a word for self-indulgence with at best a slightly naughty flavor, like having a second slice of cake. This doesn't mean that people are amoral: indeed, many non-Christians do believe that certain things are deeply wrong, and have an entirely correct horror of what we would call the sins of racism or greed or sexual exploitation—but this meaning is not attached to the word "sin," and it lacks its spiritual dimensions as well. Therefore, when Christians talk about "the forgiveness of sins" and so on, this vital and living truth is not received, because the words are empty of real meaning.

This meaning gap has profound implications for our apologetics and evangelization. As Michael Ward explains, unless the words we use carry real meaning for our audience, our Christian terms "will just be counters in an intellectual game, leaving most readers cold. Likewise, apologetic arguments for the authority of the 'Church' or 'the Bible' or 'experience' or 'reason' itself, must all be imaginatively realized before they can begin to make traction on the reader's reason, let alone on the reader's will."[3] Too much of what passes for apologetics today is indeed nothing more than the playing of intellectual games: scoring points, posturing, without substance. We must do better: we must help people to *imaginatively realize* the meaning of the words we use, so that they can discover the reality to which those words point.

Fortunately for our work, the imagination is a basic human faculty, and it is highly responsive when the proper nourishment and stimulation are provided. Consider the aardvark once again. As I have written this piece, the image I have in mind remains somewhat unclear (for the sake of my own point, I refrained from looking it up online), but my own reflection about it has made me curious—it has, in short, invested "aardvark" with additional meaning. Now, I *will* look up pictures of aardvarks online and read about them; and when I'm next at the zoo, I will be inclined to pay a particular visit to its exhibit—because "aardvark" now has a significance it formerly lacked. This meaning is, of course, entirely idiosyncratic in this case, but it is real, and conducive to further meaning-making. What happened in this instance can happen for any concept, at much higher levels of significance.

We must embrace the challenge of helping people to generate robust, accurate, full meanings for every aspect of the faith—a task that will benefit believers and skeptics alike. Those who serve as apologists, catechists,

---

3. Michael Ward, "The Good Serves the Better and Both the Best: C.S. Lewis on Imagination and Reason in Apologetics," in *Imaginative Apologetics: Theology, Philosophy, and the Catholic Tradition*, ed. Andrew Davison (Grand Rapids, MI: Baker Academic, 2011), 72.

preachers, and teachers should recognize that the words they use, *especially* if they are familiar, need to be invested with fresh meaning for their audiences.

And every Christian should cultivate a healthy, strong faculty of the imagination, and nourish it with materials that partake of truth, goodness, and beauty. In this way, we will have a solid grasp of the meaning of our own faith, and thus be better able to share it, in word and witness.

PART III

NEW MODELS

12

Socrates

Trent Horn

If you listen to the radio program *Catholic Answers Live*, then you've probably heard me or one of my colleagues answer questions about the faith from not just Catholic callers, but also non-Catholics and even non-Christians who listen to our show. In fact, my favorite programs are the ones where Catholics aren't even allowed to call in. These shows have titles like "Why are you an atheist?"; "Why are you pro-choice?"; and "Why are you Protestant?"

I like these shows because they give me an opportunity to model one of the most effective methods of defending the faith. In these interactions, I focus not so much on peppering the caller with facts and Scripture citations (though I do include them when appropriate) but on asking the caller questions. I want this person to rethink his argument against Catholicism or even his entire non-Catholic worldview.

In doing this I am modeling a *Socratic approach* to conversations about the faith.

Socrates lived about five hundred years before Christ was born and, according to legend, his friend Chaerephon visited a mystic named the Delphic Oracle and asked her, "Is anyone wiser than [Socrates]?" She answered, "There is not one wiser."[1] But this confused Socrates, because he believed that he had no special knowledge that made him wiser than other people.

So, he tried to prove the oracle wrong by finding other people who were

---

1. Plato, *Apology* 20e–21a, trans. Henry Cary, in *Plato's Apology, Crito, and Phaedo of Socrates* (Philadelphia: David McKay, 1897), 18.

wiser than he was. But unfortunately, when Socrates asked these "wise people" questions about their beliefs, he discovered that they were not wise at all. These "sophists" were good at *sounding* wise, but the actual content of their proposals didn't make logical sense.

And that's when Socrates had his epiphany. His pupil Plato recorded him as saying this: "I am wiser than this man, for neither of us appears to know anything great and good; but he fancies he knows something. . . . I appear to be wiser than he, because I do not fancy I know what I do not know."[2]

Instead of saying, "I'm right, you're wrong, and here's why," Socrates employed a more powerful method of asking his opponent questions and letting the poor guy hang himself with his own words. Now, we shouldn't use this method to merely embarrass someone in a conversation. But we should use it to help them escape the fog of their own incorrect belief system. That's because we might tell this person a hundred times, "That doesn't make sense," and it wouldn't have the same impact as his own subconscious asking him, "Does this actually make sense?"

This approach also has the benefit of being easier than always trying to come up with the perfect answer or argument in a discussion. The Christian apologist Greg Koukl says that asking questions is "a virtually effortless way of putting you in the driver's seat of the conversation."[3] If you're not sure what to say in a conversation about the faith, you can always fall back on two questions: "What do you think?" and "Why do you think that?"

Too often, we just assume that we know what other people think, and we don't bother to ask them what they actually believe. Also, sometimes we let people's beliefs go unchallenged and only defend what we believe. That's why another good question to ask along the lines of "Why do you think that?" is "How do you know that's true?"

When the subject of atheism comes up, for example, you might feel nervous that you can't perfectly articulate a proof for God's existence. Then don't. Instead, you could ask your atheist friend questions like:

---

2. Plato, *Apology* 21d, p. 19.
3. Greg Koukl, *Tactics* (Chicago: Zondervan, 2009), 56.

1. What do you mean when you say you are an atheist?
   a. Do you think there's no God or do you think God might exist but there's no good reason to think he exists?
      i. If you say there are no good reasons to believe God exists, then how do you know that's true?
         1. What's the best (or least bad) argument for God's existence and what's wrong with it?
            a. If you can't think of any, then how do you know they don't prove God exists?

Notice in this exchange you don't have to have a proof for God memorized (though it's certainly helpful if you do). You're just challenging your atheist friend's assertion about the evidence for God and gently insisting he shoulder the burden of proof by defending what he believes (even if he says he merely "lacks belief" in God).

So, we need to focus more on asking questions than giving answers, but we also can't forget to *listen* to what the other person tells us. Too often, we ask a question and then spend our time thinking about what we want to say next instead of actually comprehending what the other person is saying. In fact, sometimes merely restating what another person has told us, but in a more straightforward way, can help them reconsider their worldview.

For example, during a presentation on abortion to high school students, a young woman named Kelsey consistently gave me the "evil eye." After my talk, she raised her hand and, instead of asking a question, she made this triumphal statement: "Look, I don't see what the big deal is. I don't like abortion, but I don't go around forcing my views on other people like you do." The other students waited for my reply. Instead of giving a lengthy rebuttal, I asked her a simple question: "Kelsey, why don't you like abortion?"

Everyone fell silent as Kelsey struggled to answer the question. She finally said, "Well, I know it kills babies and all that. But what about women who will die or be stuck in poverty and can't feed their children? I don't like it, but I can't take away someone else's choice."

I replied, "Kelsey, is this your position: You don't like abortion because it kills babies, and yet you think it should be legal for other people to kill those babies? Did I understand you correctly?"

Kelsey's face grew red. "Well, it sounds terrible when you put it that way."

"But Kelsey," I said, "I didn't put it that way—you did. I'm just trying to understand where you're coming from."

Now, remember that when it comes to finding the truth, it's a journey, not a race. It's okay to take time to gather all the facts and arguments and then make an informed decision about what we should believe. If someone asks *you* a question and employs the Socratic method, don't bluff your way through an answer you don't know. You can say, "That's a really good question and I want to get you a really good answer from people who've thought about it more than I have. What's a good way to send you that answer?"

Finally, a lot of people ask me, "How do you keep your composure when you talk about these tough issues with strangers?" I always give them the same answer. Prayer and practice. Prayer because at the end of the day it is the Holy Spirit that gives us the right answers to people's questions. In Mark 13:11, Jesus tells those who will be prosecuted, "Do not worry beforehand about what you are to say; but say whatever is given you at that time, for it is not you who speak, but the Holy Spirit."

Even without study, you can ask questions, listen, and pray. If you practice these three—well, let's make it four—essential skills, then I think God will say to you what the master says in Jesus' parable in Matthew 25: "Well done, good and faithful servant. . . . Enter into the joy of your master" (RSV-CE).

13

St. Augustine

Matthew Levering

To discuss the ways in which Augustine of Hippo contributes to evangelization would require multiple books! In this short essay, I will focus solely on the evangelistic insights of Augustine's three greatest books: *Confessions, City of God,* and *The Trinity.* I will argue that each book offers a crucial evangelistic contribution. Put simply, Augustine's contributions to evangelization today are threefold: (1) he demonstrates that God is infinitely good and that human happiness can only be found in relationship with God (*Confessions*); (2) he explains how the fact of the ongoing history of sin and suffering accords with the fact that Christ reigns even now (*City of God*); and (3) he shows that the Trinity answers our deepest yearnings (*The Trinity*).

Let me begin with Augustine's *Confessions.* In the early chapters, he sets up the key evangelistic tensions. The first is the disquiet he feels within himself. Why does he get pleasure from doing wicked things with his friends, such as knocking down a neighbor's pears for no reason? Second, there is the depth of agony he experiences when a beloved friend dies. Could it be that his friend has been annihilated by death, so that all the communion that he and his friend shared is eternally gone? Third, there is the problem of God and evil. He imagines God to be a tremendously big entity, but still finite. Since he knows that there is evil, he assumes that "God" cannot be present where evil is, and so he concludes that God is limited. Fourth, he reads Scripture but finds himself offended by what he views as silly stories about polygamous patriarchs and a violent God who commands his people to kill all the people in a conquered city. Fifth, there are his ambiguous life experiences: he is caught up in a career based upon lying and flattering; he has a mistress and loves using her for sex; and he inclines first toward dualistic Manicheanism and then toward the truth-rejecting philosophy known as Academic skepticism.

I can here only briefly indicate how Augustine addresses these five problems, which remain urgent today for evangelization. The key is his discovery of a better way to think about God and evil. Evil is parasitic upon good; evil is a lack or disorder within something that in itself (in its being) is good. There is no evil being. Rather, there is a lack of what should be present, so that the particular being or action is not fully what it should be. Having come to this understanding of evil as a privation, he is able to apprehend that the good God truly is infinite, the absolute plenitude of being. Around the same time, he discovers how to read the Old Testament, aided by the preaching of Ambrose of Milan. He learns to read the Scriptures of Israel in the light of the revelation of divine love in Jesus Christ, and this aids him in discerning the spiritual meanings of troubling passages. Through his newfound love of Scripture, he also discovers the solution to the interior misery that had plagued him. The solution is Christ's humility, which overcomes our pride, restores our relationship to God, and enables us to be transformed so that we can again be what we should be. When we embrace the one Mediator in faith, the grace of his Holy Spirit heals and elevates our will. Even though we are still weak, our relationship to God is restored and we are no longer enslaved to sin and death. We are thereby freed to love our neighbor without the pride, lust, and desire to dominate that otherwise plague our relationships. We begin the process of becoming the people God wills us to be, preparing for an everlasting communion with God.

Augustine the individual is not the center of God's work in Christ. Rather, the center is the Bride of Christ, the Church that will be fully manifest in the consummated new creation when Christ comes in glory. The fundamental problem with human communal life, however, is that it is so filled with sin, suffering, and misery. Put simply, why didn't Christ come to reign over the whole world rather than to die on a Cross? It seems that the last thing the world needs, filled as it is with suffering (especially the suffering of the poor and the dying), is a crucifixion! Moreover, the Roman Empire promised people a good lifestyle, reasonably well protected and well ordered; but the presence of Christianity did not strengthen the empire but instead seemingly weakened it to such a degree that the empire collapsed.

Augustine responds to this evangelistic challenge—Why did Jesus not come as a political ruler to give us security, health, and wealth?—in his *City of God*. He begins by arguing that the promises of Rome, and the worship of its gods, were illusory. Like all empires, the empire was built upon violence and injustice, and these attributes were mirrored by its gods. To the degree that Romans were virtuous, they achieved some good, but their virtue never rose to the level necessary for true justice or enduring peace. Indeed, the pride and ambition that drove Rome could not sustain an enduring city.

While Rome represents the fleeting "city of man" built upon pride and power, the Church is the enduring "city of God"—God's inaugurated kingdom—built upon Christ's humility and self-sacrificial love. Augustine shows that the Bible records the progress of the "city of man" and the "city of God" over the course of history. Time is not cyclical; it has an origin (creation) and a goal (the fullness of the city of God). Due to the fallen condition of humanity, the life of the citizens of God's "city" will inevitably be one of suffering. But there is a purpose to this suffering—namely, humanity seeks enduring peace, life, and happiness, and these things can only be found in an enduring way in a "city" built upon self-sacrificial love, since only in such a city are true communion and true justice possible. The enduring "city," the Church of Christ, is not a city that competes with the earthly city in pride and power; rather, it is a city that instantiates a completely different politics, rooted in dependence upon the humble Lord, who is even now reigning in self-sacrificial love. The final consummation will

bring about the perfection of the city of God in the risen and glorified bodies of the blessed, who will know God as he is, and who will rejoice in the
infinite Triune love.

The third and final evangelistic step taken by Augustine can be seen in his
work *The Trinity*. Here, the challenge is whether communion with the Father,
Son, and Holy Spirit, one God, is actually the fulfillment and perfection of
human life. It might seem that the Trinity has little that would attract us; why
not just stick with the one God? In response, Augustine shows that our
souls—our conscious interiority, our remembering, knowing, and loving—
can be understood as an image of divine "triunity." He then shows that as the
"image of God" (Gen. 1:27), we are perfected when we are remembering
God, knowing God, and loving God. Put simply, he shows that our spirit is
made to be caught up into the glorious reality of the Holy Trinity, in which
the Father speaks his Word and breathes forth Love. Our perfect happiness is
to know and love the God revealed in Christ and his Spirit, because this is the
communion that the human image of God has been created for.

In sum, Augustine offers crucial evangelistic resources for today's questions that arise about sin and death, the existence of God, the problem of evil,
the nature of lasting human happiness, the fact that the coming of Christ and
the Church does not seem to have improved the world much, the contrast
between humble self-sacrificial love and proud self-centered power, and the
meaning of life as consummated by the enjoyment of Trinitarian communion. By means of his insights into these questions, he helps us to make a
strong case for the truth of Christianity.

14

St. Thomas Aquinas
John DeRosa

St. Thomas Aquinas (1225–1274) wrote a prodigious amount. Known for his impressive intellect, he excelled as a student, teacher, preacher, theologian, and philosopher. Aquinas devoted his life to Jesus and the Church and became a canonized saint. Thankfully, he left behind a treasure trove of philosophy and theology that is useful for apologetics.

We can carve up Aquinas' apologetics material into preambles of faith, motives of credibility for faith, and defenses of the articles of faith (fig. 1). Due to the excellence of his method and rigor of his content, Aquinas' corpus remains the most fitting source to consult when engaging in apologetics. What follows is a broad survey of central elements of Aquinas' *method* and *content*.

Figure 1

Category	Description	Examples
Preambles of faith	Truths that are accessible by the natural light of human reason and predispose one to faith.	• God exists • God is one • Human beings have an immaterial intellect
Motives of credibility for faith	Markers of special revelation that confirm and point to its divine source.	• Miracles • Fulfilled prophecies • Holiness and endurance of the Church

Defenses of the articles of faith	Explanations of the coherence and fittingness of Christian doctrine. Taken on divine authority, the articles of faith are not *proven*, but they are *defended*.	• The Trinity does not entail contradictions • Jesus' divinity is compatible with his statement "The Father is greater than I" (John 14:28)

St. Thomas' writings include multivolume works, disputed questions, commentaries, and other pieces.[1] A Thomist of strict observance must display sufficient command of these sources, but the apologist need not read them all. Instead, consult Aquinas on the occasion of researching a topic.

A great place to start is his best-known work, the *Summa theologiae*. Each article of this work has a memorable format. It consists of (1) a specific yes-no question, (2) objections to the answer Aquinas will give, (3) a response from an authority, (4) an overall, principled answer, and (5) replies to the specific objections. Each step matters for our craft.

First, formulating a specific query requires clear thinking. It's easy to bloviate in general about some topic, but it takes a concentrated effort to corral meanderings into a specific question. Second, Aquinas presents objections on behalf of intellectual opponents. Nowadays, we call this "steel-manning," where one sets up strong versions of an interlocutor's arguments, rather than knocking down "straw men" or weak caricatures. Third, each article contains a quote from an authority in favor of the position St. Thomas takes. As Catholics, we should cite Scripture, Tradition, and the Magisterium in support of our conclusions.

Fourth, Aquinas argues clearly for his answer. Similarly, apologists should marshal the best evidence supporting their views. Fifth, St. Thomas answers each objection directly. His replies are terse, content-based, and free of unnecessary polemics. In an age of social media sophistry and combox chaos, the

---

1. His major multivolume works include his *Commentary on the Sentences*, *Summa contra Gentiles*, and *Summa theologiae*. His disputed questions include *De veritate* (*On Truth*), *De potentia* (*On Power*), *De malo* (*On Evil*), and many others. He wrote philosophical commentaries on almost all of the works of Aristotle. His biblical commentaries cover the Gospel of Matthew and the Gospel of John as well as all of St. Paul's letters and some Old Testament works.

temptation looms to hurl insults, grandstand, or utter dismissive, sarcastic remarks. Avoid all of that. Use *concise* replies that address *the substance* of objections. Point out ambiguous terms, false premises, invalid inferences, or other flaws. Lay aside fluff and fury. Aquinas handles many objections in *two* or *three* sentences. Nothing superfluous. If Aquinas were a sports announcer, he's doing play-by-play without the color commentary. Let these five points guide our style. Consult the *Summa* frequently and absorb the best of Aquinas' method.[2]

Having examined elements of Aquinas' *style*, we turn to his *content*. At the beginning of the *Summa contra Gentiles*, St. Thomas reveals his apologetic purpose: "I have set myself the task of making known, as far as my limited powers will allow, the truth that the Catholic faith professes, and of setting aside the errors that are opposed to it."[3]

He accomplishes this purpose by *advancing* positions (i.e., preambles of faith and motives of credibility) as well as *defending* positions (i.e., showing that objections to articles of faith do not succeed). In the present chapter, I focus on the former. With an eye on the preambles of faith, consider three common modern opinions:

> (M1) Human beings are advanced animals that are purely physical.
>
> (M2) There are no good reasons to believe in God.
>
> (M3) God is a person without a body who has many advanced superpowers.

In responding to such ideas, we note that Aquinas held, respectively:

> (A1) Human beings are *rational* animals with an *immaterial* intellectual power.

---

2. For further tips on methodology in crafting arguments, see Bishop Robert Barron, *Arguing Religion: A Bishop Speaks at Facebook and Google* (Park Ridge, IL: Word on Fire, 2018).

3. Thomas Aquinas, *Summa contra Gentiles* 1.2.2, trans. Anton C. Pegis (Notre Dame, IN: University of Notre Dame Press, 1955), 62.

(A2) God's existence can be metaphysically demonstrated.[4]

(A3) God is *pure act* or *ipsum esse subsistens*.[5]

In defending (A1), one can challenge the materialism assumed in (M1). Aquinas offers Aristotelian-inspired arguments in this regard.[6] These involve discussions of matter, form, and knowledge-acquisition, which entail the intellect's immateriality. One new shift in this area involves an argument developed by the Thomistic philosopher James Ross. He deploys philosophical ideas from the twentieth century to show that formal thought cannot be reduced to purely material processes.[7]

Regarding (A2), the apologist should study Aquinas' five ways and other arguments for God's existence.[8] Natural theology, the philosophical subdiscipline concerned with arguments for God's existence, typically proceeds in two stages:

> Stage 1: Arrive at some *ultimate reality* such as an unmoved mover or uncaused cause.
>
> Stage 2: Deduce attributes of this *ultimate reality*.[9]

---

4. The notions of "metaphysical demonstration" or "rational demonstration" or "metaphysical proof" have occasionally come under fire as being inappropriate, grandiose, triumphalist, in-your-face attempts to show that interlocutors who disagree with the proofs are irrational, stupid, or intellectually removed from the field of play. But the terms "metaphysical demonstration," "rational demonstration," and "proof" do not characterize *people* (who may assent to or dissent from the demonstrations), but rather the *kind of argument* under consideration.

5. For example, Aquinas refers to God as *actus purus* (pure actuality) in *Summa theologiae* 1.3.2 and as *ipsum esse subsistens* (subsistent existence itself) in *De ente et essentia* 4.

6. Aquinas defends the immateriality of the intellect in *De anima*, lectio 12, section 377. Edward Feser also explains Aquinas' arguments for the immateriality of the intellect in *Aquinas: A Beginner's Guide* (Oxford: OneWorld, 2009), 151–162.

7. For James Ross' article, see "Immaterial Aspects of Thought," *The Journal of Philosophy* 89, no. 3 (March 1992): 136–150. For a further defense of Ross' argument see Edward Feser, "Kripke, Ross, and the Immaterial Aspects of Thoughts," *American Catholic Philosophical Quarterly* 87, no. 1 (2013): 1–32.

8. Thomas Aquinas elaborates the five ways in *Summa theologiae* 1.2.3. Various arguments for God's existence can be found in Edward Feser, *Five Proofs of the Existence of God* (San Francisco: Ignatius Press, 2017); Peter Kreeft and Ronald Tacelli, *A Handbook of Catholic Apologetics: Reasoned Answers to Questions of Faith* (San Francisco: Ignatius Press, 1994); *The Blackwell Companion to Natural Theology*, ed. William Lane Craig and J.P. Moreland (Hoboken, NJ: Blackwell, 2012), and *Two Dozen (or so) Arguments for God: The Plantinga Project*, ed. Jerry L. Walls and Trent Dougherty (Oxford: Oxford University Press, 2018).

9. Aquinas unpacks various divine attributes in *Summa theologiae* 1.3–26.

That one can argue for God is Catholic teaching,[10] but *which arguments* one can use will vary. Recent trends in natural theology concern different *interpretations* of Aquinas' arguments. For example, Gaven Kerr defends Aquinas' existential reasoning in *On Being and Essence* as foundational for proving God's existence.[11] Other Thomists defend particular versions of the five ways without invoking such existential reasoning.[12] The key: Focus on a *few* arguments, dive *deep* into their defense, and practice presenting them alongside helpful illustrations of key terms and principles.

In (M3) and (A3), we turn to God's nature. Aquinas is a *classical theist*, which means in addition to attributes like omnipotence, omniscience, and omnibenevolence, he holds that God is simple, immutable, eternal, and impassible. God is "pure act," which means he has no passive potency—that is, no aspect of his being needs switching from *off* to *on*. God is also *ipsum esse subsistens* (subsistent existence itself), which refers to the idea that, unlike all other beings, God's essence (*what* he is) is not distinct from his existence (*that* he is—or, *the act* by which he is). Hence, Thomists say God is identical to his existence.[13]

Emphatically, God is not *a being among beings*, but rather the transcendent Creator and sustainer of all other beings. As *classical theists*, we maintain God's utter uniqueness and independence, resisting the temptation to envisage him as a super-creature.[14]

---

10. "Created in God's image and called to know and love him, the person who seeks God discovers certain ways of coming to know him. These are also called proofs for the existence of God, not in the sense of proofs in the natural sciences, but rather in the sense of 'converging and convincing arguments,' which allow us to attain certainty about the truth" (*Catechism of the Catholic Church* 31).

11. Gaven Kerr, *Aquinas's Way to God: The Proof in the De Ente et Essentia* (Oxford: Oxford University Press, 2015).

12. Thomists debate whether a real distinction between essence and existence *in creatures* can be shown philosophically prior to proving God's existence. All Thomists agree there is such a real distinction, but some argue that the real distinction can be used as a *premise* in an argument for God, whereas others think it is only known as a *corollary* after establishing the ultimate and primary Cause (i.e., God). Thomists who think the real distinction can be known prior to showing God's existence include Steven A. Long, Edward Feser, Gaven Kerr, and Fr. John Wippel. Thomists taking a different view include Fr. Joseph Owens, John F.X. Knasas, and Robert A. Delfino.

13. Aquinas discusses this further in *De ente et essentia* 4.

14. For more exposition on how classical theists think about God, see Brian Davies, *An Introduction to the Philosophy of Religion*, 4th ed. (Oxford: Oxford University Press, 2020).

In this arena, many contemporary theists reject *classical theism* by denying God's infinity, simplicity, eternity, or immutability. Following Aquinas, we should maintain a classical view of God and respond to objections from those who reject it.[15]

Finally, we turn briefly to modern takes on faith and reason. In this area, apologists confront both skeptics who levy objections against the rationality of faith as well as fellow Christians who wish to modify the concept of faith. Consider these opinions:

> (M4) Faith is irrational since it involves naive acceptance and/or firm belief without sufficient evidence.
>
> (M5) Faith need not include *belief* but can be satisfied by a different mental attitude such as *wishing, assuming, hoping, trusting* and/or *committing.*[16]

Aquinas disagreed with those views and held instead:

> (A4) Motives of credibility confirm God's revelation, and God's grace works interiorly to facilitate a firm act of faith.
>
> (A5) The supernatural virtue of faith does include *belief.*

(A4) contains a twofold response to faith's alleged irrationality. First, if one worries that faith entails a blind leap or naïve acceptance of any old superstition, pointing to motives of credibility can alleviate the concern. As examples, Aquinas refers to miracles, the transformation of "unlettered and simple" men, fulfillment of prophecy, and the world's conversion to the Christian

---

15. Many Thomists have responded to critiques of God's simplicity, immutability, and eternity. Some books in this vein include Eleonore Stump, *Aquinas* (New York: Routledge, 2003); Michael Dodds, *The Unchanging God of Love: Thomas Aquinas and Contemporary Theology on Divine Immutability*, 2nd ed. (Washington, DC: The Catholic University of America Press, 2008); and James Dolezal, *God Without Parts: Divine Simplicity and the Metaphysics of God's Absoluteness* (Eugene, OR: Pickwick, 2011).

16. Some contemporary Christian philosophers who defend a view of faith that need not include belief are Daniel Howard-Snyder, Daniel McKaughan, and Lara Buchak.

faith.[17] While these motives do not *demonstrate* the faith, they serve as *sufficient signs* that God has revealed things to us. And if *God* has revealed things to us, his divine testimony deserves our full assent.[18]

The second prong of (A4) concerns faith's *firmness*. Critics object that it's unreasonable to hold tenaciously to what one cannot demonstrate. But, for Aquinas, supernatural faith is a gift from God who works interiorly to solidify our adherence.[19] The critic's concern presupposes that God cannot work with our wills to establish in us the certainty of faith.[20] Yet, if the Christian God exists, he is capable of doing just that. So, this objection cannot work independently of other arguments against Christianity.

Turning briefly to (A5), Aquinas follows Augustine in describing *belief* as "thinking with assent."[21] "Thinking" refers to an act of the intellect and "with assent" refers to "cleaving firmly" to an idea.[22] Now, just as some Christian thinkers have opted to modify *classical theism*, others have opted to modify *faith*. They replace *belief* with weaker attitudes such as trusting, committing, or hoping.[23] Aquinas would not mind trust, commitment, or hope accompanying faith, but he stands with the tradition in affirming that faith also includes *belief*. Catholics should do likewise.

Catholic apologists must hold the line on important issues. We hold the line on *method*: upholding well-sourced explanations, rigorous arguments, and content-based replies. We hold the line on *classical theism*: upholding a conception of the God who dramatically transcends the created realm in his

---

17. Thomas Aquinas, *Summa contra Gentiles* 1.6.1–3.

18. For a recent defense of the idea that our firm assent is "right and just" as it honors God as a testifier, see Dr. Gregory P. Stacey's article "Is Catholic Faith Worth Having?," *Religious Studies* (December 2020): 1–20.

19. For a beautiful, sound unpacking of this point, see Wojciech Giertych, *The Spark of Faith: Understanding the Power of Reaching Out to God* (Irondale, AL: EWTN, 2018).

20. For more on the "certainty of faith" in St. Thomas Aquinas, see Matthew Ramage, "Unless You Believe, You Will Not Understand: Biblical Faith According to Thomas Aquinas and Benedict XVI," in *Thomas Aquinas: Biblical Theologian*, ed. Roger Nutt and Michael Dauphinais (Steubenville, OH: Emmaus Academic, 2020).

21. Thomas Aquinas, *Summa theologiae* 2-2.2.1.

22. See Thomas Aquinas, 2-2.2.1.

23. For an in-depth look at Aquinas on the nature of faith and belief as well as its harmony with reason, see James Brent's doctoral dissertation, "The Epistemic Status of Christian Beliefs in Thomas Aquinas" (PhD diss., Saint Louis University, 2008).

pure actuality. We hold the line on *supernatural faith*: upholding the virtue that works in harmony with reason and includes *belief*. In these arenas, we can turn to the writings of St. Thomas Aquinas, our most fitting source, to unearth a wealth of riches. It is no surprise Pope Leo XIII declared to the whole Church, "We exhort you, venerable brethren, in all earnestness to restore the golden wisdom of St. Thomas, and to spread it far and wide for the defense and beauty of the Catholic faith."[24]

---

24. Leo XIII, Aeterni Patris 31, 1879, Vatican.va.

15

Blaise Pascal

Peter Kreeft

Søren Kierkegaard, the greatest Protestant philosopher who ever lived, is usually credited for inventing modern existentialism. But Blaise Pascal, two centuries earlier, should get the credit. Indeed, I find echoes of Pascal in almost every point of Kierkegaard's.

But Pascal himself only echoes Augustine, especially his *Confessions*. Indeed, when he knew he was dying, Pascal gave away all of his many books except two: the Bible and the *Confessions*. ("A wise choice," comments Malcolm Muggeridge.[1]) The *Confessions* is the most astonishingly and uniquely "modern" book in the premodern era. It is "existential," in the broad sense of "experiential" or "personal" or "subjective."

But Augustine is not the first existentialist, only the second. Jesus is the first.

Pascal's most famous idea, the "wager," is merely an unpacking of one of Jesus' sayings, the most practical sentence any man ever spoke about economics, the science of profit and loss: "What shall it profit a man, if he gain the whole world, and suffer the loss of his soul?" (Mark 8:36 DRA).

Pascal married his two sources, Jesus and Augustine, and presented the baby to the newly pagan world of scientism, skepticism, and secularism.

Traditional apologetics begins with two kinds of arguments for God's existence: *cosmological* and *psychological*.

---

1. Malcolm Muggeridge, *A Third Testament: A Modern Pilgrim Explores the Spiritual Wanderings of Augustine, Blake, Pascal, Tolstoy, Bonhoeffer, Kierkegaard, and Dostoyevsky* (Ossining, NY: Orbis Books, 2004), 30.

The first kind, typified by Aquinas' famous "five ways," uses premises from our observation of the cosmos, such as motion, causal dependence, contingency, imperfection, and teleological order. Like most premodern apologists, Aquinas preferred these because he thought their premises most indubitable.

The second kind uses premises from our own inner life, for instance, from the ability of our fallible and temporal minds to know infallible and eternal truths (e.g., "7+5=12"); or, from our conscience's awareness of objectively real moral law, and thus, implicitly, a Lawgiver; or, from our innate and universal natural desire for perfect happiness, coupled with the premise that no natural desire is vain and meaningless.

A third kind of argument is Anselm's *ontological* argument, which has no premises at all except a universally accepted definition of the concept of God, but which convinces only a very small percentage of philosophers, who in turn make up only a very small percentage of (at least apparently) human beings. So, I feel free to ignore it here.

Pascal uses no cosmological arguments at all (because he lived in a time when the cosmological premises were no longer secure), and among the psychological arguments he uses only the argument from desire.

But the apologetical argument his contemporaries found most impressive, and the one that is still the most famous, is the "wager," which is not an argument that claims to prove God's existence at all, but an argument for making the "leap" of faith. It is not theoretical but practical, not logical but psychological.

The *Pensées* are divided by Pascal himself into two halves: the "bad news" and the "good news"; "man's unhappiness without God" and "man's happiness with God." The first half is essentially a modernization and interiorization of book 19 of Augustine's *City of God* or of *Ecclesiastes*.

Both halves are about man rather than about God. That is one way the *Pensées* are both typically "existential" and typically modern. It thus makes contact with and responds to the modern crisis—the crisis which, as the greatest man in the worst century in history, Pope St. John Paul II, clearly saw, was a crisis of anthropology, not theology. This crisis is what Pope Benedict XVI called "the dictatorship of relativism," and what C.S. Lewis called, prophetically, "the abolition of man."

No matter how clear and strong one's purely theoretical arguments are, whether cosmological or ontological, they do not bite into the heart of modern man as does the psychological argument about unhappiness and happiness. There is no refutation of data, and both the joy of the saint and the misery of the sinner are data. In both cases, when the world sees this double data, it says (at least in its heart): "What you are speaks so loud I can hardly hear what you say." Chesterton rightly said that there is only one irrefutable argument against Christianity: Christians. Joyless Christians. There is also one irrefutable argument for Christianity: joyful Christians.

But saints are not sweets. Pascal's joy is all the more impressive because it shines through his pessimism, his psychological skepticism, his curmudgeonliness, and his medical miseries. Tolkien described Pascal as well as himself when he called himself a pessimist by temperament and an optimist by conviction. We see the same pattern in Flannery O'Connor, Walker Percy, Malcolm Muggeridge, C.S. Lewis, Fyodor Dostoyevsky, Kierkegaard, Augustine, and Jesus himself.

Unlike Augustine, Pascal does not write about himself. But he does write about another self: ours. He is "existential" because he talks about that self so transparently that, as one of my students wrote, "This man seems to be speaking to me from inside my own soul, not from outside. He comes at me through the heart, not through the eyes or the ears."

This is especially true of the sections Pascal labeled "diversion" and "indifference." Whenever we read and discuss them in class, my students get so quiet that they literally stop breathing. As a professor, I'm very sensitive to many different levels of quiet in the classroom (I distinguish five) because they are levels of attention. "No breathing" is the rarest, the quietest, and the most valuable of the five. I have taught philosophy for sixty years now, and I have never found any other philosopher who can do that to class after class of ordinary modern pagan students.

Many of them are challenged to test Pascal's suggestion that we can discover the cause of all the ills of the world if we seriously attempt to remain quietly in our own room for one hour with no distractions or diversions. They never succeed; and that is precisely their success, their learning. It is very useful for the slave to notice his sweet, sticky chains. It is an illuminating commentary on the difference between the premodern mind and the modern mind to realize that the thing many contemplative saints and sages would crave as a gift is for us the torture that we use as punishment for our most wicked prisoners: solitude.

An even higher Everest of non-diversion for most of my students to attempt to climb is to go without any screens or smartphones for twenty-four hours. For many, that is literally impossible. The fly cannot escape the interior flypaper in its brain. Their souls have melted into their screens, and when their screens are removed, they sense the terror of the emptiness that is left. But this experience can be positive. Addicts often have to hit bottom before they can bounce up.

Pascal does not construct screens, or masks, or systems; he removes them. He is not an engineer, a builder. He is a spelunker, a cave explorer. He moves down and in, not up and out.

And he is not a reductionist. Like Augustine, he lives among paradoxes, and loves them. The wretchedness and vanity of man is always juxtaposed with the greatness of man. Man's very wretchedness shows his greatness. It is as far from nihilism or despair as it is from presumption, pop psychology, self-esteem, and self-help. "Do they exalt themselves? I will abase them. Do they abase themselves? I will exalt them." That's exactly what the first existentialist did: immediately after he called Peter's confession "blessed," he called Peter's correction "Satan" (Matt. 16:13–23).

For many, Pascal's content may be disturbing to read, but his style is a joy. Most philosophers' writing styles are notoriously unreadable: ponderous, technical, wordy, abstract, difficult, and dull. But not Pascal's. He is never platitudinous, pandering, patronizing, preachy, or pacifying. He jabs, jokes, and jibes. His words are not soft; they are lightning-like lasers. They hit you in the head and the heart at once. I suspect that one reason professional philosophers ignore him is his style, and philosophers' prejudice against bright and witty thinkers, as if deep down, they must be shallow.

Pascal is the single most effective apologist I know. Why? Just as the only answer to what a novel is about is the novel itself, the only answer to that question is the *Pensées*. Read them, and weep, laugh, and leap into faith.

16

G.K. Chesterton
Dale Ahlquist

A Catholic is a person who has plucked up courage to face the incredible and inconceivable idea that something else may be wiser than he is.[1]
—*G.K. Chesterton,* The Well and the Shallows

In the opening years of the twentieth century, nothing could have been considered less fashionable than defending Christianity, and the unlikeliest place to defend it would have been in the daily newspapers. But G.K. Chesterton (1874–1936) rose to fame as a London journalist by doing just that. He provided a striking contrast to the surrounding skeptics and critics, the materialists and the modernists, the intellectuals with their sneering cynicism about faith. He answered them with a good-natured nettling of their doubt, adeptly dismantling their arguments, and showing them—and everybody else who happened to be reading—that faith is fundamental, not just for religion but for everything else. Even mathematics. You cannot start a logical proof without an assumption, a given. "You cannot prove your first statement, or it would not be your first statement."[2]

Chesterton was never afraid of a good argument, whether it was about something as paltry as local politics or as far-reaching as the other side of the universe. He started by defending God against the atheists, faith against the

---

1. G.K. Chesterton, *The Well and the Shallows* (San Francisco: Ignatius Press, 2006), 40.
2. G.K. Chesterton, *Daily News*, June 22, 1907.

agnostics, Christianity against other religions, and finally, Catholicism against everything else.

His apologetics seem to come easy because they are secondary to a greater task at hand. He points out that Nehemiah, the Old Testament hero who rebuilds the walls of Jerusalem, commanded his workers to have a sword in one hand and a trowel in the other. The sword represents reason, a weapon of defense. The trowel represents imagination, the creative tool, the work of love. Defense is an act of reason, but it is a sword. You cannot build with a sword. In this sense, apologetics is not evangelization. The trowel is the instrument for building up. As with all creation, it is the act of love. The sword defends the trowel, but the trowel does the work.

However, reason is always at work too, because the faith is always under attack. But even while parrying with his sword, Chesterton emphasizes the positive, the creative and constructive approach, building a case for the faith that is appealing and welcoming, eye-opening and arm-opening. Loving your enemy means not defeating him but getting him to come over to your side.

Chesterton's two greatest books of apologetics are *Orthodoxy* and *The Everlasting Man*. The first one presents some of the freshest, most original arguments for Christianity that have ever leaped from the page. He begins by describing his own experience with modern philosophies, finding them narrow and self-defeating, trapped in "the clean, well-lit prison of one idea."[3] Not just a prison cell, but a padded cell. He tells of how he becomes convinced of the truth of Christianity because the arguments against it are so bad and so contradictory and so desperate. He then looks at Christianity from all sides, revealing it as the sanest of all philosophies. He shows how truth is paradoxical, the opposite of what we expect, which is the basis of surprise and wonder. He demonstrates how the popular objections to Christianity have one thing in common: they're not true. He deftly dispenses with the sects and heretics and paints a lively picture of the historic Church

---

3. G.K. Chesterton, *Orthodoxy*, 2nd ed. (Park Ridge, IL: Word on Fire Classics, 2018), 16.

riding through history, swerving to avoid error, but carefully not leaning too far so as to fall into the opposite error, "the wild truth reeling but erect."[4]

Many readers are amazed that *Orthodoxy* was written fourteen years before Chesterton became a Catholic. Yet you would never know that unless for some reason you already knew it.

In *The Everlasting Man*, another coup of original thinking, Chesterton compresses the history of the world between two covers of a book. He demonstrates that man is a creature different from all other creatures because of his creativity. He is an artist. He is also religious. Civilization is as ancient as history and has always revealed the religious element in man. It has also revealed the reality of sin and shame. Then history changes utterly when Jesus steps onto the stage. Chesterton calls it "The Strangest Story in the World"— the miracle-worker, exorcist, and storyteller who made the audacious claim to be God. He was put to death for his efforts.[5] But his followers claimed he didn't stay dead. And they went from being "important enough to be ignored"[6] to causing the greatest civilization on earth to devise newer forms of public torture and persecution with which to silence them. But instead, Christianity would conquer Rome.

Chesterton says that what Jesus started was something distinct and different from a new religion: it was a Church. And it was that Church that drew Chesterton in. And he led in myriads more, who discovered, as he did, that the Church is larger on the inside than on the outside. "Becoming a Catholic," he says, "broadens the mind. It especially broadens the mind about the reasons for becoming a Catholic. Standing in the centre where all roads meet, a man can look down each of the roads in turn and realise that they come from all points of the heavens."[7]

Though *Orthodoxy* and *The Everlasting Man* are used to defend the Catholic faith, they have a broad ecumenical appeal as well. Non-Catholics

---

4. Chesterton, *Orthodoxy*, 100.
5. G.K. Chesterton, *The Everlasting Man*, 5th ed. (London: Hodder & Stoughton, 1926), 227.
6. Chesterton, 187.
7. G.K. Chesterton, *The Catholic Church and Conversion* (San Francisco: Ignatius Press, 1990), 80.

are attracted to Chesterton by his positive approach (as well as his profound and quotable one-liners), and that is the reason he is a maker of converts. There are other books that are considered to be more overtly Catholic: *The Catholic Church and Conversion*; *Where All Roads Lead*; *The Thing: Why I Am a Catholic*; and *The Well and the Shallows*. These include chapters that refute specific anti-Catholic arguments, but others filled with multiple examples where the Catholic perspective on an issue is more reasonable than any other. Again, Chesterton uses reason not just to refute the attacks on the faith, but to reveal the reasonableness of the faith: "Ours . . . is the most rational of all religions. . . . Those who talk about it as being merely . . . emotional simply do not know what they are talking about. It is all the modern religions that are merely emotional. . . . We alone are left accepting the action of the reason and the will without any necessary assistance from the emotions. A convinced Catholic is easily the most hard-headed and logical person walking about the world today."[8]

Chesterton's outstanding and unique biographies, *St. Francis of Assisi* and *St. Thomas Aquinas*, can also be regarded as works of apologetics. He makes the point that St. Francis is a universal saint, appealing even to non-Christians, but that he cannot be understood apart from his Catholic faith. And he uses St. Thomas in a surprising way: to refute Martin Luther.

As a convert, Chesterton understands the perspective of both the insider and the outsider in a way that neither of the other two can. He knows how to address both audiences at once. The goal is not only to get the outsider in, but to get the insider to really see what is inside, perhaps for the first time.

At the end of his prolific career, G.K. Chesterton found himself in much the same position as at the beginning: taking the unfashionable stand. He argued that all the reasons for being Catholic amounted to one reason: it is true. And no one seems to like that part of it. But the truth indeed sets you free. "The Catholic Church is the only thing that saves a man from the degrading slavery of being a child of his age."[9]

---

8. G.K. Chesterton, *The Thing* (London: Sheed & Ward, 1957), 194.
9. Chesterton, *The Forum*, January 1926.

17

C.S. Lewis

Fr. Michael Ward

C.S. Lewis was perhaps the most effective Christian apologist of the twentieth century, and his influence continues strongly today. In this short chapter, I cannot possibly do justice to the talents that informed his apologetic writings.[1] Instead, I will examine how Lewis himself defined the heart of the apologetic task. In "Christian Apologetics" (1945)[2] and in his preface to *Mere Christianity* (1952),[3] he helpfully outlines his approach.

A distinctive aspect of his approach is its nondenominationalism. Although Lewis was an Anglican, he never attempts to persuade his readers to join the Anglican Church. Lewis is not promoting anything "peculiar to the Church of England or (worse still) to myself." Rather, he is defending "the belief that has been common to nearly all Christians at all times," a faith "which is what it is and was what it was long before I was born and whether I like it or not."[4]

His willingness to defend a belief that he might not personally like in every particular speaks to his honesty. Though he is willing to accept even those parts he finds rebarbative, he is not going to pretend that they are

---

1. One such talent lay in his understanding of the relationship between imagination and reason. For more on this, see Michael Ward, "The Good Serves the Better and Both the Best: C.S. Lewis on Imagination and Reason in Apologetics," in *Imaginative Apologetics: Theology, Philosophy, and the Catholic Tradition,* ed. Andrew Davison (Grand Rapids, MI: Baker Academic, 2011).

2. Now published in C.S. Lewis, *God in the Dock: Essays on Theology and Ethics,* ed. Walter Hooper (Grand Rapids, MI: Eerdmans, 2014).

3. For more on this, see George M. Marsden, *C.S. Lewis's Mere Christianity: A Biography* (Princeton, NJ: Princeton University Press, 2016).

4. C.S. Lewis, *Mere Christianity* (HarperOne, 2015), viii–xi.

necessarily easy to accept. This is a good example to follow. Non-Christians are more likely to listen to us if they can see we are not simply parroting a spiritual "party line." Which is not to endorse a cafeteria mentality: Catholics are under an obligation to believe all that the Church teaches as *de fide* (of the faith). But we are free to find—and acknowledge that we find—certain elements tricky even as we loyally embrace their truth. As Newman said in a similar vein: "Ten thousand difficulties do not make one doubt."[5]

Lewis' approach also speaks to his intellectual objectivity. Modern audiences, he says, are surprised to learn that you are defending Christianity "solely and simply because you happen to think it true." Too many people assume that Christians adopt the faith for no other reason than that they were raised in it or think it good for society. Maintaining a clear distinction "between what the faith actually says and what you would like it to have said or what you understand or what you personally find helpful or think probable, forces your audience to realize that you are tied to your data just as the scientist is tied by the results of the experiments." Your interlocutor can thus more easily realize that what is being discussed "is a question about objective fact—not gas about ideals and points of view."[6]

Another reason for focusing on "mere" Christianity is that it foregrounds the crucial issue. The primary matter to get straight in any apologia is that "there is one God and that Jesus Christ is His only Son."[7] Tackle that issue, Lewis advises, and only later address areas of disputed doctrine, such as pertain to ecclesiology. Get people into the hallway of the house of faith and let them choose which room (i.e., which denomination) they want to occupy once they are inside the building. Crossing the threshold of faith in Jesus is the first and most important step to take. This "unwavering Christocentrism," as Bishop Barron describes it,[8] was certainly practiced in Lewis' apologetic.[9]

---

5. John Henry Cardinal Newman, *Apologia Pro Vita Sua* (London: Longmans & Green, 1889), 239.
6. "Christian Apologetics" in Lewis, *God in the Dock*.
7. Lewis, *Mere Christianity*, ix.
8. For more on this, see Robert Barron and Brandon Vogt, "Unwavering Christocentrism," *Word on Fire Show* podcast, May 2, 2017, https://www.wordonfireshow.com/episode73/.
9. See, for example, "What Are We to Make of Jesus Christ?" in Lewis, *God in the Dock*.

Admittedly, his somewhat *laissez faire* approach to ecclesiology would have to be regarded by a Catholic as a product both of his own Anglicanism and of Protestantism more generally. Catholics do not find it so easy to distinguish "the faith" from "the Church." As Ian Ker notes in a probing discussion of *Mere Christianity*, "From the Catholic point of view, to say that Christianity comes first and then the Church is to put the cart before the horse. The Catholic belief is that Jesus Christ came into this world first and foremost to found a Church, not to propagate a religion called Christianity."[10] Furthermore, there is a practical problem inherent in the very concept of "mere Christianity," for who is to decide the boundaries of "the belief that has been common to nearly all Christians at all times"? Newman again: "The chief difficulty obviously lies in determining what *is* the fundamental faith."[11]

Notwithstanding these two potential weaknesses in Lewis' approach, Catholic apologists would do well to learn from it. The effectiveness of his work indicates that he was doing something right, for a tree is known by its fruit (Luke 6:44).[12] As the Second Vatican Council's decree on ecumenism, *Unitatis Redintegratio*, teaches, "Catholics must gladly acknowledge and esteem the truly Christian endowments from our common heritage which are to be found among our separated brethren. It is right and salutary to recognize the riches of Christ and virtuous works in the lives of others who are bearing witness to Christ."[13] Moreover, a remarkably high proportion of those converted to Protestantism by reading Lewis have gone on to become

---

10. Ian Ker, "'Mere Christianity' and Catholicism" in *C.S. Lewis and the Church*, ed. Judith Wolfe and Brendan Wolfe (London: T&T Clark, 2011), 132.

11. John Henry Newman, *Essays Critical and Historical*, vol. 1 (London: Longmans & Green, 1895), 209–210.

12. Huge numbers of people have attributed their conversion to Lewis' writings, and especially to *Mere Christianity*. See, for example, *Mere Christians: Inspiring Stories of Encounters with C.S. Lewis*, ed. Mary Anne Phemister and Andrew Lazo (Grand Rapids, MI: Baker Books, 2009); also "Books of the Century," *Christianity Today* 44:5 (24 April 2000), https://www.christianitytoday.com/ct/2000/april24/5.92.html.

13. Vatican Council II, *Unitatis Redintegratio* 4, Vatican.va. The decree goes on: "Nor should we forget that anything wrought by the grace of the Holy Spirit in the hearts of our separated brethren can be a help to our own edification. Whatever is truly Christian is never contrary to what genuinely belongs to the faith; indeed, it can always bring a deeper realization of the mystery of Christ and the Church."

Catholics later.[14] This again indicates to a Catholic the value of his apologetic, because Christ himself prayed for his followers "that they may be one" (John 17:21)—not just in baptism but also at the table of the Lord.

I trust that Lewis' example will not lead any Catholic toward indifferentism about ecclesiology. Lewis himself was not indifferent on that point, as it happens.[15] The takeaway is threefold: to be honest, to be objective, and to focus always on the person of Jesus Christ.

This latter point is the most crucial, and not only in our interactions with non-Christians, but also in our relations with apologists from other traditions. Lewis himself found that his approach, though it was not undertaken for the purposes of reunion, helped to show why Christians ought to be reunited: "It is at her centre, where her truest children dwell, that each communion is really closest to every other in spirit, if not in doctrine. And this suggests that at the centre of each there is a something, or a Someone, who against all divergencies of belief, differences of temperament, all memories of mutual persecution, speaks with the same voice."[16]

If we train our eyes upon our Lord, in the manner of the forgiven Edmund Pevensie who "just went on looking at Aslan,"[17] our apologetic won't go far wrong. Lewis retained that Christocentric focus, and as a result, his ministry was richly blessed. As Pope John Paul II observed, "C.S. Lewis knew what his apostolate was, *and he did it!*"[18]

---

14. For more on this, see Joseph Pearce, *C.S. Lewis and the Catholic Church* (Charlotte, NC: St. Benedict, 2013), 173–205.

15. As he writes in the preface to *Mere Christianity*, one's choice of church must be as much governed by intellectual objectivity as one's initial faith in Christ: "Above all you must be asking which door is the true one; not which pleases you best by its paint and panelling. In plain language, the question should never be: 'Do I like that kind of service?' but 'Are these doctrines true: Is holiness here? Does my conscience move me towards this?'" (Lewis, *Mere Christianity*, xvi).

16. Lewis, xii.

17. C.S. Lewis, *The Lion, the Witch and the Wardrobe* (HarperCollins, 2008), chapter 13.

18. Gregory Lippiatt, "Requiem eulogy," Edinburgh University Press website, https://www.euppublishing.com/doi/full/10.3366/ink.2021.0096.

18

Flannery O'Connor

Matthew Becklo

Flannery O'Connor was a great writer of fiction—arguably one of the greatest in America's history. And her grotesque, quirky, and often violent stories about outcasts and fundamentalists in the deep South were informed by a deep Catholic sensibility. But was she an *apologist* for the Christian faith?

The designation seems odd—even more so when we consider that the only two direct references to apologetics in her letters are rather negative in tone. In one letter, she writes that "the prevailing tenor of Catholic philosophy . . . is too often apologetic rather than dialogic. . . . Thomism usually comes in a hideous wrapper."[1] In another, she decries the desire of many Christian readers for "an apologetic fiction" that presents a formulaic, respectable faith through straightforward allegory. "Our Catholic mentality is great on paraphrase, logic, formula, instant and correct answers," she writes. "We judge before we experience and never trust our faith to be subjected to reality."[2]

Flannery O'Connor was not opposed to apologetics itself; after all, she read the innovative apologists of her time who paved the way for the *ressourcement* movement—theologians like Jacques Maritain, Etienne Gilson, and Romano Guardini, and even "dangerous"[3] thinkers like Teilhard de Chardin. Rather, what likely irked her was the staid and even smug presentation of the

---

1. Flannery O'Connor, *The Habit of Being: Letters of Flannery O'Connor* (New York: Farrar, Straus & Giroux, 1979), 303.
2. O'Connor, 516.
3. O'Connor, 571.

faith, rooted in decades of neo-scholasticism in the Church, with which "apologetics" had become associated. It was tidy, abstract argumentation that lacked the concrete realities of history and human experience, a disincarnate "defense" that lacked "reverence" and "gentleness," or awe and humility (1 Pet. 3:15, 16). To borrow from the title of her collection of essays, it was an apologetics that lacked *mystery* and *manners*.

Of course, in our own time, Catholics tend to face exactly the opposite problem: we so valorize dialogue, gentleness, and reverence that we forget to make a defense! This is why the balance between head and heart defined by St. Peter is so crucial; indeed, Flannery O'Connor's life and work can be understood as a striking example of exactly this balance.

O'Connor was not shy about explaining and defending the Catholic faith in her letters and essays. This is especially true of her 150 letters to Betty Hester (identified as "A" in *The Habit of Being*), a credit company clerk who first caught O'Connor's attention with a thoughtful fan letter. That Hester was an agnostic with same-sex attraction and a troubled past makes their friendship feel all the more contemporary, and O'Connor's intellectual and spiritual support in her letters all the more instructive. In one letter to Hester, she refers playfully to her own "high powered defense reflex whateveritis," demurring, "I know well enough that it is not a defense of the faith, which don't need it, but a defense of myself who does."[4] But O'Connor—who alludes to great thinkers like Edith Stein, John Henry Newman, and Thomas Aquinas in their correspondence—was clearly very eager to convince her interlocutor of the truth of Catholicism.

In fact, some of her greatest one-liners can be found in her apologetical letters to Hester. She defends objective truth: "The truth does not change according to our ability to stomach it emotionally."[5] In the same letter, she defends the Incarnation and Resurrection: "For you it may be a matter of not being able to accept what you call a suspension of the laws of the flesh and the physical. . . . For me it is the virgin birth, the Incarnation, the resurrection

---

4. O'Connor, 131.
5. O'Connor, 100.

which are the true laws of the flesh and the physical."[6] She defends the Church as a force against nihilism: "If you live today you breathe in nihilism. In or out of the Church, it's the gas you breathe. If I hadn't had the Church to fight it with or to tell me the necessity of fighting it, I would be the stinkingest logical positivist you ever saw right now."[7] And she tells the famous story of how she defended the Real Presence of the Eucharist to a lapsed Catholic at a fancy dinner: "Well, if it's a symbol, to hell with it."[8]

But throughout the letters, O'Connor roots these convictions in her own personal experience, and answers Hester's inquiries with warmth, honesty, and humor. In short, she makes her defense with "manners." That it had an effect is evidenced by the fact that Hester did indeed become Catholic, with O'Connor serving as her Confirmation sponsor. Sadly, she eventually back-pedaled and left the Church. But even then, O'Connor continued to write to her, offering a defense surrounded with kindness: "I don't think any the less of you outside the Church than in it," she admits, "but what is painful is the realization that this means a narrowing of life for you and a lessening of the desire for life. . . . Faith comes and goes. It rises and falls like the tides of an invisible ocean. If it is presumptuous to think that faith will stay with you forever, it is just as presumptuous to think that unbelief will. Leaving the Church is not the solution."[9] In her last letter to Hester, sent just days before dying, O'Connor offers one final defense of Catholicism by referencing the "heresy" that you can "worship in pure spirit."[10]

While O'Connor's nonfiction is rich with apologetic insights and arguments, her stories are also, in a sense, one long defense of the faith. As Bishop Barron points out in *The Pivotal Players*, the master idea of her writing is "the juxtaposition of sin and grace"—the "fallen and compromised world" we human beings occupy and the "wrenching" experience of God breaking into

---

6. O'Connor, 100.
7. O'Connor, 97.
8. O'Connor, 125.
9. O'Connor, 451–452.
10. O'Connor, 594.

that world to set things right.[11] As O'Connor herself admitted, "All my stories are about the action of grace on a character who is not very willing to support it."[12] The drama of human depravity encountering divine grace—or, as she writes at the end of *The Violent Bear It Away*, "the terrible speed of mercy"[13]— is the unifying idea behind all her work. And she knew she was writing for secular people who didn't believe in or even particularly care about these truths, so she strategically drew "large and startling figures" precisely to shock her readers into seeing them.[14]

But O'Connor doesn't approach these religious themes in a didactic or moralizing way; rather, she displays them in their great mystery, with a holy reverence, awe, or fear. A refrain of O'Connor's essays is the need for the writer, especially the Catholic writer, to explore reality as it truly is—and this means an exploration of mystery. "When fiction is made according to its nature, it should reinforce our sense of the supernatural by grounding it in concrete, observable reality," she explains. "If the writer uses his eyes in the real security of his Faith, he will be obliged to use them honestly, and his sense of mystery, and acceptance of it, will be increased."[15] The religious writer who thinks "that the eyes of the Church or of the Bible or of his particular theology have already done the seeing for him" fails to really get at the heart of the matter, and what results is the "sorry religious novel."[16]

Thus, her stories enter into the mystery of iniquity—ignorance, dysfunction, cruelty, loneliness, rage, murder, rape, deceit, and the whole dark and disorienting terrain of sin and suffering. Amid this darkness, the light of grace comes, and "where sin increased, grace abounded all the more" (Rom. 5:20). Even the devil, as O'Connor writes in one essay, frequently becomes "the

11. Robert Barron, *The Pivotal Players: 12 Heroes Who Shaped the Church and Changed the World* (Park Ridge, IL: Word on Fire, 2020), 234, 219.

12. O'Connor, *Habit of Being*, 275.

13. *Flannery O'Connor Collection*, ed. Matthew Becklo (Park Ridge, IL: Word on Fire Classics, 2019), 368. Many of the letters quoted here, as well as the quoted essay from *Mystery and Manners*, are available in this collection.

14. Flannery O'Connor, *Mystery and Manners: Occasional Prose*, ed. Sally and Robert Fitzgerald (New York: Farrar, Straus & Giroux, 1970), 34.

15. O'Connor, 148.

16. O'Connor, 163.

unwilling instrument of grace."[17] Yet this grace, too, is a mystery; it does not look like we might expect it to. Whether it be the restless atheist Hazel Motes preaching a "Church Without Christ" only to become an ascetic for Christ, or the pious Mrs. Turpin who looks down on her neighbors only to be knocked down to see a strange revelation in the skies, O'Connor's characters are, as Chesterton once quipped, turned upside down in order to be given the chance to see things right side up. As she put it, "All human nature vigorously resists grace because grace changes us and the change is painful."[18] In all of this—the light of God breaking into the darkness of sin and death—O'Connor's writing takes its cue from the central mystery of the Christian faith: the Incarnation.

Flannery O'Connor was indeed an apologist, but one with a keen sense of mystery and manners. In this, she is a forerunner and model for apologetics in our time. She knew that defending the faith requires more than just ready-made answers; it requires a willingness to meet people where they are, to explore reality as it truly unfolds, and to orient the skeptical soul—even if it means a shock to the system—to its great need for the greater mercy of "the God Who Is."[19]

---

17. O'Connor, 118.
18. O'Connor, *Habit of Being*, 307.
19. O'Connor, 93.

19

René Girard

Grant Kaplan

René Girard (1923–2015) is the most unlikely of apologists, having been trained as an archivist in France before writing a dissertation in modern history while in the United States, where he would develop a theory of the novel in 1961. Such an inauspicious beginning did not portend his future as an apologist, and as someone whom Bishop Barron predicted might one day be remembered "as one as one of the great Fathers of the Church."[1]

Girard's most central contribution to Christian apologetics comes at the level of anthropology. Girard's anthropology is linked to two ideas—mimetic desire and the scapegoat mechanism—which he unfolded in his work on modern novels (*Deceit, Desire, & the Novel*) and his subsequent exploration of human origins through studies in anthropology and ethology. According to Girard, we desire according to the desires of others; we are, in other words, hardwired for imitation. Above the appetitive level, our higher desires are most primarily learned and lie below the level of conscious awareness. Girard's theory cut against the dominant grain of "romanticism," a worldview in which one's authenticity was best marked by being free of all influence—think of Emerson's epigrammatic line from his famous essay "Self-Reliance": "Imitation is suicide."[2]

Girard then asked whether the human capacity for imitation and

---

1. Blurb for Cynthia L. Haven, *The Intellectual Vision of René Girard* (Milwaukee: Wiseblood Books, 2017).

2. Ralph Waldo Emerson, "Self-Reliance," in *Nature and Selected Essays*, ed. Larzer Ziff (London: Penguin Books, 2003), 176.

escalation could go wrong. In his second major work, *Violence and the Sacred* (1972), Girard launched the theory of the scapegoat mechanism—that early human societies avoided mimetic escalation by stumbling into scapegoating, in which the collective energy of a community focused on a singular group or person. This spontaneous act of violence initiated a strange and unexpected peace, which could be re-presented through reenactment (ritual) or story (myth). The diversity of myths and rites were born of one event: group scapegoating. And the diverse gods that the world's earliest cultures attested to were deified victims.

Girard's theory of scapegoating was both a social theory and a theory of religion. Girard's naturalistic theory of religious origins argued both for and against religion. Arising from the scapegoat mechanism, religion—older even than agriculture—proved far from superfluous or detrimental; it kept human cultures from collapsing under the weight of escalating violence. Yet these archaic religions could only promise a false transcendence built upon a divinized victim, resulting in structures that frequently demanded further victims. Girard's theory explains how religion—regarded by skeptics as at best useless—could occupy such a central space in almost all ancient cultures of record. He concludes, "Humanity, in my view, is the child of religion," by which he means that religion allows humanity to outlive the threat of collapse by finding a way to build a new culture not available to its nearest animal relatives.[3]

Not unlike the great Swiss theologian Karl Barth, Girard casts Christianity as an anti-religion: "Christianity," Girard states laconically, "demystifies religion."[4] Girard recalls that when he turned from his study of ancient myths to the biblical texts, he had expected to discover the same phenomenon for which many critics had maligned Christianity: the concealment of an original violence through stories that soften the founding murder, and the projection of a victimizing group's violence onto a divinity. Instead, Girard was struck by

---

3. René Girard, *I See Satan Fall Like Lightning* (Maryknoll, NY: Orbis Books, 2001), 93.
4. René Girard, *Battling to the End: Conversations with Benoît Chantre* (East Lansing, MI: Michigan State University Press, 2009), x.

a remarkable difference: rather than telling stories from the perspective of victimizers, the Bible told the story from the victim's viewpoint. Already in the tale of Cain and Abel, Abel's blood cried out from the ground. Girard noticed symmetries between the stories of Job and Joseph, and the Oedipus cycle by Sophocles, but these symmetries made their difference all the more striking—only the biblical text insisted on the innocence of the victim. In the New Testament, the Gospels not only told the story from the perspective of the victim—it identified God with the victim. This further iteration accounted for the fundamental difference between the two Testaments.

Christian revelation, then, offers to humanity more than a simple set of facts about God. It re-veals—in the sense of pulling back the curtain on—the mythic concealment of archaic religion, upon which all human culture rests. More than simply deconstructing archaic religion, Christianity, in Girard's reading, offers a true transcendence and reveals a God who creates freely and has nothing to do with the violent sacred that confuses the human need for blood with a bloodthirsty God. Christ's death on the cross unmasked sacred violence once and for all. Later critics of religion simply swim in Christianity's wake and, even worse, confuse the biblical and the archaic. Girard's apologetic, therefore, pulls the rug out from under so much anti-Christian atheism: "These [critics] do not see that their skepticism [toward Christianity] itself is a by-product of Christian religion."[5]

Girard's project can be described as an anthropological apologetic. Girard develops a theory of the human being as driven by mimetic desire, and unites the human sciences (the social sciences—i.e., psychology, anthropology, sociology) with a single theory that explains both interpersonal and group dynamics. Although he discovered this in great literature, he writes that the Bible already foresaw many of his own conclusions. In his exegetical hands, the story of Joseph, the friendship between Pilate and Herod, the death of John the Baptist, and the "woes" against the Pharisees all take on new

---

5. Girard, *Battling to the End*, xvi.

meaning by revealing the pull of the mimetic impulse and the solidarity made possible through scapegoating.

By calling it an anti-religion, Girard grants Christianity an exalted status because it offers humanity salvation from endless sacrificial repetition and shows a path to channel mimetic desire in ways that allow for pacific, rather than escalatory, mimesis: "Be imitators of me, as I am of Christ" (1 Cor. 11:1). Other religions and philosophies, of course, articulate elements of this (most obviously Buddhism), but none reveals the scapegoat mechanism as explicitly as Christianity does. Girard writes, "Christianity has good reason to consider itself absolutely unique. You can believe that without being an ethnocentric simpleton."[6] Girard would confirm the Second Vatican Council's reminder that "the Catholic Church rejects nothing that is true and holy in these religions."[7] But there is a fullness of revelation in Christianity that lets Girard insist on the superiority of the Gospel.

Girard's unique apologetic permits a different kind of engagement with modernity. Girard reads modernity as iterative of biblical religion, meaning that the basic values of the Enlightenment are given space to grow within a Christian environment. By blaming a scapegoat for any ill that befalls a community, prebiblical societies short-circuit the question of causality. Once one abandons the idea that a scapegoat could lie at the root of the problem, one must search elsewhere for a solution. Girard thinks Christianity's anti-scapegoating, however imperfect and delayed it was, birthed modern science. Rather than science being the reason that Western societies ceased witch hunting, Girard thinks that the cessation of witch hunting caused modern science.[8] Girard's apologetic demands that modern critics confront the biblical roots of their most dearly held convictions.

Although Girard began his career barely mentioning Christianity, he considered himself an apologist—at least dating from his reconversion to

---

6. René Girard, *When These Things Begin: Conversations with Michel Treguer* (East Lansing, MI: Michigan State University Press, 2014), 92.

7. Vatican Council II, *Nostra Aetate* 2, Vatican.va.

8. René Girard, *The Scapegoat* (Baltimore: Johns Hopkins University Press, 1986), 96.

Catholicism in 1959—while writing his first major work. He later admitted, "Since the beginning of the 'novelistic conversion' in *Deceit, Desire, and the Novel*, all of my books have been more or less explicit apologies of Christianity."[9] His unique form of apologetics offers several largely untrod paths into different conversations and promises bountiful possibilities for unbelievers and skeptics to discover the things "hidden from the foundation of the world" (Matt. 13:35).

9. Girard, *Battling to the End*, xv.

20

Joseph Ratzinger

Richard DeClue

Joseph Ratzinger—known eventually as Pope Benedict XVI—served as a professor of both dogmatic and fundamental theology. The latter, while distinct from apologetics, is a close relation to it. Ratzinger often addresses contemporary issues involving obstacles to faith, which is part of the work of an apologist. Thus, Ratzinger is a fitting model and resource for those interested in apologetics.

Ratzinger's approach to apologetics is very personal. The I-You relationship is a hallmark of his theology in general, and this is no exception. He addresses the nonbeliever as a whole person, which is always more than the sum of one's syllogistic argumentation. His approach, then, can aptly and accurately be described as a *personalist* one.

Here, we will not be concerned with detailed arguments so much as with presenting major themes and broad outlines of Ratzinger's approach to modern skepticism about the faith. We begin by establishing a commonality between believers and nonbelievers that forms a basis for dialogue. Characteristics of authentic dialogue are then discussed. Next, Ratzinger's criticism of epistemological reductionism is presented with a consideration that truth is more than mere fact. That leads to the final consideration: faith leads to understanding. The basic conclusion is that, in the light of faith, everything makes more sense.

Faith and Doubt: A Shared Experience

While apologetics is a defense of the faith, one need not be *defensive*. The better move is to be humble, not placing oneself over one's interlocutor as the all-knowing master teaching the ignoramus,[1] but as a fellow seeker of truth. Such humility can be disarming, allowing hostilities to cease and real discussion to take place.

It is sometimes presupposed that people of faith are always faced with challenges of doubt, while the unbeliever has neither faith nor doubt. Ratzinger rejects this and insists that both believers and unbelievers have a common experience. He challenges unbelievers to recognize that they, too, are faced with doubts: "Just as the believer knows himself to be constantly threatened by unbelief, which he must experience as a continual temptation, so for the unbeliever faith remains a temptation and a threat to his apparently permanently closed world."[2]

Ratzinger further suggests that belief, too, is a commonality between persons of faith and those who deny or reject God: "In other words, both the believer and the unbeliever share, each in his own way, doubt *and* belief, if they do not hide from themselves and from the truth of their being. Neither can quite escape either doubt or belief; for the one, faith is present *against* doubt; for the other, *through* doubt in the *form* of doubt."[3]

For Ratzinger, this honestly shared commonality can be a starting point for communication between the believer and the unbeliever. In order to have a real conversation, there must be *personal* openness to communication. Such communication, properly called "dialogue," requires the willingness to listen as well as to speak.[4] We will treat aspects of such authentic dialogue next.

---

1. See Joseph Ratzinger, *Introduction to Christianity*, trans. J.R. Foster and Michael J. Miller (San Francisco: Ignatius Press, 2004), 40–41.

2. Ratzinger, 45.

3. Ratzinger, 46–47.

4. See Joseph Ratzinger, *The Nature and Mission of Theology*, trans. Adrian Walker (San Francisco: Ignatius Press, 1995), 32–33.

Authentic Dialogue

Dialogue is of fundamental importance to Ratzinger. It is more than an exchange of ideas. If it is properly conducted, it leads to a true, personal exchange that leaves its mark deeply on those involved. Dialogue must be an *encounter*, and "this encounter is the condition of an inner contact which leads to mutual comprehension. Reciprocal understanding, finally, deepens and transforms the being of the interlocutors."[5]

Ratzinger makes a distinction here between having a conversation about external, impersonal matters and an authentic dialogue that is truly an interpersonal exchange: "When we speak of dialogue in the proper sense, what we mean is an utterance wherein something of being itself, indeed, the person himself, becomes speech."[6] Because dialogue is an openness of persons to one another, it has the potential to have a profound, enriching, and deepening effect on the persons involved.

At the same time, Ratzinger insists that this personal encounter called dialogue is also only possible if it is not merely subjective or relativistic. Drawing upon the records of St. Augustine's own process of conversion, Ratzinger notes that authentic dialogue can only take place by a prior and mutual commitment to the reality of truth, which is not determined by the people involved but is the condition of the possibility of a dialogue to take place at all. Reflecting on the conversations St. Augustine had with his dialogue partners, Ratzinger writes, "Augustine concludes that the community of friends was capable of mutual listening and understanding because all of them together heeded the interior master, the truth. Men are capable of reciprocal comprehension because, far from being wholly separate islands of being, they communicate in the same truth. The greater their inner contact with the one reality which unites them, namely, the truth, the greater their capacity to meet on common ground. Dialogue without this interior obedient listening

---

5. Ratzinger, *The Nature and Mission of Theology*, 33.
6. Ratzinger, 33.

to the truth would be nothing more than a discussion among the deaf."[7] If there is no truth which both parties are committed to seeking and to obeying, then no dialogue is possible. Dialogue presupposes that the truth can be sought, acquired, and shared, that *logos* is the basis of *dia-logos*. This *logos* is more than brute fact, as we shall see.

Truth Is More Than Fact

Despite the preponderance of relativism today, there is—rather ironically— also a preponderance of positivism based upon (over)confidence in the hard sciences. Technological advancement serves as both the evidence for and the goal of dedication to scientific knowledge. Science is empowering; it lets humanity shape the world.

The danger is a tendency to reduce truth to mere fact and *techne*, what Ratzinger calls the knowledge of "makability" [*Machbarkeitswissen*].[8] Myopically, this leaves no room for other levels of truth, such as meaning, which is both higher and deeper than brute knowledge of facts. Ratzinger opposes the reduction of knowledge to scientific positivism, not because he is opposed to science and technology, but because science and technology are not self-sufficient.

Let me give an example. The mere fact that chemical compound A reacts with chemical compound B to result in C is not nearly as important as understanding that compound A is an antidote to poison B that results in the saving of a human life (C). Thus, even the value of medical science is dependent upon a level of meaning that scientific positivism itself cannot determine or supply. To view a particular technology as a good is to make a value judgment or even a moral judgment. Furthermore, mere technological power without judgments of value or ethics is dangerous. Growth in scientific knowledge

---

7. Ratzinger, 34. The original context of these words is in a chapter "On the Essence of the Academy and Its Freedom," in which Ratzinger tackles the question of the nature, value, and extent of academic freedom.

8. See Ratzinger, *Introduction to Christianity*, 63–69, here 66.

and technical power at a time when moral reasoning is on the decline is alarming. "By thinking of the practicable, of what can be made, [man] is in danger of forgetting to reflect on himself and on the meaning of his existence."[9]

Human persons cannot really thrive without meaning. Thus, Ratzinger thinks that a commitment to pure scientific positivism leads inevitably to dissatisfaction: "The world of planned economy, of research, of exact calculation and experiment is quite obviously not enough to satisfy people";[10] for man "is insecure most of all at the point where exact science abandons him, and it is the measure of his abandonment that first makes him aware of how narrow the slice of reality is in which science gives him security."[11] Faith, on the other hand, provides a deeper vision.

Faith and Understanding

Faith is not just about the affirming of this or that fact. It is also about seeing the meaning of the whole. God is the ground of all that exists; he is the intelligence that makes possible our own intelligence. God is also personal, someone who can be addressed as a "thou." "What is so striking here is, of course, the fact that this whole ground of being is, at the same time, relationship; not less than I, who know, think, feel and love, but rather more than I, so that I can know only because I am known, love only because I am already loved."[12] The relationship with God that faith entails gives a vision of the whole; it enables one to see the meaning and purpose of reality. The light of grace enables one to understand, not just know.

Everyone, whether implicitly or explicitly, must take a stance on the question of God. What one can see is determined by where one stands. Faith "does not belong to the relationship of 'know-make'. . . but is much better

---

9. Ratzinger, 71.
10. Joseph Ratzinger, *Faith and the Future* (Chicago: Franciscan Herald, 1971), 25–26.
11. Ratzinger, 28.
12. Joseph Ratzinger, *Principles of Catholic Theology: Building Stones for a Fundamental Theology*, trans. Sister Mary Frances McCarthy (San Francisco: Ignatius Press, 1987), 74.

expressed in the quite different relationship 'stand-understand.'"[13] In this view, "faith in God appears as a holding on to God through which man gains a firm foothold for his life. Faith is thereby defined as taking up a position, as taking a stand trustfully on the ground of the word of God. . . . 'If you do not believe, then you do not understand, either.'"[14] In the light of faith, everything—including science—makes *more* sense, not less. That, itself, is a reason to believe.

---

13. Ratzinger, *Introduction to Christianity*, 68.
14. Ratzinger, 69. The final quote is a reference to Isa. 7:9.

PART IV

NEW ISSUES

SCIENCE AND FAITH

21

Theology and Science: How and Why

Christopher Baglow

Over the past fifteen years, I have received and answered countless questions from skeptics and believers alike about the Catholic faith and modern science: questions about science and the Bible, the Big Bang and creation, etc. Offering reasonable answers to such questions is a vital element of proposing the Gospel in the context of our scientifically advanced culture, and upcoming chapters will address some of the most common faith-science questions. But an equally important task is to address a question that one rarely, if ever, encounters, for it regards the deeply entrenched, false assumption of our culture that faith and science are antagonistic "forces" at war with each other. This most important "unasked question" is about the very nature of faith and science as ways of knowing reality: Are faith and science, to one degree or another, trying to answer the same kinds of questions in incompatible ways, placing them in intractable conflict? Or are they unique, noncompetitive perspectives on reality?

If we are to show that "relational unity" between faith and science is possible, we must first distinguish them. Only in doing so can we hope to overcome the conflict model of faith and science, which often undercuts attempts to relate theology and science to each other at the level of specific topics. For example, it avails little to show that the first creation account (Gen. 1) is not a scientific treatise when one's interlocutor is left thinking that, even if it weren't, it very well could have been. Calling a stalemate on one battlefield does not end a war. It simply shifts its focus.

In this short essay, I will introduce an imprecise yet helpful way of distinguishing faith and science as two ways of knowing, using the words "how" and "why." Then, I will explore the very different ways each attains to certainty and to making judgments; here, we will understand how not simply faith and science, but also theology and science, are noncompetitive, mutually enriching approaches to reality.

In the words of Rabbi Jonathan Sacks, "Science takes things apart to see *how* they work; religion brings things together to see *what they mean*."[1] Or, as St. John Paul II once said, "The theological teaching of the Bible, like the doctrine of the Church . . . does not seek so much to teach us the *how* of things, as rather the *why* of things."[2] Here, clarity is important, for we often use the word "why" as a synonym for "how." For example, the question "Why is there an element called oxygen?" can be answered with an explanation about *how* oxygen was first formed—in the process of helium fusion in the cores of stars. In the how-why distinction we are developing here, we are using "why" in regard to questions of meaning and purpose, as in "Why did you go to Mass last Sunday?" or "Why did Michelangelo paint the Sistine Chapel?" With that qualification, the how-why distinction is a helpful way to begin.

Let's illustrate this difference with a thought experiment. Imagine enjoying an outdoor concert on a sunny afternoon. Afterward, an alien spacecraft lands and an alien (who strangely can understand and speak English) approaches you and asks about the noise that had been coming from the stage. You begin by explaining what the music being played is called (blues, folk, rock and roll), and you go through the type of music it is, the instruments it involves, a little music theory about harmony, keys, and octaves, etc. Once you have said enough for the alien to understand, he responds, "Now I

---

1. Jonathan Sacks, *The Great Partnership: Science, Religion and the Search for Meaning* (New York: Schocken Books, 2011), 2 (emphasis added).

2. "L'enseignement théologique de la Bible—comme la doctrine de l'Eglise qui l'explicite—nous apprend moins le comment des choses que leur pourquoi." (John Paul II, "Discours aux Participants au Colloque sur le Thème: Science, Philosophie et Théologie," September 5, 1986, Vatican.va [emphasis added]).

understand *how* the music is played. But I don't understand *why* it is being played."

Now, you have an entirely different task of explanation. You might say that people love music because it moves them by putting the experience of being human into beautiful sounds—music is about experiencing your ordinary life from a new perspective. You might add that it unites the music fans into a common experience—music is about relationships. You might conclude your explanation by remarking that, through poetry and musical artistry, music draws listeners out of ordinary life for a moment—music is about transcendence. The meaning of music is outside the music: to discover it, you have to step outside the details of its composition into its human context, the context of the artist and her audience, and ponder why the music was created.[3] Then, you can begin to relate what one knows of how the music is played to that larger, perhaps more difficult, question of meaning.

Notice that, in order to explain music, you have at least two choices. You can explain the internal logic of the music, describing *how* it is composed and played. But in order to explain the *meaning* of music to those who play it or enjoy it, you have to answer *why* questions about it. Science is about answering *how* questions: it approaches the physical universe according to its internal patterns, telling us *how* it works. Faith approaches the universe according to what the whole system of the universe means: *why* it exists, its role in human happiness, and the intentions of its Creator. Just as in the case of understanding music, the answers to why questions and how questions about the universe are very different, but taken together they can provide a fuller picture, a deeper understanding, of reality.

This approach is helpful as a start, but it does not address the prevalent impression that faith only involves reason as a kind of "rearguard action" to defend its assertions.[4] Here, a further distinction can help us, one that is noteworthy precisely because of the greatness of its originator—St. Thomas

---

3. Sacks, *The Great Partnership*, 29.
4. Joseph Ratzinger, *'In the Beginning . . .': A Catholic Understanding of the Story of Creation and the Fall*, trans. Boniface Ramsey (Grand Rapids, MI: Eerdmans, 1986), 6.

Aquinas—and of its modern advocate Joseph Ratzinger.[5] Both science and faith can be described as "thinking with assent." That is, both are the use of reason by which one reaches a conclusion about reality—"thinking." And both of them involve an assent to truth, a response of "Yes, this is true." What makes them different from each other is the order in which thinking and assent occur. In science, thinking occurs first and makes assent possible and almost necessary—the evidence forces us to say "yes" to what it reveals. But in faith, assent comes first, and from there assent and thinking, will and intellect, walk hand in hand; they balance each other.[6] Understanding this difference is crucial.

In science, assent must be rigorously suspended in the development of a hypothesis—you can't decide in advance what you'll find out in the lab or the field before experimentation. Assent should only come when investigation has demonstrated that one's hypothesis is correct. But in faith, assent comes first, as a response to God's offer of himself and of salvation. What remains is the struggle to honestly face the myriad questions that arise from this encounter, in which the mind must follow the heart's assent, much as Bartimaeus, cured of his blindness, "followed [Jesus] on the way" (Mark 10:52). As Ratzinger says, "[In faith] thought has not attained to assent in its own way, but on the basis of the will, it has not yet found its rest; it is still reflecting and still in a state of seeking (*inquisitio*). It has not yet reached satisfaction. It has been brought to an end only 'from outside.'"[7] And this is why faith seeks understanding—this is why we have theology.

And it is here that the relationship between science and theology becomes clear—and it is the antithesis of conflict. When theology faces science, it does so not to oppose its discoveries but to incorporate them into its seeking. It can do so because God is not another being in the universe that science

---

5. Joseph Ratzinger, "Faith and Theology," in *Pilgrim Fellowship of Faith: The Church as Communion* (San Francisco: Ignatius Press, 2005). In this lecture, Ratzinger masterfully interprets and applies St. Thomas Aquinas' distinction between faith and "discursive thought" (*cogitationem*) to the distinction between theology and science.

6. Ratzinger, 22–24.

7. Ratzinger, 25.

studies, but the universe's Author: "The whole of the cosmos, coming to be and passing away in time, is His speaking to us."[8] St. John Paul II captured this when he wrote that theology "must be in vital interchange today with science," and mused positively about how cosmology and evolutionary science might enrich theology when fruitfully engaged by theologians, and even contribute to the development of doctrine.[9] This means that theology not only has boundaries, but also new horizons. Acknowledging this is not to deny the transcendent perfection of God's self-revelation in Christ. It is the humble recognition, in Ratzinger's words, that "the Word of God is always in advance of us and our thinking."[10]

Theology and science, with their radical differences in the types of questions they answer and the order in which they engage the mind and the will in reaching conclusions and making judgments, are not in conflict. Together, they can and do flourish. In theology, faith is challenged by science to probe more deeply the contents of faith and to engage new questions. Science is challenged by faith to move beyond itself from the how to the why. In admittedly different ways, they need each other.

---

8. Frederick Crosson, "Structure and Meaning of Augustine's *Confessions*," *Proceedings of the American Catholic Philosophical Association* 63 (1989): 92.

9. John Paul II, "Letter of His Holiness John Paul II to Reverend George V. Coyne, SJ, Director of the Vatican Observatory," June 1, 1988, Vatican.va.

10. Ratzinger, *Pilgrim Fellowship of Faith*, 26.

22

Defending a Historical Adam and Eve in an Evolving Creation

Fr. Nicanor Pier Giorgio Austriaco, OP

In recent years, an increasing number of Christians have struggled to believe that an original couple named Adam and Eve, from whom all of us are descended, really existed. They are challenged by the claims of biologists who have concluded that we are descended from an ancestral human population that never dropped below ten thousand individuals. Some are even tempted to give up the Gospel because it appears irreconcilable with an evolutionary picture of the world.

In this chapter, I respond to this challenge by providing a "fittingness" argument for why God may have chosen to create through an evolutionary process. I then provide a possible account that defends a historical Adam in light of the genomic discoveries we have made about the origins of *Homo sapiens*.

The Fittingness of Evolutionary Creation

Since Charles Darwin first described his seminal ideas in 1859, it has become certain, with supporting evidence from disparate fields of the natural sciences, that God used evolution to bring about the diversity of life on Earth. For Christians, this raises a profound question: Why would God have chosen a strategy of evolutionary creation rather than one of special creation, as the book of Genesis appears to describe?

To answer questions that seek to penetrate the mystery of God—and our question about God's motives behind creation is certainly one such question—theologians appeal to arguments from fittingness. Arguments of this kind have been utilized throughout the history of the Church to illustrate the coherence, intelligibility, and beauty of the Christian faith. St. Thomas Aquinas used these arguments in his work. As Joseph Wawrykow observes, for Aquinas, arguing from fittingness involves understanding why an end is attained better and more conveniently with the choice of a particular means rather than another.[1] In this sense, and as St. Thomas himself explains, choosing to ride a horse is more fitting than walking if one seeks to quickly reach one's destination on a journey.

Since fittingness arguments examine the appropriateness of a particular means to attain a certain end, we begin by asking: What is the end of creation? Why did God choose to create at all? The *Catechism of the Catholic Church* provides the following answer: "Scripture and Tradition never cease to teach and celebrate this fundamental truth: 'The world was made for the glory of God'" (CCC 293). Later, the *Catechism* explains: "We believe that God created the world according to his wisdom. . . . We believe that it proceeds from God's free will; he wanted to make his creatures share in his being, wisdom and goodness" (CCC 295). God created to reveal his glory, his power, and his perfection! This is the end of creation.

We can now ask whether or not evolutionary creation attains this end in a more fitting manner than special creation. I propose that it does.

We begin by acknowledging that God could have created everything in the world directly and immediately without using other causes. He could have done everything himself. And yet, when we look at the history of creation and the history of salvation, we discover that God has preferred to act

---

1. Joseph Wawrykow, *The Westminster Handbook to Thomas Aquinas* (Louisville: Westminster John Knox, 2005), 58. In his magisterial examination of theological fittingness and beauty the Dominican scholar, Gilbert Narcisse, OP, describes fittingness arguments this way: "Theological fittingness displays the significance of the chosen means among the alternative possibilities, and the best reasons for which God in his wisdom effectively realized and revealed, freely and through his love, the mystery of salvation and the glorification of mankind." (See his *Les Raisons de Dieu* [Fribourg: Editions Universitaires Fribourg Suisse, 1997], 572 [author's translation from the French]).

through his creatures. He generates infants through their parents. He heals the sick through their doctors. He forgives sinners through his priests. Whenever the circumstances require it, God acts directly, but whenever it is possible and fitting, he acts through his creatures. Why does God do this? Why does he prefer to work with and through his creatures rather than without them? St. Thomas explained that this mode of action allows God to give his creatures a share of his causality.[2] And in doing this, he reveals his power.

To understand this claim, consider two teachers who are working with a student who is struggling with a calculus exam. One teacher simply completes the questions for the student. He acts directly on the exam; he writes down the answers. The other teacher teaches the student enough calculus so that the student can complete the exam himself. Instead of acting directly, this teacher answers the exam with and through her student. Who is the better teacher? Clearly, the second teacher. She was able to share her knowledge of calculus in a way that made the student a knower and doer of calculus himself.

Similarly, God could have created all living kinds himself. However, I propose that he chose to create through evolution because he wanted to better reveal his power through the use of creaturely causes in the same way that a teacher reveals her expertise by forming excellent students. Maybe surprisingly for some, evolutionary creation reveals God's unparalleled glory in a way that special creation does not.

The Historicity of Adam and Eve

By all accounts, the *Catechism* appears to affirm the existence of an original couple from whom all of us are descended. This magisterial text refers to Adam and Eve as our "first parents" who are created in an original state of justice and holiness (§375). Though it affirms the use of figurative language in the creation narrative, it also explicitly concludes: "Revelation gives us the

---

2. Thomas Aquinas, *Summa theologiae* 1.103.6.

certainty of faith that the whole of human history is marked by the original fault freely committed by our first parents" (§390). Finally, it teaches that all human beings are Adam's descendants and implicated in his sin (§404).

In apparent contrast, the current scientific narrative for the origins of our biological species, *Homo sapiens*, would go something like this.[3] Anatomically modern humans first evolved in East Africa from a more ancient African hominin population around 200,000 years ago. Significantly, the ancestral population of humans never shrank below a number of approximately 10,000 individuals. These modern humans eventually spread, first across Africa and then, around 80,000 to 60,000 years ago, out of Africa into the rest of the world. Today, every human being is descended from the ancestral African population.

How can we reconcile this scientific consensus with the theological account of a unique beginning for our kind in an original human couple? I propose three steps.

First, contemporary anthropologists acknowledge that the *Homo sapiens* living today—that is, us—are anatomically modern humans that have an additional suite of behavioral and cognitive traits that set us apart from our recent human ancestors, also members of *Homo sapiens*, who lived about 100,000 years ago. These traits have been linked to symbolic behavior, and their revolutionary emergence in recent human history has been called the Great Leap Forward.[4] This suggests that there are actually two populations of individuals in the biological species *Homo sapiens*: those who can think symbolically, and those that do not. We belong to the former group, the natural

---

3. For details and citations to the scientific literature for the narrative given here, see the following reviews: Bastien Llamas et al., "Human evolution: a tale from ancient genomes," *Philosophical Transactions of the Royal Society B: Biological Sciences* 372.1713 (2017): 20150484; Christ Stringer, "The origin and evolution of Homo sapiens," *Philosophical Transactions of the Royal Society B: Biological Sciences* 371.1698 (2016): 20150237; and Marta Mirazon Lahr, "The shaping of human diversity: filters, boundaries and transitions," *Philosophical Transactions of the Royal Society B: Biological Sciences* 371.1698 (2016): 20150241.

4. Ian Tattersall, "The Great Leap Forward," *Weber: The Contemporary West* 28.1 (2011): 40–47. Also see Ian Tattersall, "Human evolution and cognition," *Theory in Biosciences* 129.2-3 (2010): 193–201. For an opposing minority perspective, see Sally McBrearty and Alison S. Brooks, "The revolution that wasn't: a new interpretation of the origin of modern human behavior," *Journal of Human Evolution* 39.5 (2000): 453–563.

kind I will call *Sapiens*, within the population of individuals that evolutionary biologists have called the biological species *Homo sapiens*.

Next, though it is difficult to prove at this time, distinguished anthropologist Ian Tattersall has proposed that the human capacity for language is what distinguishes behaviorally modern humans from their anatomically modern ancestors. For Tattersall, the evolution of the language capacity would explain the recent revolutionary appearance of symbolic behavior and, thus, culture, which occurred in the past 100,000 years.

Finally, though much work remains to uncover the mystery of language evolution,[5] distinguished linguist Noam Chomsky has proposed that the capacity for language arose in a *single* human individual who was living among our ancestral population of anatomically modern humans in East Africa.[6] Some genetic modification rewired this individual's brain such that he was born capable of language. He was the first speaking primate.

Therefore, I claim that it is still reasonable to trace the origin of our kind to an original individual. He would have been the first anatomically modern human to have evolved the capacity for language that allowed him to think symbolically and abstractly. He would have been the first individual person belonging to *Sapiens* as a natural kind, living among a population of nonlinguistic individuals belonging to the biological species *Homo sapiens*. His name was Adam, and since we are all born with the capacity of language, we are all descended from him. Finally, it would have been fitting for God to have raised up another linguistic individual to be Adam's mate. Her name was Eve. She was the mother of all those living today.

---

5. For discussion, compare Johan J. Bolhuis, Ian Tattersall, Noam Chomsky, and Robert C. Berwick, "How Could Language Have Evolved?" *PLoS Biology* 12 (2014): e1001934; and Marc D. Hauser, Charles Yang, Robert C. Berwick, Ian Tattersall, Michael J. Ryan, Jeffrey Watumull, Noam Chomsky, and Richard C. Lewontin, "The mystery of language evolution," *Frontiers in Psychology* 5 (2014): 401.

6. Noam Chomsky, *The Science of Language: Interviews with James McGilvray*, ed. Noam Chomsky and James McGilvray (Cambridge: Cambridge University Press, 2012), 12.

Conclusion

As Pope St. John Paul II put it so well, "faith and reason are like two wings on which the human spirit rises to the contemplation of truth."[7] Consequently, we must strive to reconcile all apparently contradictory theological and scientific claims—including the claims about the origins of our rational kind—though the task may often be onerous and, sometimes, seemingly intractable. However, we do so knowing that the intellectual struggle is itself an act of worship that gives honor to God, the Creator of all things. To him be the glory for ever and ever. Amen.

---

7. John Paul II, *Fides et Ratio* 1, Vatican.va.

23

Free Will and Its Challenges from Neuroscience

Daniel De Haan

This chapter confronts the influential Libet-style experiments on the neural antecedents of conscious volition and their challenge to free will. Before exploring these experiments, we need to examine the concept of free will. There are many incompatible concepts of "free will," and there are independent philosophical grounds for rejecting the particular concept of free will assumed in the Libet-style experiments.

What is free will? Why should we believe free will exists? The existence of free will isn't obvious. It's never mentioned by Plato or Aristotle, and explicit concepts of free will only show up later in the Stoics and Church Fathers.[1] Why then does free will's existence seem obvious? The confusion arises from conflating free will with the activities it enables us to do. Free will isn't an activity we *do*. It's the *power* exercised whenever we perform activities like deciding and freely acting or refraining from acting. These voluntary activities are obvious facets of human life, but distinguishing the different powers that enable human activities is difficult business. We identify powers by first identifying their activities or operations. Acts of seeing visible things reveal the power of vision. Acts of understanding and reasoning disclose the power of intellect.

The power of free will is identified by *voluntarily* or *freely* conducted

---

1. Michael Frede, *Free Will: Origins of the Notion in Ancient Thought* (Berkeley, CA: University of California Press, 2012); John M. Rist, *Augustine Deformed: Love, Sin and Freedom in the Western Moral Tradition* (Cambridge: Cambridge University Press, 2014).

activities. Because voluntary operations, like choice, are so tightly bound up with practical reasoning[2] and motivation, it's hard to establish that free choice, and the power of free will, are in fact distinct from the activities and powers of practical reason and sentient appetite. St. Thomas Aquinas drew attention to this latent interconnection in Aristotle's own ambivalent characterization of choice as "an appetitive intellect or an intellectual appetite."[3]

Our fully voluntary actions exhibit rational control over their initiation, continuation, and termination. We also perform voluntary actions that aren't freely initiated, even though we can control their outcomes. I cannot sneeze at will, but I can often freely control whether I sneeze into a tissue after I feel an urge to sneeze.[4] Voluntary actions are free insofar as they are *up to us*, which is why we are accountable and responsible for the actions we rationally and voluntarily control. Free will is best conceptualized as a two-way power enabling humans either to act or to refrain from acting in light of their practical reasons for acting.[5]

The interdependency of practical reason and free will has been stressed here because some "libertarian" conceptions of free will mistakenly believe free will is only free if choices occur without being causally influenced. In an effort to escape the errors of determinism, they leap to another extreme, hoping to secure freedom by indeterminism. Such conceptions of free will confuse liberty with arbitrary indeterminacy. But indeterminism cannot secure the rational self-control and responsible agency that truly characterizes human freedom.

Another related error is the view that actions can only be voluntary if one

---

2. Thomas Aquinas, following Aristotle, distinguishes two ways of reasoning and understanding. We exercise theoretical reasoning whenever our intellectual judgments and inferences aim at knowledge of the truth. We exercise practical reasoning whenever our intentions, deliberations, and judgments of choice aim at the goods of action. See Thomas Aquinas, *Summa theologiae* 1.79.11.

3. Thomas Aquinas, *Summa theologiae* 1.83.3. Stephen Brock, *Action and Conduct: Thomas Aquinas and the Theory of Action* (Edinburgh: T&T Clark, 1998).

4. M.R. Bennett and P.M.S. Hacker, *Philosophical Foundations of Neuroscience* (Oxford: Blackwell, 2003), 224–228.

5. *Catechism of the Catholic Church* 1730–1748; Yves R. Simon, *Freedom of Choice*, ed. Peter Wolff (New York: Fordham University Press, 1999); Robert Sokolowski, *Moral Action: A Phenomenological Study* (Washington, DC: The Catholic University of America Press, 2017).

is conscious of an explicit decision or volition to act prior to acting. It claims that if we don't first consciously plan a future action or experience a prior "sense of agency," then the ensuing action cannot be voluntary. This is clearly false, but this mistaken conception of free will was assumed in the famous Libet-style experiments on free will. We can see why it's false by considering the three distinct ways practical reason informs our voluntary actions.

Practical reasoning pertains to activities of intending good ends and deliberating about the best means to achieve them.[6] We sometimes consciously exercise practical reason before we act, like when we deliberate about whether to attend a concert or how to get to a venue. But we don't always need to deliberate overtly about how to achieve our ends prior to acting voluntarily, like when we commute to work, carry on a conversation, or enjoy a family meal. These quotidian examples of intentional activities belong to a second form of practical reasoning.

This second form occurs whenever we consciously act for reasons and achieve our ends without explicitly deliberating beforehand. In most conversations, we don't rehearse or plan ahead of time what we are going to say before we say it; rather, we simply say what we consciously intend to say.

A third form of practical reasoning takes place retrospectively after we have voluntarily acted. A daily examination of conscience, for example, involves reflecting on prior actions and considering what one has done or failed to do, whether one should have chosen a better means to achieve one's end, or whether one should not have pursued certain ends or actions at all. It is the second form of practical reasoning in particular that demonstrates why it's false to hold that all voluntary actions require prior conscious volitions or decisions. Unfortunately, this flawed concept was assumed and operationalized in the Libet-style experiments on free will.

In the early 1980s, Benjamin Libet conducted a number of experiments that purportedly showed "the brain evidently 'decides' to initiate or, at the

---

6. Alasdair MacIntyre, *Dependent Rational Animals: Why Human Beings Need the Virtues* (Chicago: Open Court, 1999); Alasdair MacIntyre, "What is a human body?," in *The Tasks of Philosophy* (Cambridge: Cambridge University Press, 2006), 86–103.

least, prepare to initiate the act at a time before there is any reportable subjective awareness that such a decision has taken place."[7] Subjects were instructed to watch a special clock and wait for a conscious urge, decision, or volition to move their finger. If they experienced a conscious volition to move, then they were to move their finger and note the time on the clock when they felt this conscious volition. This time was compared with the time that their finger moved and the time of a neural signature in the motor cortex of their brain, called a *readiness potential*, detected by an EEG cap worn on the head. Surprisingly, the readiness potential in the brain consistently occurred around 350 milliseconds before "the appearance of a reportable time for awareness of any subjective intention or wish to act."[8] Subsequent and more advanced Libet-style experiments on free will continue to get similar results. Some have concluded that these experiments demonstrate that free will is an illusion because the brain initiates decisions or volitions before we consciously decide to act. But scores of theorists have argued that these experiments don't challenge the existence of free will. We have space to consider three fundamental problems with these experiments.[9]

First, these experiments assume and operationalize a flawed conception of free will. We can voluntarily act without waiting for a prior experience of a volition to act. Even when we do deliberate prior to acting, it is practical reason, not free will, that we enlist to deliberate concerning what we should do. Furthermore, subjects were told *to wait for* an urge or volition to move. But unlike *willing*, which is *active*, this targets a quintessentially *passive*

7. Benjamin Libet et al., "Time of Conscious Intention to Act in Relation to Onset of Cerebral Activity (Readiness-Potential): The Unconscious Initiation of a Freely Voluntary Act," *Brain* 106.3 (1983): 623–642, at 640.

8. Libet, "Time of Conscious Intention," 640.

9. Parashkev Nachev and Peter Hacker, "The Neural Antecedents to Voluntary Action: A Conceptual Analysis," *Cognitive Neuroscience* 5.3-4 (2014): 193–208; Parashkev Nachev and Peter Hacker, "The Neural Antecedents to Voluntary Action: Response to Commentaries," *Cognitive Neuroscience* 6.4 (2015):180–186; Alfred Mele, ed., *Surrounding Free Will: Philosophy, Psychology, Neuroscience* (Oxford: Oxford University Press, 2015); Alfred Mele, *Effective Intentions* (Oxford: Oxford University Press, 2009).

phenomenon that nonvoluntarily happens to someone, like feeling an urge to sneeze.[10] Consequently, these experiments mistakenly target a phenomenon that's both misdescribed as voluntary and is categorically unlike willing.

Second, the Libet-style experiments only study arbitrary movements like finger flicking. But these aren't *choices* informed by reasons for acting; they are more aptly characterized as *picking* for no reason at all. Consequently, at best, these experiments might show our brain initiates our arbitrary *picking*, but they say nothing about the rational choices relevant to moral responsibility and free will.[11]

Third, these experiments overlook—and so fail to control for—a major confound. Voluntary actions are informed by our reasons or intentions for acting, and intentions for acting are typically subordinated to further intentions. For example, volunteers in Libet's experiments must intend to follow Libet's instructions, and that intention will influence everything volunteers intend to do and experience while participating in the experiment. This includes intentionally watching a clock and introspectively waiting for an ersatz experience characterized by the experimenters as a volition, decision, or urge to move. A volunteer's intention to follow instructions might also influence their brain, including neural events or the readiness potential detected by the EEG. In short, these experiments fail to control for how volunteers' intentions to follow instructions might be causing the very readiness potential in the brain claimed to threaten free will.[12]

These responses focus on major problems with Libet-style experiments. But what about future experiments claiming to undermine free will? One lesson of this chapter is that we should always raise two questions for any past

---

10. "Strikingly, Libet's theory would in effect assimilate all human voluntary action to the status of inhibited sneezes or sneezes which one did not choose to inhibit. For, in his view, all human movements are initiated by the brain before any awareness of a desire to move, and all that is left for voluntary control is the inhibiting or permitting of the movement that is already underway." Bennett and Hacker, *Philosophical Foundations of Neuroscience*, 230.

11. Alfred Mele, *Free: Why Science Hasn't Disproved Free Will* (Oxford: Oxford University Press, 2014).

12. Raymond Tallis, *Aping Mankind: Neuromania, Darwinitis and the Misrepresentation of Humanity* (Durham: Acumen, 2011), 51–59, 247–256.

or future challenges to free will: Which concept of free will is being challenged? Is that concept the most accurate concept of free will? We should also consider whether any radical challenges to voluntary agency based on experiments might self-defeatingly undermine all scientific experiments. Consider the fact that all experiments require experimenters to wield rational embodied control over relevant phenomena. So, no scientists can consistently conclude that experiments have demonstrated that rational embodied control is an illusion without undermining all experiments. Now, the kind of voluntary agency exhibited in rational embodied control is precisely the kind of agency enabled by the power of free will. Consequently, if this is the right conception of free will, and free will is indispensable to rational embodied control, then no experiments could ever demonstrate that free will is an illusion.[13] We therefore have solid grounds for concluding that scientific experiments presuppose the existence of free will.

---

13. Daniel De Haan, "The power to perform experiments," *Neo-Aristotelian Metaphysics and the Theology of Nature*, ed. William M.R. Simpson, Robert C. Koons, James Orr (London: Routledge, 2021).

24

The Quantum Revolution and the Reconciliation of Science and Humanism

Robert C. Koons

Quantum mechanics is one of the most successful theories in the history of science. In some form, it is here to stay. The quantum discoveries of the twentieth century transformed our understanding of the natural world. In fact, the quantum revolution is a theologically wholesome development, reconciling our scientific view with the possibility of human agency and knowledge.

The Greek philosopher Aristotle (384–322 BC) had a theory of nature that offered a number of advantages from the Christian viewpoint. While Aristotle recognized a profound difference between human beings and other "substances" (i.e., fundamental entities), based on our unique rationality, he avoided dualism, and he conceived of human aspirations as continuous with the striving of all natural things to their essential ends (i.e., teleology), providing an objective basis for norms in ethics, aesthetics, and politics.

The perennial philosophy understood nature in terms of form and matter. Substances contain a principle known as "substantial form," which plays the following three roles:

1. Substantial form determines the *natural kind* of a substance by fixing its essential causal powers.
2. Substantial form is the ultimate principle of unity that secures the existence of composite and transitory entities (including organisms) as substances.

3. Substantial form undergirds the possible possession of the secondary qualities that we rely upon to identify entities, affirming the reliability of our sensory knowledge.

The postulation of substantial forms gives rise to Aristotle's four "causes." The form of a substance is its formal cause. The substance's material components are its material cause. Aristotle accepts both top-down (formal) and bottom-up (material) explanations. The form supports the existence of a set of causal powers for each substance. These causal powers orient the substance toward acting in a particular way in the world (final causation), and they enable substances to effect change in one another (efficient causation).

1. The Quantum Revolution

In the modern revolt against Aristotle, dominant from the time of Galileo until the quantum revolution, all fundamental material entities are simple and microscopic in scale. No composite thing (like you and me) is a true substance. Instead, we are mere heaps, wholly reducible to the natures and interactions of our ultimate constituents.

The quantum revolution of the last one hundred years has transformed the image of nature in profound ways, reviving Aristotelian modes of understanding. Physicists first discovered in the early twentieth century that the energy of isolated systems cannot vary continuously but must jump from one discrete level (quantum) to another. This apparently modest discovery has profound implications for all of science. It actually constituted a kind of "Scientific Counter-Revolution," reviving the Aristotelian conception of nature in at least three ways: rehabilitating teleology, unseating the microscopic world from its privileged position, and securing the ontological autonomy of chemistry and thermodynamics (and potentially also the autonomy of biology and psychology) from mere physics.

1.1 The Revival of Teleology

Classical mechanics can be formulated in either of two ways: in terms of differential equations, based on Newton's laws of motion, or in terms of integral equations, relying on the conservation of energy (the Hamiltonian method). The Newtonian model is completely bottom-up, but the Hamiltonian is Aristotelian, being both holistic and teleological. The total energy of a closed system is a holistic property: it cannot be reduced to the properties of the system's constituents, taken individually. More importantly, the Hamiltonian method relies on so-called "variational principles," like the least-action principle (and the use of the least-action principle is a form of *teleological* explanation, as Leibniz recognized).[1]

In classical mechanics, either model can be used, and they are probably equivalent in that setting. However, with the quantum revolution, the Hamiltonian picture becomes mandatory, since the particles can no longer be imagined to be moving in response to the composition of forces exerted at each moment from determinate distances. Teleology reigns supreme over mechanical forces, as Max Planck noted.[2]

1.2 Unseating the Micro-Physical: The Measurement Problem

A quantum particle doesn't typically have any position or momentum at all: it has merely the *potential* to interact with macroscopic systems in various locations. Thus, the quantum world cannot be a complete basis for the macroscopic world.

Of course, this situation gives rise immediately to a puzzle: What, then, is the relationship between the macroscopic and quantum worlds?

---

1. Jeffrey K. McDonough, "Leibniz's Two Realms Revisited," *Noûs* 42 (2008): 673–696; "Leibniz on Natural Teleology and the Laws of Optics," *Philosophy and Phenomenological Research* 78 (2009): 505–544.

2. See Max Planck, "The Principle of Least Action," in *A Survey of Physical Theory*, trans. R. Jones and D.H. Williams (New York: Dover, 1960), 69–81; Val Dusek, "Aristotle's Four Causes and Contemporary 'Newtonian' Dynamics," in *Aristotle and Contemporary Science*, vol. 2, ed. Demetra Sfendoni-Mentzou, Jagdish Hattiangadi, and David M. Johnson (New York: Peter Lang, 2001), 81–93; Mariam Thalos, *Without Hierarchy: The Scale Freedom of the Universe* (Oxford: Oxford University Press, 2013), 84–86.

Presumably, macroscopic physical objects are wholly composed of quanta. How, then, can the quanta fail to be a complete basis for them?

Aristotle offers a ready answer to this puzzle. The microscopic constituents of macroscopic objects exist only as potentialities for interaction. They are only virtually present, except when they are activated.

Quantum mechanics has given rise to a dizzying variety of "interpretations," each offering its own solution to the measurement problem. Some involve monstrously exotic hypotheses. The *many-worlds* interpretation posits the existence of an unimaginably large number of parallel universes, each splitting off from a common history at every moment. David Bohm's model supposes that the entire cosmos is instantaneously involved in guiding the movement of each particle, making it impossible to isolate any interaction from remote and uncontrollable factors. *Objective collapse* theory postulates new and so-far undetected mechanisms for producing mostly determinate results at the macroscopic scale. The *transactional* interpretation supposes that the future can influence the past, and the *Copenhagen* interpretation supposes that phenomena are real only when we observe them.

But only the *Aristotelian* interpretation preserves our common-sense knowledge without speculative add-ons. And the very existence of multiple interpretations reflects the fact that quantum mechanics, unlike "classical" mechanics, no longer provides unambiguous support to materialism.

1.3 Thermal Substances: The Irreducibility of Quantum Chemistry

I have developed and defended a theory of thermal substances in some recent work,[3] building on the pioneering work on quantum chemistry by the

---

3. Robert C. Koons, "Hylomorphic Escalation: A Hylomorphic Interpretation of Quantum Thermodynamics and Chemistry," *American Catholic Philosophical Quarterly* 92 (2018a): 159–178; Robert C. Koons, "Powers ontology and the quantum revolution," *European Journal for Philosophy of Science* 11, no. 1 (2020): 1–28; Robert C. Koons, "Thermal Substances: A Neo-Aristotelian Ontology for the Quantum World," *Synthese* 198 (2021): 2751–2772, doi:10.1007/s11229-019-02318-2.

theoretical chemist Hans Primas.[4] William Simpson ably lays out the case for the existence of such substances in his doctoral thesis,[5] building on the work of cosmologist George Ellis and physicist Barbara Drossel.[6]

On this theory, the world consists of thermal-chemical *substances* (typically macroscopic in scale) and their virtual microscopic *parts*. Each thermal substance has a full complement of "classical" properties, such as temperature, entropy, and chemical composition. In contrast, the class of *quantal* properties are typically found in apparently contradictory states called "superpositions." The neo-Aristotelian theory thus avoids the paradox of Schrödinger's cat, which is supposed to be simultaneously dead and alive. As an Aristotelian substance, the cat and its biological and chemical properties never enter into such contradictory conditions.

Quantum chemistry and thermodynamics are demonstrably irreducible to quantum microphysics, in contrast to the situation in prequantum science, which favored a bottom-up determination of everything by physics. This can be seen in two ways. First, as we have just seen, the quantum world is incomplete, a realm of mere potentiality, in contrast to the fully actual and determinate character of thermal and chemical properties. Second, pure quantum physics cannot explain *spontaneous symmetry breaking*, which is needed to explain chemical structure and phase transitions (like melting or evaporating).[7] The Stone-von Neumann theorem demonstrates that no finite quantum system can have multiple, "unitarily inequivalent" states, which are

4. Hans Primas, "Foundations of Theoretical Chemistry," in *Quantum Dynamics for Molecules: The New Experimental Challenge to Theorists*, ed. R.G. Woolley (New York: Plenum Press, 1980), 39–114; Hans Primas, *Chemistry, Quantum Mechanics, and Reductionism: Perspectives in Theoretical Chemistry* (Berlin: Springer-Verlag, 1981).

5. W.M.R. Simpson, "What's the Matter? Toward a Neo-Aristotelian Ontology of Nature," (PhD diss., University of Cambridge, 2019).

6. Barbara Drossel, "On the relation between the second law of thermodynamics and classical and quantum mechanics," in *Why More Is Different: Philosophical Issues in Condensed Matter Physics and Complex Systems*, ed. Brigitte Falkenburg and Margaret Morrison (Berlin: Springer, 2015), 41–54; George F.R. Ellis and Barbara Drossel, "Contextual Wavefunction Collapse: An Integrated Theory of Quantum Measurement," *New J. Phys.* 20 (2018): 113025.

7. R.G. Woolley, "Quantum Theory and the Molecular Hypothesis," in *Molecules in Physics, Chemistry, and Biology*, vol. 1, ed. Jean Maruani (Dordrecht: Kluwer Academic, 1988), 45–89; Laura Ruetsche, *Interpreting Quantum Theories: The Art of the Possible* (Oxford: Oxford University Press, 2011).

needed for symmetry breaking.[8] Quantum theorists overcome this result by using the "continuum limit," treating quantum systems as composed of an infinite number of virtual parts. The fact that we must use such an "unrealistic" procedure rules out in principle the possibility of an exhaustive, bottom-up explanation of chemical and thermodynamic facts in terms of quantum particles and their states. The inequivalent states (or *superselection* sectors) of quantum chemistry and thermodynamics correspond to irreducibly chemical and thermodynamic properties.

2. Prima Facie Problems

2.1 Violations of the Law of Noncontradiction or Excluded Middle

In the classic two-slit experiment, individual electrons seem to take multiple, incompatible paths between the source and the screen, going simultaneously through both the right and left slit of the barrier. It is only when the electron is detected at the screen that the wave-function "collapses" into one definite path. The theorem of John S. Bell (commonly referred to as "Bell's theorem") demonstrated that, if quantum theory is correct, we cannot suppose that individual particles take definite paths before detection—that is, we cannot assume that quantum probabilities merely reflect our ignorance of which path is already actual. Some take quantum theory to require a revision of classical logic: either supposing that the electron *both is and is not* passing through the left slit (violating the law of noncontradiction), or that the electron *neither is nor is not* passing through that slit (violating the law of excluded middle).

However, from the perennial philosophy, these erroneous conclusions result from failing to distinguish between *actuality* and *potentiality* (or act and potency, to use the traditional terms). The electron is not a substance—it is rather a potential *action* of the substantial source that generates the electrons.

---

8. Geoffrey L. Sewell, *Quantum Mechanics and Its Emergent Macrophysics* (Princeton, NJ: Princeton University Press, 2002).

This source has the potential of affecting either the left or right slit. However, when actualized, the electron will always be detected in exactly one place.

Werner Heisenberg first noted that quantum mechanics had simply revived Aristotle's notion of potentiality.[9] In prequantum physics, we did not need to refer to potentialities at all. We could simply describe and predict the actual trajectories of particles using deterministic laws of motion. In quantum theory, as in Aristotle's philosophy of nature, a complete description of nature requires us to include also the merely potential states and locations of things.

2.2 Violations of the Causal Principle: Natural Ex Nihilo?

All quantum theory incorporates an element of indeterminism. We could never predict with certainty where and when a quantum effect will be detected by our instruments, even if we were to know all physical facts with perfect precision, and even if we were able to perform all necessary calculations instantaneously. The world's evolution is irreducibly *probable* in nature.

But being undetermined should not be confused with being *uncaused*, as Elizabeth Anscombe pointed out in her inaugural Cambridge lecture.[10] Aristotle's philosophy of nature always recognized that rational agents are undetermined. Quantum mechanics has simply revealed that natural agents are more like rational agents than Aristotle had supposed.

Here is an extreme case of this indeterminism: the spontaneous appearance of virtual particles in the quantum vacuum. At first glance, this seems a violation of the ancient principle, *ex nihilo nihil fit* (nothing comes from nothing). However, appearances are deceiving.

Remember, quantum particles, including virtual particles, are not substances. They are only *potential actions* of substances. When a virtual particle is produced in the so-called "vacuum," the particle is generated by a quantum

---

9. Werner Heisenberg, *Physics and Philosophy: The Revolution in Modern Science* (London: George Allen and Unwin, 1958).

10. Elizabeth Anscombe, "Causality and Determination," in *Collected Philosophical Papers of G. E. M. Anscombe*, vol. 2: *Metaphysics and the Philosophy of Mind* (Oxford: Basil Blackwell, 1981), 133–147.

field, which represents the potential action of one or more macroscopic substances in the environment. When a virtual particle is detected, the detector helps to actualize some active power of these substances. The causal principle is fully respected at all times.

2.3 Nonlocal Spookiness

As Bell's theorem demonstrated, quantum mechanics requires a certain kind of instantaneous influence at unlimited distances. This is illustrated by the Einstein-Podolsky-Rosen (EPR) thought experiment, in which a decision about what property to measure at one point in space can have an instantaneous effect on the probabilities of results at a distant measurement site. This is a serious problem for mechanistic forms of materialism, which is why it worried Einstein so much. But it poses no difficulty at all for Aristotelians.

Aristotle believed in instantaneous influence at a distance: he thought, for example, that a light source illuminates an extended body of air instantaneously. Aristotle was wrong about the propagation of light, but he was right in thinking that one substance can influence a distant substance instantaneously. The power of a substance to act propagates outward at a velocity no greater than the speed of light, but the actualization of a power at one point in space can affect instantaneously the way in which that same power manifests itself at a distant point, as the EPR experiment illustrates.

3. Back to Aristotle's Philosophy of Nature

Quantum mechanics reaffirms what Aristotelians have known all along: that the world's ultimate constituents are not the extremely small and simple particles of physics, but much larger, composite bodies with irreducibly holistic and teleological properties and powers. This puts us firmly on the path toward recognizing that even more complex bodies—namely, persons and other living organisms—can also be metaphysically fundamental entities, with irreducibly biological and psychological properties and powers. Once we have accepted top-down determination of parts by wholes in chemistry, it is not at all hard to accept what common sense teaches about the top-down determination of my body's behavior by *me*. The indeterminism of quantum mechanics leaves plenty of room for human free will to make a real difference in the natural world, without violating any laws of nature or requiring any special élan vital or mental force.

Moreover, Aristotelianism provides the best foundation for science, since it is the only philosophy of nature that fully secures the reliability and accuracy of our senses, something that is absolutely needed if experimental science is to be a source of knowledge. The so-called secondary qualities of color, smell, and solidity are real and irreducible features of reality, properties of thermal substances. Our sense of vision, hearing, and smell are all simply adaptations of real chromatic, acoustic, and osmotic interactions between nonliving thermal substances. They are not, as modern scientists like Galileo and Descartes supposed, mere appearances in the mind. The natural world is not fundamentally colorless, soundless, smell-free, and intangible, but a world rich in qualities as well as quantities.

25

Creation and the Cosmos
Jonathan Lunine

Cosmology is the study of the origin and structure of the universe or cosmos (these two words are interchangeable). It is a branch of astronomy that stands at the boundary between physics and metaphysics, because to ask how the universe began is just a small step from asking why there is something rather than nothing. And the latter question is in fact the purview of metaphysics: the question of why there is something rather than nothing isn't answerable by the scientific method, as this article will explain later in some detail.

Today, we know from many precise astronomical observations that the universe is expanding—not in the sense that the collections of stars known as galaxies are moving apart from each other through fixed space, but rather that space itself is expanding, causing the distances between clusters (gravitationally bound groups) of galaxies to increase. The rate at which space is expanding is itself increasing with time—that is, the expansion is accelerating. The cause of this acceleration is unknown, but that unknown is given the name "dark energy." And there is another major unknown in cosmology—"dark matter." Entirely distinct from dark energy, dark matter does not absorb, reflect, or scatter light, and so is literally invisible. Its presence is deduced from the motion of normal matter—stars and clouds of gas and dust—as they orbit around the centers of their galaxies. While candidates exist for dark matter—possible exotic forms of subatomic particles quite different from the electrons, protons, and neutrons that make up the bulk of normal matter—no definitive identification has yet been made.

Cosmologists do know two important facts: dark matter is much more abundant than normal matter, thus determining the spatial distribution of material in the universe, and dark energy dominates over all other sources of matter and energy, including dark matter. Put simply, the identity of most of the matter and energy content of the universe—our reality—is not known.

The situation of cosmology today is similar to what it was one century ago. Back then, humanity's understanding of the cosmos was in the throes of a true revolution. Einstein had published his theory of general relativity in 1916, at a time when many astronomers thought the universe was small by today's standards, static, and quite likely, eternal. Einstein's theory, which visualized gravity as the distortion of space caused by the presence of matter, created a big problem for eternal universes, because it seemed that matter would cause space to collapse in on itself. To counter this unpleasant tendency, Einstein inserted what he called a "cosmological constant" into his basic equation of relativity, to provide an arbitrary repulsive effect that would balance the attractive effect of matter. Einstein didn't like such an ad hoc solution, and shortly thereafter, others proposed alternatives—that the universe might be expanding or be so empty of matter that collapse could be avoided.

A young cosmologist and Catholic priest, Georges Lemaître, entered this debate in the mid-1920s. By then, astronomers using a new generation of large telescopes had begun to find evidence that the galaxies—or strictly speaking, clusters of galaxies—were flying apart from one another. By splitting up the light from these collections of billions of stars into their component wavelengths, astronomers could see the telltale fingerprints of different elements making up the stars of these galaxies—but the fainter (and hence farther from us) the galaxy, the more the fingerprint pattern was shifted in color toward the red. An elementary interpretation of this was that the galaxies were moving away from us, causing their light to be stretched out in what is called the Doppler effect.

Lemaître was familiar with the astronomical data. He was also an expert in the theory of general relativity, which, in 1927, was an almost unique combination. Others, notably the Russian mathematician Alexander Friedmann, had invented solutions to the equations of general relativity that included expanding and contracting universes. But Lemaître was the first to formulate a solution that fitted the astronomical data and tied the red shift of the light from galaxies to the expansion of space itself. He also showed that the universe had no center to the expansion and should look more or less the same on large scales in all directions. These are properties of the cosmos that are accepted today.

In 1931, Lemaître published his famous paper asserting that the expanding universe had to have had a beginning from a primordial ultradense state—and the initiation of the expansion came to be known by the 1950s as the "Big Bang." The Big Bang model received spectacular confirmation in the 1960s when astronomers first detected a nearly uniform electromagnetic energy emanating from every direction of the cosmos. This "cosmic microwave background radiation" is the echo—receding with the expanding universe and thereby cooling—of a time soon after the Big Bang when the universe became dilute enough that matter and light could decouple from each other, allowing the latter to freely move through space. The pattern of that light is not quite uniform in temperature around the sky, suggesting that the very early universe was lumpy. The scale and degree of lumpiness are important constraints cosmologists use to construct models of the earliest moments of the Big Bang—when the universe may have expanded enormously in an event called cosmic inflation. It is also possible that the background radiation contains clues to the nature of dark energy.

Cosmologists today wrestle with the same questions that the brilliant Catholic priest Lemaître did in evaluating the implications of his revolutionary idea: Did the universe begin at the Big Bang, or was it the start of an episode in a cyclic evolution of the cosmos? Might there be a way to probe beyond the Big Bang to determine what was there "before"? Some say yes; others, for example the famous theoretical physicist Stephen Hawking, assert that the question makes no sense—that it is like asking what is north of the

North Pole. Lemaître himself speculated that time itself began at the Big Bang. And was our Big Bang a unique event, or one in an innumerable budding of new universes from some sort of larger reality? If it exists, what is the nature of that larger reality, which is referred to by the term "multiverse"? Unless the other universes of the multiverse have some effect on our own universe, such a question must lie outside the realm of science, which strictly relies on observations to ground hypotheses in data that allow them to be tested.

One of many models for a larger reality beyond the universe envisions an extra spatial dimension, large enough to have an effect on the way gravity works in our universe, but not directly accessible to us. Our universe of three spatial dimensions exists as a "brane" within this four-dimensional "bulk," and collisions between branes would create signatures in the cosmic microwave background that in principle are observable. Even were that to be the case (and no such signatures have been found to date), this seemingly elevates the metaphysical question of why there is something rather than nothing to a higher ontological level—from our universe to the multiverse, if the latter exists.

One current idea for the origin of universes within a multiverse is that these universes arise as small fluctuations at the subatomic level in a so-called "false" or "quantum" vacuum—an emptiness in which energy can spontaneously appear. Such fluctuations could initiate the inflation of space and energy into the universe we see today, and innumerable other universes. However, such a model does not provide a means of leaving God out of the creation of everything (as some cosmologists have argued), because the false vacuum is itself a physical reality of some sort. The "nothing" in the *creatio ex nihilo* of St. Thomas Aquinas is an absolute, ontologically complete absence of reality—of any reality whatsoever, no matter how alien to our own cosmos today. That metaphysical "nothing" is not the false vacuum of the cosmologist. To borrow an analogy from the physicist Stephen Barr, a false vacuum is like a bank account with an average balance of zero, but which on occasion spontaneously develops a positive balance (on which one might collect interest!). The ontological nothing of metaphysics, on the other hand, is the non-existence of the bank account itself.

The contributions of Lemaître and many other Catholic scientists to modern cosmology show that there is no intrinsic conflict between understanding the structure and origin of the cosmos on the one hand, and belief in a Creator God on the other. All that we observe, and the processes by which those things we observe appear and evolve in the universe, represent the physical reality that God is bringing into existence at every moment and every place, in his eternal now.

26

Artificial Intelligence: Religion of Technology

Fr. Anselm Ramelow, OP

Technology fascinates contemporary minds. Tools—means for the ends in our lives—are treated as ends in themselves; the medium has become the message. And as even the tool user himself is in the process of being replaced by his tools, we no longer have a clear idea why we should not think that computers can be people too. Or even why the computer should not become some super-person subsuming us into the "hive mind" as so many bits of information.

If faith and apologetics want to address the modern mind, this imaginary would seem to be a prime target.[1] Here is where we find energy and imagination and great openness for input and reflection. Initially, though, we will have to talk about the soul and the place and origin of *immateriality*. For modern people tend to think that computers can become conscious or self-conscious because we have already begun to think of *ourselves* as machines, as purely material entities. We reduce our mind to the brain (understood as a carbon-based computer) and consider our dignity merely in terms of our performance.

Therefore, a first step would be to show that we cannot reduce mind to

---

1. There is surprisingly little connecting the topic to faith in substantial ways. From a religious, cultural, and ethical perspective, see Noreen Herzfeld, *Technology of Religion* (West Conshohocken, PA: Templeton Press, 2009); Albert Borgmann, *Power Failure: Christianity in the Culture of Technology* (Grand Rapids: Brazos Press, 2003); and Anselm Ramelow, "Can Computers Create?," in *Evangelization & Culture* 1 (2019): 39–46.

matter. Here, we may need to argue that *qualitative states* of the mind, called "qualia" by philosophers (e.g., how blue looks, how the clarinet sounds, how coffee tastes), are not themselves physical: nothing in the brain turns blue or sounds like a clarinet or tastes like coffee when we have those perceptions. Nor is the *unified character* of the mind anything observable in the brain. We are always aware of many things at once, in one mind, while our material brains consist of extended parts that are not united by anything observable. What, indeed, makes the brain *one* thing in the first place?

Moreover, we can describe physical processes as causes producing effects, but the "intentionality" of our mind is of a different kind: our *awareness of things* that affect us causally (e.g., light waves) is "causally upstream" and not itself a physical phenomenon.

Further, anything material is a *particular* entity, including brain states. Yet, we are aware of *universal* concepts and of laws of nature that are *universal* (or general) in scope. Nothing material can account for the universality of such thoughts (this is why Aristotle maintained that thought, unlike the senses, cannot have a physical organ) because everything material is particular. Such universals include algorithms: as a process or rule to be followed by the operations of the machine, it is a universal for all the particular operations that it governs. Here, too, the particular material processes that we observe in the computer are underdetermined with regard to this universal. In the long run it could turn out to be something else than we think; or the particular case may even be a mistake. It has therefore, surprisingly, been argued that there are not even algorithms in computers; there is no fact of the matter in the computer with regard to which algorithm is being executed: the algorithms exist only in our interpretation. And only in that interpretation (i.e., in a mind) are they universal.

Higher states of mind such as *reflexivity* (e.g., the ability to relate to ourselves by the first-person pronoun) cannot be explained materially either. Parts of a machine can move other parts, but something material cannot reflexively relate to itself as a whole, and all at once, and at the same time (for this would be like trying to put a briefcase into itself). Accordingly, a thermostat cannot change its own setting unless it is by a further, higher algorithm that, on the highest level, is not itself subject to reflection and self-evaluation. Reflexivity implies a kind of distance from ourselves that is neither temporal nor spatial; it is immaterial. This self-transcendent distance, it can be argued, is also a root of our *free will*—another aspect that cannot be accounted for by material states.

Once we have gotten our own immaterial mind in view again, we can then ask why we should think ourselves capable of making machines with immaterial aspects. Everything we know about computers can be accounted for materially. We know this because we have made them, and we know that we have not put anything else into them. We also know that we cannot create *life* from the bottom up; for everything living comes from something else that is living (*omne vivum ex vivo*). Now in the natural world, minds exist only in living things, and can indeed be considered a higher form of life. If, then, we cannot make life, why should we expect to be able to make consciousness?

From a Christian perspective, we can point out that (contrary to Alan Turing's or Dr. Frankenstein's aspirations) God has already provided a way for bringing other minds into existence: procreation. Unlike computers, we as animals are begotten, not made. And for our *rational* minds, not even begetting is enough: as we have said, a material substratum is underdetermined with regard to the states of rational minds. It is inexplicable therefore how such a mind could arise from matter alone, without a spiritual cause. This cause turns out to be God—or so tradition has held.

Such arguments would need to be spelled out in more detail, but to a certain extent even the modern mind seems to know this intuitively. This is why theological "memes" always resurface and, in fact, permeate the modern technological imagination. They provide an important entry point for apologetics, even if more on the level of the imagination than on the level of logical argument. Here are some examples:

The place into which we now upload our minds and our information and indeed most of our existence is called the "Cloud." It is there that our infor-mation ascends, and in some accounts even we ourselves—when we will be able to "upload" ourselves into a Cloud-based immortal existence. From this Cloud, we also consult the voice of an AI agent or receive information and are inspired by new data as if from a revelation—downloading it like Moses on "tablets."

Is it a coincidence that the Apple headquarters looks like a coiled-up snake in a garden and that the building is transparent, made out of glass, like the jeweled walls of the heavenly Jerusalem? Is it not curious that its products feature as their logo an apple from which a bite has been taken, and that one is invited to eat from an apple tree in the middle of the head-quarters? Or that the first Apple computer cost $666? This is not meant to be a conspiracy theory or accusation but an indication that even the tech-nological mind is still imbued with imagery that it has received from the Christian tradition.

And technology promises to produce effects that are somehow biblical as well: through the Cloud, the internet not only connects people but also things in an automated fashion. It is like a tower of Babel that makes all things and people interconnected and transparent to each other. But also like the tower of Babel, our algorithms now confuse our language and com-munication by enclosing us in echo chambers; technological globalization turns into a new parochialism and partisanship.

We build these towers, not into the sky (like "skyscrapers"), nor into interstellar space, but into *virtual* space, cyberspace. What is supposed to emerge here is the "Singularity," a technological tool that has become self-conscious, not merely a self-driving car, but a fully automated self-conscious world into which we are subsumed as into a "hive mind." Thus we form one mystical body in this electronic Pentecost (which then also may repair the incident of the tower of Babel). This process will not transfigure our bodies like those of the blessed in heaven, but it promises to make them exchangeable and upgradeable. There are Protestant and

151

Catholic versions of this story (Mormons tend to be fascinated by it too): even a secular thinker like Jaron Lanier suggests that it is a version of the Rapture: some are left behind, but others are taken up. The Catholic version appeals to Jesuit Teilhard de Chardin and his "noosphere," which, according to him, is at least in part to be achieved by technology as well.

Apart from theological presuppositions, though, adherents cannot answer the question of why we should expect this entity to be *benevolent*. Aquinas could argue that God must be benevolent for metaphysical reasons, and faith confirms this. But a material entity is indifferent toward good and evil; after all, we can use a tool for good or ill. So, why should we trust those algorithms that we cannot understand anymore? In the absence of trust, we must *placate* this entity. Accordingly there was, until recently, even a Church of AI, Anthony Levandowski's "Way of the Future," in which the "Transition" was to be anticipated in worship: the idea was to get on the good side of this entity so that it will be benevolent toward us and treat us at least as its pets.

This is literally a page from the Old Testament: we worship the work of our own hands. The Singularity is a monotheist idol. But as in the Old Testament, those worshiping it become as hard of heart and as deaf and dumb (no qualia here!) as the material entities they worship.

Technology is not the solution to our problems, as much of the modern age since Bacon and Descartes has thought and as Pope Benedict XVI critiqued in *Spe Salvi*. Moreover, it is a means, not an end in itself. It cannot give us an account of what it is to be used for. Without a true account of our end, of who we ought to be, of where we come from and where we are going, our sinful free will is going to rule this technology with disastrous consequences. Technology cannot sin because, as we have said, it does not have free will. But it certainly will reinforce our own sinful tendencies.

Technology cannot redeem us (and therefore does not deserve our worship). But if faith redeems us, we can hope to give technology its proper place in turn. Heaven, after all, is not a garden but a city: the heavenly Jerusalem. The cities that Cain founded can indeed be redeemed and even serve to glorify God, who wants to be their light. But unlike the tower of Babel, this city "comes out of heaven"; it requires a self-surrender to God, to his grace and his providence. Technology, by contrast, teaches us that *we* can be in control. Faith may grow where this expectation is disappointed, where people become aware that technology has created new kinds of dependencies and an increasingly de-skilled humanity, and that it has diminished our sense of agency. Technology at present rather controls *us*—not least our minds and imaginations—by a sort of mirage from which we need deliverance. Here, the Catholic faith in the Real Presence may prove to be helpfully counter-cultural. Not only can the real presence of a Catholic priest never be replaced by robots (or screens), but Eucharistic Adoration is the perfect antidote to virtual reality: virtual reality is all appearance and no reality, while the Eucharist is all reality and no appearance. It is the only means which is also an end in itself, the only means that is to be worshiped. For it makes present the God Who Is—the God who alone can save us.

PSYCHOLOGY AND ANTHROPOLOGY

27

Psychology and Religion

Christopher Kaczor

We can identify rival approaches to the relationship of psychology and religion, ranging from hostile opposition to enthusiastic appropriation. A first approach develops Sigmund Freud's antipathy to religion and is represented today by figures such as Steven Pinker.[1] A strategy used by these atheist psychologists is to explain away religious beliefs as byproducts of evolution (spandrels) or as evolutionary adaptations, such as providing comfort in suffering or bringing a community together to enhance the possibility of survival. These psychologists seem to think that to explain the *origin* of a belief is to also undermine the *truth* of the belief. If religion developed through evolutionary means, then religion must be false.

One trouble with such dismissals of Catholic belief and practice is that they often do not actually explain the beliefs in question. If Catholic teaching on contraception is aimed at producing as many babies born to Catholics as possible, then why would the Church also teach many things that do not maximize procreation, such as celibacy for priests and nuns, monogamy rather than polygamy, a prohibition on adultery (which would in some cases lead to pregnancy), and an allowance of natural family planning for purposes of avoiding pregnancy? If religion is aimed at bringing about comfort, then why do Catholics have beliefs that are not comforting, like hell? If religious belief

---

1. Steven Pinker, "The Evolutionary Psychology of Religion," October 29, 2004, Freedom from Religion Foundation website, https://ffrf.org/about/getting-acquainted/item/13184-the-evolutionary-psychology-of-religion.

and practice is simply a means for survival, why celebrate martyrs who died rather than deny the faith?

Moreover, even if it were true that Catholic belief and practice arose from evolutionary forces, the *genetic fallacy* states that the origin of a belief does *not* determine the truth or falsity of a belief. Dmitri Mendeleev discovered the relationship between the chemical elements and atomic weight that make up the periodic table through a vivid dream. August Kekulé gained insight about the structure of atoms in benzene when he dreamed of intertwining snakes. Alexander Fleming discovered antibiotics because he didn't properly clean his lab. The origin of an idea does not determine the truth or falsity of an idea. So, even if it were true (which remains highly debatable) that some ideas about religion arose from evolutionary forces, it does not follow that these ideas are false. Indeed, God could use any means God wants (including evolutionary forces) to help human beings come to deeper knowledge of the divine.

A second significant approach to the relationship of psychology and religion is represented by the thought of Martin Seligman. He notes:

> For half a century after Freud's disparagements, social science remained dubious about religion. . . . About twenty years ago, however, the data on the positive psychological effects of faith started to provide a countervailing force. Religious Americans are clearly less likely to abuse drugs, commit crimes, divorce, and kill themselves. They are also physically healthier and live longer. Religious mothers of children with disabilities fight depression better, and religious people are less thrown by divorce, unemployment, illness, and death. More directly relevant is the fact that survey data consistently show religious people as being somewhat happier and more satisfied with life than non-religious people.[2]

Indeed, religious practice normally enhances positive emotion, engagement

---

2. Martin Seligman, *Authentic Happiness: Using the New Positive Psychology to Realize Your Potential for Lasting Fulfillment* (New York: Simon and Schuster, 2002), 59.

with activities, relationships with others, meaning making, and achievement in a number of ways.[3] Contemporary psychological research provides decisive evidence against the old canard that religious faith and practice damages mental health. Rather than repressing sexuality, married couples who practice a faith together are more likely than nonreligious people to report satisfying sex lives.[4] Although Seligman sees the psychological and social utility of practicing faith, he is still skeptical of God's existence (at least God as traditionally understood).[5] Seligman views religious practice as (on the whole) healthy and beneficial for human well-being, and yet in his efforts as an amateur theologian and philosopher he also views traditional religious belief as irrational and unjustified.

Another approach to psychology and religion is found in the work of psychologists who are also practicing Catholics, such as Paul Vitz.[6] This psychological approach manifests an intentional integration of psychology and Catholic Christianity similar in some ways to St. Augustine's integration of the pagan philosopher Plato with biblical Christianity. This approach involves appropriating what is legitimate and useful from secular psychology but modifying or rejecting what is contrary to true faith and practice. Careful discernment is needed to distinguish what is true from what is false, what is useful from what is counterproductive for the person of faith. Yet because God is the ultimate author of both the truths of faith and the truths of reason as found in the created order (including in the minds of human persons), there is no ultimate contradiction between the true, the good, and the beautiful as found in psychology and as found in theology. Indeed, this synthesis of truth was envisioned by the fathers of the Second Vatican Council in their document *Gaudium et Spes*: "In pastoral care, sufficient use must be made not only of

---

3. Christopher Kaczor, *The Gospel of Happiness: How Secular Psychology Points to the Wisdom of Christian Practice*, 2nd ed. (South Bend, IN: St. Augustine's, 2019).

4. Stephen Cranney, "The Influence of Religiosity/Spirituality on Sex Life Satisfaction and Sexual Frequency: Insights from the Baylor Religion Survey," *Review of Religious Research* 62 (2020): 289–314.

5. Martin Seligman, *Authentic Happiness: Using the New Positive Psychology to Realize Your Potential for Lasting Fulfillment* (New York: Free Press, 2002), 12, 255.

6. Paul C. Vitz and Craig S. Titus, *A Catholic Christian Meta-Model of the Person: Integration with Psychology and Mental Health Practice* (Sterling, VA: Divine Mercy University, 2020).

theological principles, but also of the findings of the secular sciences, especially of psychology and sociology, so that the faithful may be brought to a more adequate and mature life of faith."[7] Just as Thomas Aquinas incorporated the insights of the pagan philosopher Aristotle in order to come to deeper insights about Christian theology, so too the Catholic psychologist of today can learn from the insights of secular psychologists to come to a greater understanding of the human person.

Psychology may even aid in the work of evangelization. René Girard taught that "man is the creature who does not know what to desire, and he turns to others in order to make up his mind. We desire what others desire because we imitate their desires."[8] In their book, *Yes! 50 Scientifically Proven Ways to Be Persuasive*, Noah J. Goldstein, Steven J. Martin, and Robert B. Cialdini support Girard's view by pointing to empirical evidence in psychology of the "bandwagon effect." What we think that other people want is what we tend to want. So, in evangelization, it is helpful to emphasize models of good faith and practice (the saints), and the numbers of people who are doing the right thing. All people, but especially the young, want to "fit in" and do what they perceive to be "normal." So, in speaking to people of no faith or weak faith, it is counterproductive to evangelization to emphasize how many people reject Catholic faith and practice. It is much more helpful to emphasize the fact that "the Catholic Church is larger than any other single religious institution in the United States, with over 17,000 parishes that serve a large and diverse population."[9] In evangelizing less than fully committed audiences, it is useful to speak of modern conversion stories, the more than 2 million Catholics in the United States who attend Mass more than once a week, and the many young people who are attracted to practices like Eucharistic

---

7. Vatican Council II, *Gaudium et Spes* 62, *The Word on Fire Vatican II Collection*, ed. Matthew Levering (Park Ridge, IL: Word on Fire Institute, 2021), 292.

8. René Girard, "Generative Scapegoating," in Robert G. Hammerton-Kelly, ed., *Violent Origins: Walter Burkert, René Girard, and Jonathan Z. Smith on Ritual Killing and Cultural Formation* (Stanford, CA: Stanford University Press, 1987), 122.

9. David Masci and Gregory A. Smith, "7 Facts about American Catholics," Pew Research Center, https://www.pewresearch.org/fact-tank/2018/10/10/7-facts-about-american-catholics/.

Adoration.[10] It is, of course, necessary in some contexts (among highly committed Catholic leaders) to address the "bad news" of disaffiliation from the Catholic Church, but in the work of evangelization the empirical psychological research indicates it is much more helpful to find and emphasize the "good news" of conversions, faithfulness, and good work done by the Church.[11]

---

10. There are approximately 70,412,021 million Catholics in the United States, and Pew reports that 3.3 percent of them attend Mass more than once a week.

11. US Conference of Catholic Bishops, *The Catholic Church in America: Meeting Real Needs in Your Neighborhood* (Washington, DC: Catholic Information Project, 2006).

28

Happiness and the Meaning of Life
Jennifer Frey

The Catholic Church teaches that the point and purpose of human life generally—and thus your life specifically—is perfect happiness, understood as
complete human fulfillment. Happiness both tells us what human life and
action is in its essence, and, in so doing, also provides a measure of success for
it: a life is good if it is happy. Without this defining and ordering end, human
life would have no ultimate purpose, intelligibility, or meaning—we would
simply be creatures who happen to find ourselves alive for a cosmically insignificant period of time who then pass away into oblivion.

In this chapter, I want to provide the philosophical and theological resources to address existential questions that reflective persons ask about happiness and the meaning of life in a way that reflects the wisdom of the
Catholic intellectual tradition. But before I do that, I want to address the
obstacles in our path.

The first obstacle is the profound difference between the contemporary
concept of happiness—both theoretical and cultural—and what Catholic tradition offers. Happiness today is a rather light word used in casual self-reporting
on one's own emotional states. It can mean anything from being in a good
mood to feeling positive about one's life on the whole. Etymologically, happiness is related to good fortune. If happiness is good, it's not very serious, and
it has nothing to do with either virtue (stable dispositions that enable us to
live well) or meaning in life.

This is certainly the case in theoretical, academic work, where the most prevalent view on offer is some variety of subjectivism: the view that happiness can be cashed out solely in terms of an individual's subjective, first-person experience. Whether happiness gets cashed out in terms of positive emotional states, pleasures, or the personal satisfaction one feels when one considers one's life as a whole, all forms of subjectivism reject any distinction between true and false happiness, or a happiness that is deep rather than shallow.

As apologists, we need to know that social scientists and ordinary people alike are using happiness to refer to nothing beyond a person's individual psychology, because we need to argue that not only is this a false conception of human happiness, but more importantly, a darkly dystopian one.

First, let us note that insofar as subjectivists have a conception of "a good life," they mean a life that merely *appears* good from an individual's subjective perspective. There is no objective component to these theories. Therefore, subjectivism creates a dualism in our practical reason: we must always choose between whether to pursue happiness, meaningfulness, or virtue. If these pursuits ever coincide—if doing just or deeply meaningful actions brings you joy—this is a happy accident. But if happiness has nothing to do with morality nor helping to make sense of our own lives, then there is no good reason to make happiness a priority. To do this would be both selfish and superficial.

Second, subjectivism has a narrow focus on the individual. Happiness is exclusively about you and how you feel. Insofar as anything else matters, things matter only as much as they bear upon your psychological well-being. There is no space within subjectivism for thinking of happiness as the Church does—as a common good. Now, common goods are "common" in three senses: (1) they are common to all human beings in virtue of their shared natures; (2) they are not competitive, insofar as one person's pursuit of a common good in no way detracts from another's; (3) and they are participatory, because the realization and enjoyment of such goods only happens in cooperation with others.

Here's an example to make this more concrete: think of the good of an orchestra playing Beethoven's Ninth Symphony. As music, it is a good common to humans—every human culture makes and enjoys music. It is not competitive. The French horn player doesn't compete with the harpist or the soprano; they must cooperate in order to bring the symphony into being. Finally, the activity of playing could never be identified with any single member of the orchestra; the joy comes through playing each part in unison so as to realize the beautiful whole. Whatever makes a human person ultimately happy, it must be a common good thus defined: universal, noncompetitive, and brought about with and enjoyed with others.

Third, subjectivism creates a divorce between subjective experience and objective reality. I tend to draw on a thought experiment to help my students feel the force of this problem. I ask them to imagine a virtual-reality machine that is so sophisticated that they cannot tell the difference between simulation and real life. I tell them they can plug into the machine and experience happiness as the subjectivist defines it. Of course, in reality, they will not really be experiencing any human goods; they will be floating in a nutritive jelly, kept alive so their brains can be externally manipulated to experience "happiness." I then ask them whether they would get into such a machine.

This thought experiment is a powerful way to get people to see that there is something missing from the subjectivist account of happiness, which is that the human desire for happiness is a desire for real communion with the ultimate good. We don't just want to *feel* good; we want what *is* good. Therefore, we need an account of happiness in which *subjective* well-being is achieved through communion with what is *objectively* good.

Now that we have gone over some problems with subjectivism and some strategies for teasing out these problems, we need to turn to the positive vision the Church offers us about happiness and the meaning of life. The main point is this: there is no path to authentic happiness or true meaning in life without *virtue*.

The virtues are stable dispositions of thought, action, and feeling that allow us to act well *with ease and pleasure*. You can think of virtue like a certain kind of training; just as you need to train your muscles to excel at sports,

164

you also need to train your deliberation, emotions, and choices so that you can excel at human life. Virtues enable us to experience authentic human happiness, understood in terms of fulfillment of our specifically rational abilities—our desire to know the truth, love and pursue the good, and delight in what is beautiful.

What are the virtues? There are many of them, but at a very general level, there are the cardinal virtues of justice, temperance, fortitude, and practical wisdom, which allow us to live well regarding our natural end of human flourishing in friendship with others. But the happiness we can have in this life is fragile and imperfect—we get sick and wounded, we suffer the bad decisions of others, and of course, we and our loved ones die. Therefore, *perfect* happiness—a complete fulfillment that, once possessed, cannot be lost—is not possible in this life. Consequently, we need virtues that direct us to a supernatural end we cannot lose: eternal happiness in friendship with God, as realized in the beatific vision. These are the theological virtues of faith, hope, and love. Whereas we obtain natural virtue through good education and the formation of good habits, we cannot obtain theological virtue through our own efforts—these are infused in us through God's grace.

Finally, how does happiness relate to meaning in life? Well, if happiness is the architectonic end or goal that orders all of our practical reasoning, then this gives our life meaning and purpose. We do not pass into and out of existence for no reason, as many today will insist; we are meant to be happy, and we will inevitably be disappointed with our lives to the extent that we have failed to satisfy this natural desire. The Church has a vision of happiness that is intrinsically connected with the meaning of life. Alternative conceptions on offer see meaning, morality, and happiness as completely separate and unrelated topics. A vision that unifies these is surely more desirable, both practically and theoretically.

We need to flip the script on happiness, which is neither a superficial nor a selfish pursuit, but an essential and meaningful one. We have been created to be happy—deeply and permanently fulfilled as the kind of creatures we are. But what could really and truly fulfill us in a permanent way? The only plausible answer is God, who is himself the fullness of the truth, goodness, and beauty our hearts desire.

29

Matters of Life and Death

Stephanie Gray Connors

When it comes to debating matters of life and death, the pro-life position is often dismissed as being confusing and contradictory. Detractors will say:

- "If you're against abortion, shouldn't you be in favor of birth control to prevent unplanned pregnancies?"
- "If you're against birth control, shouldn't you embrace creating life through IVF?"
- "If you believe God gave us freedom, shouldn't you allow for assisted suicide and abortion?"

On the surface, what appears to be a worldview of conflicting positions is actually one that is profoundly unified and consistent. We can demonstrate this by appealing to three principles that speak to truths written on all human hearts:

1. Humans thrive in loving fellowship with others.

Why is solitary confinement a punishment—even considered torture?

As the Scriptures tell us, "It is not good that the man should be alone" (Gen. 2:18). In imaging God, man images the Trinity, a communion of persons. We were made for recognition, affection, and relationship; in short, we were made for love. But we must have life in order to give and receive love.

Assisted suicide, for example, violates this because it destroys an individual's life to which we should direct our love. Moreover, some might be tempted toward assisted suicide precisely because they feel abandoned, isolated, or even like a burden to others. What such lonely souls need is not an exit strategy from life but loving encounters in fellowship.

Part of being truly loved is not being rejected when certain aspects of us become known. That's what *unconditional* love is. Birth control, however, is withholding the life-creating part of oneself while rejecting the same in another. Opposing birth control doesn't lead to more abortion, because the pro-life mindset involves only having sex with one's spouse and always embracing the child of our beloved, rejoicing that one's marital love has the capacity to physically manifest in an unrepeatable and irreplaceable individual.

Further, love views another person as a subject, not an object. A human is not a commodity to be bought, sold, or weeded out for being less desirable, and yet the IVF industry does just that in the process of trying to make some humans. Whereas sex brings spouses together—always focusing on a communion of persons—IVF separates and isolates the family relationships: man and woman do not come together but instead give their most sacred power to a stranger instead of a lover, all the while leaving their child to begin life alone in a glass dish, instead of beneath the mother's heart.

Healthy and happy relationships involve tenderness, and we see that being especially necessary when one party is weaker. In particular, civil societies acknowledge that parents have a special responsibility to nurture their needy children. The dependency of a preborn child should heighten a parent's responsibility toward her, not lessen it; but abortion is the opposite of that, destroying the most sacred of all relationships. It turns mothers and fathers against each other and against their very progeny.

2. Life, not death, attracts us.

What lover gives his beloved a bouquet of wilted, rotting flowers?

Consider that when a woman has a miscarriage there is much grief, and when a woman gives birth there is great rejoicing. One laments death whereas the other celebrates life. Of those two situations, abortion is more like miscarriage (although worse, because it is intentionally inflicted); it is death that should be grieved.

Similarly, when it comes to those who are sick and dying, assisted suicide involves inflicting death instead of nourishing and comforting life. Even IVF, which might appear to be oriented toward life, often creates a human life at the expense of destroying other human lives, by killing "excess" embryos or selectively reducing tiny humans deemed genetically unfit. Birth control can even be connected to this mentality because it embraces an attitude of "I can have sex without babies," so that if pregnancy arises, abortion might be considered in the hearts of some, due to that prior belief. In each way, we see an orientation against the very thing that magnetizes humans—life.

3. Good designers design for flourishing.

When a person designs furniture that requires assembly, do they give instructions for our benefit or to oppress us?

Clearly, when they tell us how to put the pieces together, it is so the item can be used safely and effectively. Rather than take offense at the designer's instructions, we are grateful for guidelines. So it is with life principles. We humans have design features that our Creator implemented. We need to trust his judgment. If we don't look to an all-knowing, all-loving God as our authority, then who are we looking to? Whether it's ourselves or another human, there is no denying that either option involves imperfect beings who are not omnipotent. Do we really want to trust a flawed and weak source?

We can look to the design of our bodies to reveal what leads to our flourishing. For example, if an eye cannot see, we know that, because of its nature, there is a problem requiring correction. But if a healthy eye has 20/20 vision, we should not intentionally maim it. Likewise, fertility is a sign of the body working correctly, and it shouldn't be intentionally thwarted or maimed through birth control. In contrast, infertility is a sign of something gone wrong in the body, and it's therefore reasonable to correct such problems at their root—for example, surgery to clear a fallopian tube, so sperm, eggs, and embryos can pass through as designed. Such an approach aids the sexual act in achieving its designs. One of the problems with IVF is that instead of correcting an underlying problem, it bypasses it entirely. It replaces sex and our design to become one with another, manufacturing a human into existence. Because humans are subjects and not objects, this is not how we are meant to come into existence. Love is the mark of successful human relationships, and harm is the mark of destructive ones. Not only does treating humans as objects involve harm, but more obviously, so does direct killing, which is at the heart of abortion and assisted suicide. These violate our design to be in communion with others.

We are living at a time when those opposed to a sanctity-of-life ethic embrace a type of extreme autonomy where they uphold personal "choice" at all costs. It is perhaps best captured in their phrase "My body, my choice," which is used to justify everything from birth control to IVF, from abortion to assisted suicide. In response, pro-lifers should point out the insight of poet John Donne, who mused, "No man is an island." We are affected by the actions and omissions of others. Instead, what we propose to the world's selfishness is *selflessness*, a perspective grounded in the design of our bodies and our human nature: We are made for relationship. A better mantra would be "My body, for you," echoing the sentiment of Jesus as well as our own mothers who gave birth to us. This isn't slavery; it is servant leadership.

To dive deep into these conversations, we can ask questions that draw out key principles, as the above three examples provide. Then, we help connect the dots for the listener about how humans thrive in relationship, when focused on life, and when embracing our design.

Moreover, as we come up against another mantra, that of "freedom," we need to ask who is more free: The person who can choose anything or the person who chooses what is right? If we consider the success of a musician who declines a party in order to practice his instrument, or an athlete who declines dessert in order to stay healthy for competition, we see that their disciplined decision to override immediate gratification and to think long term is made in freedom and leads to flourishing. So it is when following a moral code on matters of life and death—the truly free person sees all the options and chooses the right one.

In determining that right path, we can remind people that there are some lines we simply shouldn't cross. For example, scandals in the news about parents financially bribing universities so that their children will gain access to postsecondary education are an example of what is not ethical, no matter what good the student could achieve. Likewise, the pro-life worldview doesn't just look at what is possible but at what one *ought* to do, pointing out that some lines should not be crossed, particularly in matters of life and death.

In revealing to the public how various pro-life positions actually complement and commend each other, and how they are designed for human flourishing, we aim to present the worldview as attractive. In doing so, we want the hearer to experience what the disciples did after they encountered Jesus on the road to Emmaus: "Were not our hearts burning within us while he was talking to us?" (Luke 24:32).

30

Anthropological Fallacies

Ryan T. Anderson

"It's not a baby, it's just a clump of cells." "Okay, sure, what I mean is that even if it's a human being, it's not a person."

"That's not my wife anymore, that's a vegetable." "Okay, sure, that's her body, but she left the body a long time ago when she started losing her mind."

"Love is love, the plumbing doesn't matter." "Okay, sure, we can't literally unite as one-flesh, but that's just poetry anyway. All that matters is that we express our love—how we do it isn't important."

"I'm a woman trapped in a man's body; the doctors got my 'sex assigned at birth' wrong." "Okay, sure, maybe sex isn't technically 'assigned,' but the real me is a woman and modern medicine can affirm my 'gender identity' through hormone therapy and surgery."

Perhaps you've heard various versions of these arguments in recent years. We could undoubtedly multiply them—both on these four issues and on countless others. To be intelligible—let alone plausible—they assume a single anthropological fallacy: "body-self dualism." Whether you're discussing abortion or euthanasia, same-sex marriage or transgender ideology, it is highly likely that body-self dualism will be either explicitly appealed to, or implicitly assumed, as the conversation plays out.

Here's how.

Any number of honest pro-choicers have to recognize the now-irrefutable biological reality that the life of a human being begins (at the very latest) at the completion of fertilization, when the two gametes (sperm and egg) that give rise to the newly formed embryo cease to exist, their pronuclei line up, and a new organism begins its integral self-directed growth from the embryonic stage of human existence to the fetal, newborn, toddler, child, teenager, and reader-of-this-book stage. Each of these terms—embryo, fetus, newborn, toddler, child, teen, reader—describes one and the same organism, just at different ages or stages of development. Honest pro-choicers can't deny this.

Likewise, most pro-choicers are reluctant to give up on human dignity and equality. They want to affirm that it's wrong to devalue—let alone kill—individuals of any class of humanity. But if a human being begins at conception and all human beings have equal dignity, how could you justify abortion? Simple: you explain that human dignity and equality are for "persons" and the unborn human being is not yet a person. To be a person—to be a "self," to matter morally—is to have self-awareness, self-consciousness, and a higher mental life. All entities with *that* have dignity, or so the argument goes. I'm a self, but I was never really a fetus—that was just the physical preparation of me.[1]

And so, too, there might be living physical remains of "me" before my body dies and leaves behind a corpse. That is, even as my heart continues pumping and my lungs continue breathing, the real me, the conscious "self," might depart from my body. What's left might be called a "vegetable"—in a revealing attempt at dehumanization. No one denies that the patient in a so-called "persistent vegetative state" is a living human being, they just deny that it's a human person, a self. The same is true for children—like Alfie Evans and Charlie Gard—whom the powerful view as having lives unworthy of living. Yes, they're living human beings, but they're not human persons in the way that matters. Why not? Because they aren't capable—here and now—of personal actions, of self-awareness and consciousness and the acts that manifest such "higher" mental life.

---

1. There are important nuances between "moral" dualism and "personal" dualism discussed in Robert P. George and Christopher Tollefsen, *Embryo: A Defense of Human Life* (New York: Doubleday, 2008), but here we can gloss over them. On the similarities, especially in terms of response, see Sherif Girgis, "The Wrongfulness of Any Intent to Kill," in *National Catholic Bioethics Quarterly* 19, no. 2 (2019): 221–248.

What's true of these debates at the beginning and end of life is also true of our debates about human sexuality: dualism plays a foundational role. This was evident during the debate over the very nature and definition of marriage, but it undergirds the entire sexual revolution. If our bodies are just instruments of our conscious, desiring "self," then bodily union just as such is insignificant. What matters is "personal" union—understood as an emotional or romantic thing—where the body is a mere instrument at the service of the personal self. The "plumbing" doesn't matter, so long as the body is being used in a way that both (all?) parties to the encounter find expressive of their emotions, or at least pleasurable. Whether it be same sex or opposite sex, monogamous or polyamorous, permanent or temporary, exclusive or open— it's neither here nor there, so long as the sexual bodily action is at the service of the desiring conscious self.

And once we've said that about our sexual *actions*, why not say the same about our sexual *identity*? Though here we use the word "gender" to further separate bodily sex from an inner sense of "gender identity." But the same basic framework is at play: The "real me" is something other than my physical body; there's a real me either to be discovered or created (the various gender ideologues conflict on this point), and then my body should be transformed to align with the "gender identity" of the inner (real) me. Some go so far as to claim that sex is "assigned at birth"—with the implication being that sex can later be "reassigned." More cutting-edge gender theorists, though, use the language of "gender confirmation" and now "gender affirmation" to describe the various medical procedures performed on the (mere) body to "affirm" that inner self.

The attentive reader will have noticed that body-self dualism is intimately related to *expressive individualism*, another key anthropological fallacy of our age. If the body is a mere costume or vehicle—an instrument of the desiring self—then that self should use the body to express its inner truth. Of course, the person of the Psalms, of St. Paul's epistles, and of St. Augustine's *Confessions* was also a "self" in the sense of having an interior life. But the inward turn of the biblical tradition was at the service of the outward turn toward God. The person was a creature of God, who sought to conform himself to the truth, to objective moral standards—particularly having to do with his embodiment—in pursuit of eternal life. Modern man, however, seeks to be "true to himself." Rather than conform his thoughts, feelings, and actions to objective reality (including the body), man's inner life itself becomes the sole source of truth. The modern self finds itself in the midst of what Robert Bellah has described as a culture of "expressive individualism"—where each of us seeks to give expression to our individual inner lives rather than see ourselves as embodied beings embedded in communities and bound by natural and supernatural laws. Authenticity to inner feelings, rather than adherence to transcendent truths, becomes the norm.

Rather than seeing ourselves as what Gilbert Ryle called "ghosts in machines," where the real self is the mind or the will or the consciousness that somehow inhabits a body and makes use of the body as a mere instrument, we should see ourselves as incarnate, bodily beings—"dependent rational animals," as Alasdair MacIntyre explains. Only if my body is me, if I'm an embodied soul, or an ensouled body, a dynamic unity of mind and matter, body and soul, can we make sense of the truthful positions on these four issues. We are animals of a certain sort—with a rational nature even if and when we can't immediately exercise our rational capacities—and that explains why we're persons from the beginning to the end. And given our bodily nature—which itself is a personal nature—certain ends are naturally good for us. Body-self dualism and its social manifestation in expressive individualism underlie the rejection of our given human natures with given human goods that perfect our natures.

So, any effective apologetics agenda on anthropology would need to center on responding to body-self dualism and the rejection of natural law that expressive individualism entails. This will require work from philosophers and theologians to communicate the theoretical problems with dualism, and work from scientists and social scientists (including medical doctors) to show the practical realities of our life as embodied beings. But most importantly, it will take the work of artists to dramatize the truth of our embodiment, and of the Church to ritualize it through sacraments and liturgy. For any of this to take root in the next generation, the domestic church—the family—will need to cultivate this understanding of the embodied nature of the human person and the goodness of our created bodies in the social practices, family traditions, and daily activities that constitute family life.

31

The "Fourth Age" of Human Communications

Jimmy Akin

I was there at the dawn of the Fourth Age of human communications. Many of us were!

It began in the 1990s, when the internet became commercially available. To appreciate the magnitude of this epochal event, we need to look back in time. It is only by appreciating where we have been that we can discern where we are likely to go.

First Age: The Spoken Word

The spoken word goes back as far as the human race. In Genesis, God tasks Adam with naming the animals, "and whatever the man called every living creature, that was its name" (Gen. 2:19).

We do not know precisely when this age began. The Church leaves this question to science (*Catechism of the Catholic Church* 283), but in 2004, the International Theological Commission—under the leadership of Joseph Ratzinger (later Pope Benedict XVI)—stated, "While the story of human origins is complex and subject to revision, physical anthropology and molecular biology combine to make a convincing case for the origin of the human species in Africa about 150,000 years ago in a humanoid population of common genetic lineage."[1]

The First Age thus may have begun 150,000 years ago. At this time, the only way for information to be passed from one person to another—or from one generation to another—was orally.

Second Age: The Written Word

Early on, people experimented with recording information in non-oral formats. This included tying knots in string and making hash marks to keep track of numbers. It also included making petroglyphs, like images of people, stars, or animals.

But there was no way to document complex ideas until writing allowed people to record the equivalent of sentences. This happened a little before 3000 BC, when Mesopotamians developed cuneiform writing and Egyptians developed hieroglyphs.

Writing did not immediately catch on everywhere. Many cultures were able to function orally, and this initially included the Israelites. The earliest evidence of Hebrew writing dates to around 1000 BC, about the time of King David.

Third Age: The Printed Word

The next age began in the AD 1450s. Printing was used earlier, but only on a limited basis.

This changed when Johannes Gutenberg invented a printing press that used moveable type. Now, documents could be duplicated and distributed to people *en masse*—at least by people who had access to a printing press.

This dramatically brought down the cost of books, since scribes were no

---

1. International Theological Commission, "Communion and Stewardship: Human Persons Created in the Image of God" 63, Vatican.va.

longer required to copy documents by hand. This resulted in a global explosion of literature.

Fourth Age: The Electronic Word

The nineteenth and twentieth centuries saw communication milestones including the telegraph, telephone, radio, television, satellites, and computers. By the 1990s, these combined to produce the internet.

The internet was developed partly as a Cold War command-and-control system to allow military messages to be routed around holes that nuclear bombs could punch in the US communications grid. However, it showed great promise, and the military allowed its commercial development and release to the public.

No longer was it true that freedom of the press belonged just to those who owned a printing press. With the internet, everyone could publish their ideas to a worldwide audience.

Opportunity and Danger

From the perspective of faith, each age has brought both opportunities and dangers. God has made himself known to mankind since the very beginning,[2] but in the First Age, his word could only be passed on orally, from person to person. This meant tradition was the first and original expression of God's word.

As the human race spread, the primordial tradition was not preserved in purity. The need to communicate in person meant that, as humanity grew, its branches lost contact and formed new societies, with different religious ideas. Polytheism was prominent in these societies, and even Abraham and his family originally "lived beyond the Euphrates and served other gods" (Josh. 24:2).

In the Second Age, God's word began to take written form, and Scripture

---

2. See Vatican Council II, *Dei Verbum* 3, in *The Word on Fire Vatican II Collection*, ed. Matthew Levering (Park Ridge, IL: Word on Fire Institute, 2021), 18.

was added to tradition. Scripture is a creation of the Second Age, and by inspiring it, God took advantage of writing to further reveal himself and his will.

This allowed God's word to be more easily communicated across time and distance. But the problem of those who spread contrary ideas remained. If an Israelite insisted on worshiping other gods, the only options were for him to flee or be executed (Deut. 13:1–18).

In the Third Age, it became easier to spread God's word, as the price of books fell so that ordinary people could afford them. Previously, only the rich could. This led to the Protestant Reformation, with its principle of *sola scriptura* (Latin for "by Scripture alone"). Now that books were cheaper, the Reformers were energized by the idea of everyone having a copy of Scripture and looking to it alone as authoritative in religion.

In previous ages, a widespread movement based on ordinary people looking to Scripture as their sole religious authority would have been unimaginable, for it was impossible to provide ordinary people with copies of the Scriptures. Protestantism is thus a child of the Third Age.

In addition to Bibles, a host of other religious books began to be published, not all of which were sound. To respond, the Church took two measures: it created the imprimatur to approve quality religious works (*imprimatur* is Latin for "let it be printed"), and it created the Index of Forbidden Books to warn the faithful against unsound works.

Life in the Fourth Age

The Fourth Age also presents opportunities and dangers. The ability to share the Gospel is greater than ever, and people are being reached with the message of Jesus in countries where in-person evangelization is forbidden.

But the internet has also created a global marketplace of religious ideas, so apologists and evangelists need to address a wider array of viewpoints, concerns, and objections. The internet also will require changes in how the Church approaches publications. Even before the internet, the flood of twentieth-century publications led to a loosening of the imprimatur system, so that fewer works require imprimaturs. It also led to the abolition of the Index of Forbidden Books, though the Church still publishes warnings about influential Catholic books containing ideas contrary to the faith.

Something similar will likely emerge for the internet, with highly influential Catholic sites receiving a form of ecclesiastical approval or disapproval. Still, it will not be possible for bishops to deal individually with the flood of items being posted on the internet.

Another challenge of the age is internet censorship. Some nations have banned particular content or websites, and internet companies have "deplatformed" voices they do not approve of—either by denying them access to an internet service altogether or by downranking their search results so they are effectively unfindable.

With the spread of anti-Christian values in political and corporate culture, we should be very concerned about these trends and should do everything possible to ensure free speech on the internet.

Already, China has introduced a "social credit system" that ranks people based on their identification with party ideology. Some in the West have proposed similar systems, and it is easy to imagine a Big Data–driven equivalent that penalizes those who maintain traditional Christian beliefs and values.

Political and corporate censorship may be the greatest threat to the proclamation of the Gospel in the future. Given increasing hostility to Christian teachings and values, we may be branded a "hate group," deplatformed, and persecuted in our offline lives.

A Fifth Age?

We also should think about what comes next, as the ages have been growing shorter. The First Age lasted for tens of thousands of years, the second for thousands, and the third only for hundreds. With technological change accelerating, a new age may begin in decades. It may involve a concept known as *machine telepathy*—the transmission of information using a brain-machine interface. We currently have prototypes of this, and they are used to allow paralyzed people to communicate and interact with their environment.

As this technology matures, it will be possible in principle to fit people in general with brain-machine interfaces, connecting them directly to the internet or whatever succeeds it.

We would then be in the Fifth Age—the age of the mental word—and it also would bring opportunities and dangers.

Many will be squeamish about the idea of having the internet hooked up to their heads, especially if it is like the current internet, with pop-up ads, viruses, hacking, and privacy violations.

But the internet provides value, which is why people use it. It is hard to be successful today and *not* use the internet. The same could one day be true of machine telepathy.

In that case, Christians need to be thinking *now* about how to meet the challenges that may be ahead of us and how we can avoid Orwellian scenarios involving groupthink, loss of privacy, and mental manipulation that the advance of technology will make possible.

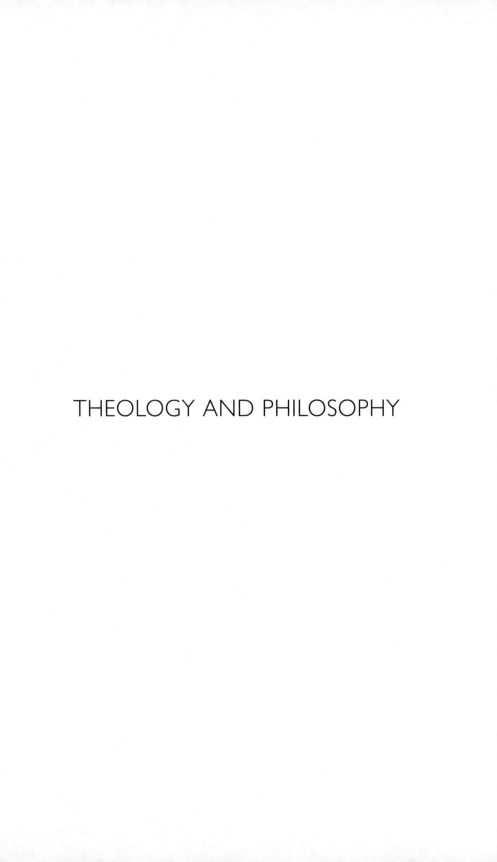

THEOLOGY AND PHILOSOPHY

32

The Threefold Way

Fr. James Dominic Brent, OP

In contemporary evangelization and apologetics, what works? Long experience in the apostolate, as well as philosophical and theological reflection, have confirmed for me that what works is the proclamation of the God of love. The simple statement, too, that "Jesus is Lord" has supernatural impact. So, too, the proclamation of the cross and Resurrection. The way to go in initial proclamation is simply to tell the Gospel story. Such a proclamation works because it reveals the eternal truth, and the Spirit of Truth works secretly in hearts to convert people. Apologetics surrounds the proclamation, and the only effective apologetic is one that speaks to particular issues raised by particular people.

Experience and reflection also confirm for me that what Catholics need now (and always) is a more profound formation in what sacred tradition calls the "threefold way." It was Dionysius who coined the expression, but in so doing, he named a certain spiritual practice common among the prophets, Apostles, and the Fathers of the Church. It is meant to become ours too. The prophets, Apostles, inspired authors of Scripture, and Fathers of the Church took over much of what was true in Greek philosophy and used it to tell the truth of God. Cosmological reasoning is one case in point.

Cosmos is a Greek word originally having two meanings. It meant the *world*—as in the world of nature around us—and it meant *order*. This single word signified both, because it is a fundamental human experience and a basic conviction of reason that the world is essentially an order. It is the orderliness of things—their arrangement, beauty, and harmony—that has impressed the human mind since days immemorial. And it impresses us still. World-order is a given of experience. Rational reflection upon it naturally leads the mind to realize there must exist a first principle of the order of the world.[1] Such reflection began among Greek philosophers and grew to a measure of rigor—especially in Aristotle, but also in others.

The author of the book of Wisdom was familiar with the cosmological reasoning of the philosophers, and offered some divinely inspired commentary on it. In Wisdom 13:1–9, Scripture teaches that world-order is how God manifests himself to *all* human beings: "From the greatness and beauty of created things comes a corresponding perception of their Creator" (Wis. 13:5). Greatness is a blend of both goodness and magnitude, and beauty is a property peculiar to order. Order alone is beautiful. And it is from the order of the world that human beings *as human* (rather than as Greek or Jew, Christian or Muslim, American or Chinese) are able to know God exists. In his summary restatement of Wisdom 13:1–9, Paul makes the same point: "Ever since the creation of the world his eternal power and divine nature, invisible though they are, have been understood and seen through the things he has made" (Rom. 1:20).

Sacred tradition tells us the literal sense of these scriptural passages. Thomas Aquinas, commenting on Dionysius, says:

> For the whole of creatures is displayed to us by God so that we may know him, for the ordered universe has some likeness and faint resemblance to the divine nature to which it is compared as an image to its principal exemplar. Thus, from the consideration of the ordered universe we ascend in degrees, so far as we are able, by our intellect to God who is above all, and this in three ways.[2]

The three ways are not three independent lines of argument, but three mo-

---

1. Thomas Aquinas, *Summa contra Gentiles* 3.38 n.1.
2. Thomas Aquinas, *Commentary on The Divine Names* 7.1.4.

ments of one life of the mind. One moment is cosmological argumentation, another moment is drawing a radical distinction between God and the world, and another moment is the acknowledgment of how all-surpassing are the perfections of God. The threefold way is a certain itinerary of the mind leading to a deeper encounter with God, so that, from out of the encounter with God, one might speak *to* God in prayer or *of* God in evangelization. The threefold way proceeds as follows.[3]

First, one notices world-order and through a process of inquiry (more or less elaborate) one infers that a principle or source of world-order exists. One might argue from world-order as a whole and offer a design argument. Or one might argue in terms of a large-scale order in the world, such as the orders of motion, causality, contingency, perfection, finality, morality, truth, or others. Or someone might receive by grace a certain non-inferential realization that there is a first principle of it all. One way or another, one arrives at the existence of a first principle of the order of the world. Since that first principle matches common (and biblical) definitions of the word "God," the conclusion is *God exists*.

Second, one then negates the conclusion *God exists* in the sense of denying that the term "exists" here means the same thing as it does in ordinary discourse about everything else. God does *not* exist in the manner in which this or that thing in the world exists—such as a dog or a mouse. The reasons for the negation vary from one argumentative context to another, but generally it is because of something discovered along the way in the first step—for example, God is immutable.

Third, one affirms anew that *God exists*, but now one is saying (with explicit awareness) that God exists in a much more sublime way than everything else. No one on earth knows just what God's way of existing is. His existence surpasses all categories and concepts whatsoever. The three ways or steps lead to knowing *that* God is, but not *what* God is, as well as to the *awareness* of not knowing what God is.

---

3. Recent research shows that in practice the order of the three ways is variable and open to creativity in different contexts.

Furthermore, a similar process is also used to interpret *every* word spoken from God, to God, and about God, either in Scripture, liturgy, private prayer, preaching, or theology. For example, God is love. Yet God is not any form of love found in this world. Rather, God is love surpassing all categories and concepts whatsoever. And *that* love—incomprehensible love—is now calling us.

Thanks to the prophets and Apostles and fathers, the cosmological reasoning of sound philosophy is now part of the Scripture and Tradition of the Church. In our sacred tradition, argumentation upward to the existence of God is always but a first step or moment on this threefold way to God. Those who take the first step, but not the second or third, remain stunted in their cognitive and theological development, often mislead people in evangelization and apologetics, and potentially fall into idolatry of their own ideas of God. The situation with the new atheists was a good example. Their thinking about God was wholly in terms of the categories and concepts of this world. Their interpretation of God-talk never entered into the second step of purification through negation or into the third step of acknowledging the ineffable sublimity of God. Many of their Christian respondents, though well intentioned, often thought on the same level and in the same terms. The practice of *all three steps*, however, helps dissolve some of the effects of what Charles Taylor called "the immanent frame," and serves to open the heart to the one who "dwells in unapproachable light" (1 Tim. 6:16).

Given the fierce cultural opposition to cosmological arguments for the existence of God, and getting stuck in the dialectics of the first step, many in the Catholic Church have despaired over natural theology—including many theologians, pastors, and catechists. Yet, the arguments work. Personally, I have witnessed secular-minded people go from critical opposition to the argument from contingency, to prolonged wrestling with it, to seeing at last the truth of the conclusion. Common sense is on the side of the arguments. And the alternative positions are deeply counterintuitive if not strictly absurd. Denial of the principles of causality and sufficient reason come with a heavy intellectual price. Many people see that. There is a new openness to metaphysics, new critiques of mechanicism and reductionism, a flourishing neo-Aristotelianism, and new interest among Protestants in Thomas Aquinas. All such trends are obvious seeds of the Word worth cultivating.

Three practical steps toward a renewal of the threefold way. First, get out of the artifact jungle, go into nature, and look around: "Scripture urges us to look at the stars, since their order (*dispositio*) maximally shows how everything is subject to the will and providence of the creator."[4] Second, study up on the basics of divine names, using the bibliography at the back of this book (see appendix). Finally, ask God daily to send forth his light and his truth to shine in our hearts, that we may all come to know him in a manner worthy of our call in Christ Jesus.

---

4. Thomas Aquinas, *Quaestiones disputatae de potentia Dei* 3.17 resp.

33

New Challenges to Natural Theology
Edward Feser

Suppose you are engaged in Catholic apologetics. Where do you start? That depends on your audience. If you are trying to convince Eastern Orthodox or Protestant Christians, you needn't argue for God's existence or the authority of the New Testament. They already agree with you about that much. If your audience is Jewish or Muslim, you will have less in the way of common ground, and thus more work to do. But at least they will be open to the general idea of special divine revelation. If your interlocutor is willing to entertain some purely philosophical form of theism but is skeptical of the very idea of special revelation, the task will be even harder. And of course, it will be harder still if he is an atheist.

Yet not all atheists are alike. Some take theism seriously as an intellectual position and are simply unconvinced by the arguments for it. But they will engage earnestly with those arguments—trying their best correctly to understand them, developing objections in a civil manner, hearing out possible responses to those objections, and so on. Contemporary atheist philosopher Graham Oppy would be an example. Other atheists are more dismissive. They consider theism a view that might reasonably have been taken at one time, but that has now been decisively refuted. Still, they will engage the arguments for it in at least a superficial way. They are not interested in investigating very carefully what theistic thinkers have actually said, will trot out hackneyed objections in an aggressive and condescending way, and have little patience for hearing out possible responses. But they will at least go through the motions of rational engagement with the other side. Richard Dawkins and some of the other new atheist writers are like this.

A third group of atheists is more dismissive still. They don't treat theism as something worthy even of a perfunctory refutation. For even that much treats the dispute between theism and atheism as a disagreement about where the evidence and argumentation ought to lead us, and thus pays the theist the compliment of taking him to be at least minimally rational. It takes the theist to have a properly functioning intellect, but one that simply hasn't yet considered all the facts. But the third kind of atheism that I'm describing takes the theist to have a *malfunctioning* intellect. Peter Boghossian's book *A Manual for Creating Atheists* reflects this mentality. Atheist encounters with theists ought in his view to be modeled on "clinical interventions" aimed at curing a pathology. Some offer a theoretical rationale for such an approach by arguing that theistic belief is a byproduct of overactive cognitive systems originally molded by natural selection to enable us to detect agency in our natural environment.

The idea that theism reflects a kind of psychological dysfunction has a long history in atheist thought, tracing back to thinkers committed to one version or another of the "hermeneutics of suspicion." There is, for example, Marx's view that religion functions as a kind of "opium" that prevents the oppressed from perceiving their oppression and rebelling against it, Nietzsche's analysis of religion as a disguised expression of the believer's "will to power," and Freud's analysis of belief in God as the projection of the infantile need for a protective father figure. This sort of view can morph into a fourth and even more hostile attitude toward theism, which sees it as a danger to mental health and social order that ought to be actively suppressed. The history of communism shows that such a militant and oppressive form of atheism is by no means merely a theoretical possibility.

So, there are four basic approaches an atheist might take toward the arguments of natural theology, each increasingly hostile: (1) substantive engagement; (2) superficial engagement; (3) refusal to engage; and (4) active suppression. Apologists in modern democratic societies are familiar with (1) and (2), and occasionally encounter relatively mild forms of (3) as well.

But there is reason to think that a more aggressive form of approach (3), and even some version of approach (4), might become more common in the future. Recent years have seen the sudden rise to prominence of various forms of critical theory, which apply a quasi-Marxist "hermeneutics of suspicion" to a variety of ideas and institutions in the name of a radical egalitarianism. For example, critical race theory claims to detect racism hidden in every nook and cranny of social life and dismisses all disagreement with its analysis as itself merely a further manifestation of racism. Among the views it claims to be "racist" are those which hold that the breakdown of the traditional family is the chief source of social problems and that the restoration of traditional sexual morality is therefore a necessary part of the solution to those problems. Other forms of critical theory posit "patriarchy" and "heteronormativity" as further omnipresent bogeymen and dismiss all defenses of traditional sex roles and traditional sexual morality as manifestations of these purportedly sinister forces. Even traditional standards of rational argumentation and debate are dismissed as part of the framework by which these oppressive forces maintain their control. The critical theorist urges that the education system, law, and public policy ought to be radically transformed so as to reflect its analysis and to root out "oppression" wherever the critical theorist claims to see it.

Since critical theorists typically regard traditional forms of theism to be bulwarks of these oppressive forces, it is not surprising that some of them apply to those religions the same "hermeneutics of suspicion." Now, an intellectual culture in which all ideas are evaluated in terms of political utility or the suspect motives their critics impute to their defenders, and in which canons of reason and objectivity are rejected, is one in which the project of natural theology (and indeed any other rational enterprise) is impossible. It is also bound to degenerate into one in which disputes are settled not by argumentation but through intimidation or worse.

Apologists may soon find themselves in a situation where much of the culture lacks even the bare minimum of common ground necessary for rational engagement—namely, respect for rational engagement itself. Now, a failure to respect and abide by standards of rationality is a moral vice, and it is closely connected to other vices. In the *Republic*, Plato argues that those individuals and societies that are the furthest from rationality are those that take every desire to be equally good, and that are dominated by sensual desires in particular. In the opening to the Letter to the Romans, St. Paul links the inability to see the evidence for God in nature to sexual immorality. In the *Summa theologiae*, St. Thomas Aquinas argues that sins of the flesh are the chief source of what he calls "blindness of mind" or an intellect's inability to reason well about spiritual things.[1]

What Plato called "misology" or hostility to reason and argument is thus very closely tied to the domination of the soul by disordered passions, and disordered sexual passions especially. It is no accident that modern societies exhibit both misology and disordered sexuality to a very high degree. Opinions about theism can indeed, as atheists of type (3) allege, be closely linked to psychological dysfunction. But from the theist's point of view, the dysfunction involves a *hostility* to theism rather than an inclination toward it—a "hatred of God" that, says Aquinas, is due to "his forbidding the desired pleasure."[2]

By no means is this to say that all atheists are so motivated. Again, there are atheists of type (1) who are willing to engage theists at the level of rational argumentation. But the more deeply contemporary culture sinks into its addiction to sins of the flesh, the more apologists will likely find that they cannot neatly separate off the defense of natural theology from the defense of natural law. Indeed, since irrationalism is the consequence of such sins, they will also find that philosophical enlightenment of the intellect may increasingly require, first, a moral reform of the soul. In the long run, effective

---

1. Thomas Aquinas, *Summa theologiae* 2-2.15.1.
2. Thomas Aquinas, 2-2.153.5.

apologetics may presuppose—though it can and should also contribute to—a more general spiritual renewal within society at large.

34

Doubt and Certainty

Tyler Dalton McNabb

Can we be certain that God exists? Vatican I makes it clear that we can possess metaphysical certainty when it states, "If anyone says that the one true God, our Creator and Lord, cannot be known with certainty by the natural light of human reason by means of the things that are made, let him be anathema."[1] What's metaphysical certainty? Roughly, a subject, call her S, is metaphysically certain that proposition p is true, if S believes p, S has no doubts about p, p is a necessary truth, and S arrives at her belief that p by either recognizing that p is a self-evident truth or by way of reasoning from other self-evident truths that p is true.[2] Notice, metaphysical certainty requires that one does not have any doubts about the proposition in question. This means that metaphysical certainty requires what philosophers call *psychological certainty*. Roughly, S is psychologically certain that p, if S thinks that the possibility of ~p (i.e., not p) is insignificant.[3] Another way to put it is that S firmly holds to p and thinks that ~p isn't remotely likely. It's this sort of certainty that I would like to take a closer look at. In this short chapter, I'll sketch out how it's possible for a subject to know, with psychological certainty, that Catholicism is true, even in light of being aware of technical objections to her faith.

---

1. Vatican Council I, *Dei Filius*, quoted in Pius X, *Pascendi Dominici Gregis*, encyclical letter, Vatican.va.
2. This is a summary of Michael James Ryan, "Certitude," *The Catholic Encyclopedia*, vol. 3 (New York: Robert Appleton, 1908), New Advent, http://www.newadvent.org/cathen/03539b.htm.
3. For this account, see Andrew Moon, *Knowledge and Doxastic*, unpublished manuscript.

Alvin Plantinga's Epistemology

Alvin Plantinga has argued extensively that a subject can know that God exists even if the subject isn't aware of good arguments for God's existence. How does he go about making his claim plausible? Plantinga argues that as far as we know, it is possible that God exists and has created in humans a cognitive faculty that is aimed toward producing beliefs about God and his activities.[4] Roughly, Plantinga thinks that if the belief in question is true, and if the cognitive faculty is properly functioning and is successfully aimed at producing true beliefs, the belief in question would constitute knowledge.

Let me further elucidate Plantinga's argument by way of an illustration. Imagine you wake up and find yourself in a beautiful forest on a sunny day. You pick up a delicate flower and see its beautiful texture and all of its intricacies. All of a sudden, you simply find yourself believing that God created this flower. This belief isn't the result of some inference such as "it looks designed so probably there is a designer"; rather, the belief is immediate. If this belief is true and it is the result of properly functioning faculties that are successfully aimed at truth, you would possess knowledge that God created this flower.

Plantinga doesn't stop here, however. He goes on to argue that it's possible that a subject could know that Christianity is true even if the subject lacked arguments for the truth of Christianity.[5] For Plantinga, accepting the testimony of someone else can lead to knowledge.[6] Specifically, the idea is that knowledge can be transferred from one person to another. For example, if my daughter Eden is told by her teacher that Christopher Columbus sailed the ocean blue in 1492, she could come to know that Columbus sailed the ocean blue in 1492 by accepting the testimony of her teacher, at least, assuming that her accepting the testimony was the result of her cognitive faculties functioning properly (which Plantinga simply terms "cognitive proper

---

4. Alvin Plantinga, *Warranted Christian Belief* (New York: Oxford University Press, 2000), 178–179.
5. Plantinga, 252.
6. Alvin Plantinga, *Warrant and Proper Function* (New York: Oxford University Press, 1993), 77.

function"). In light of this, Plantinga argues that for all we know, the Holy Spirit exists and, along with various human authors, has written Holy Scripture. Upon reading Holy Scripture, if moved by the Holy Spirit, one just finds herself believing that "Jesus died and rose again," then she could be said to know that proposition is true, again, if accepting the testimony of Scripture is the result of her faculties functioning properly.[7]

We can tell a similar story for how specifically a subject can come to know that Catholicism is true. Let's say that a priest truthfully tells my son Ezra that the Catholic Church is the one true Church, and, following this, my son finds himself believing that this is the case. If his acceptance of the testimony is the result of his faculties functioning properly, he would know that the Catholic Church is the one true Church. There are of course other ways to describe how a subject can come to know the relevant proposition. Perhaps, upon visiting a beautiful cathedral, my daughter Eva-Maria simply finds herself believing that God has established the Catholic Church. If this belief is the result of cognitive proper function, she would have knowledge.

Now, let's say that my children encounter a technical objection to their faith. It could relate to the problem of evil, the problem of divine hiddenness, the coherence of theism, or to an apparent conflict with science. Can my children know that their faith is true with *psychological* certainty? In order to answer this question in the affirmative, I will introduce an objection to faith and discuss how the objection can be rightfully dealt with.

How to Deal with Objections 101: A Case Study

The paradigm view in cognitive science is that religious belief is natural.[8] Specifically, it is a byproduct of certain evolutionary factors that are advantageous for human survival. One popular theory is that religious belief is the

---

7. Plantinga, *Warranted Christian Belief*, 252.
8. J.L. Barrett, *Cognitive Science, Religion, and Theology: From Human Minds to Divine Minds* (West Conshohocken, PA: Templeton Press, 2011).

result, at least in part, of a hyperactive agency detection device (HADD).[9] Humans detect agency so frequently that we even detect it when agency is nowhere to be found. An organism that is overly sensitive to detecting agency is more likely to survive than an organism that doesn't detect agency enough. Stephen Law has argued that we shouldn't trust HADD when it comes to forming beliefs about the supernatural, as HADD is responsible for also producing beliefs about gods, ghosts, and psychics.[10] We don't trust HADD when it produces beliefs about other supernatural entities, so why trust HADD when it comes to our faith? When confronted with this information, how can my children (or anyone else for that matter) stand firm in their faith and not think that their faith is merely the result of an overly active agency detector?

Neither they, nor anyone else, need succumb to doubt. First, it might be said that even if you come to believe that HADD is responsible for producing false supernatural beliefs in lots of people throughout time, you still might be convinced that it didn't lead *you* to have false beliefs about your faith. If you keep on believing that your faith is true, and this belief is the result of cognitive proper function, you'd still possess knowledge (assuming your faith is true!).[11]

Second, when engaging an objection to your faith, you can often explain away the objection by appealing to a story or narrative that resolves the objection. In this instance, you might come up with a story that shows that HADD is actually reliable when it comes to supernatural belief. As I've argued elsewhere, HADD's reliability could be likened to a group of people in a dark room.[12] Perhaps no one in the group could clearly perceive what's in the room and perhaps every person in the group would disagree with one another about what exactly is in the room, but every person's faculties would still lead to an

---

9. S.E. Guthrie, *Faces in the Clouds: A New Theory of Religion* (New York: Oxford University Press, 1993).

10. Stephen Law, "The X-claim Argument against Religious Belief," *Religious Studies* 54 (2018): 15–35.

11. Tyler Dalton McNabb, *Religious Epistemology* (Cambridge: Cambridge University Press, 2018), 29–32.

12. McNabb, 29–32.

awareness that there are, in fact, objects in the room. In the same way, assuming that divinity exists, HADD would be reliable insofar as it gets us to become aware of the supernatural.[13] We could then fine-tune our awareness of the supernatural through the tools of philosophy, science, and group cooperation.

Third, we might verify the truth of our faith by appealing to a circular argument. Now, you might think that all circular reasoning is bad, but that simply isn't the case. As some epistemologists have pointed out, circularity is only bad when you aren't already confident in the belief in question.[14] For example, it seems permissible to utilize your cognitive faculties when you form the belief that your cognitive faculties are reliable. Circularity would only be impermissible if there were a genuine question about the reliability of your faculties. If you are already certain that the belief in question is true, circularity can be your friend. With respect to our case study then, you might appeal to the fact that Catholicism is true and that if Catholicism is true, the Holy Spirit probably guided your belief-forming process.[15] So, HADD probably hasn't given you over to deception.

Finally, as Vatican I states, we can have certainty about God's existence by way of arguments. Thus, in order to show that HADD hasn't led us astray, we could always appeal to natural theology.[16] Whatever option you take, it seems clear that it is indeed possible to know that your faith is true and to know it with psychological certainty—no doubts required.

---

13. McNabb, 29–32; Kelly James Clark and Justin Barrett, "Reidian Religious Epistemology and the Cognitive Science of Religion," *Journal of American Academy of Religion* 79, no. 3 (2011): 639–675.

14. See Andrew Moon, "Circular and Question Begging Responses to Religious Disagreement and Debunking Arguments," *Philosophical Studies* 178, no. 3 (2021): 785–809; Michael Bergmann, *Justification without Awareness* (New York: Oxford University Press, 2006), 206.

15. Moon, "Circular and Question Begging Responses," 794.

16. For a good example of this, see Edward Feser, *Five Proofs for the Existence of God* (San Francisco: Ignatius Press, 2017).

35

The Existence of the Immortal Soul
Turner C. Nevitt

When they hear the phrase "the immortal soul," most people nowadays probably think of something like a ghost temporarily inhabiting their body but destined eventually to depart for a disembodied eternity of joy with God in heaven. Many of those who believe in the existence of the immortal soul probably think of themselves as such a ghost with such a destiny. This is not a traditional Christian belief. Traditionally, Christians have thought of themselves as bodily beings whose hope for eternal life lay, not in the immortality of their souls, but in the resurrection of their bodies from the dead. That is how the first Christians could think of death as a great enemy to be conquered, and why they saw the Resurrection of Jesus Christ from the dead as such good news of victory. Yet Christians have also traditionally believed that a spiritual part of each person continues to exist between their death and resurrection, at least by God's power if not its own. This spiritual part of each person is commonly called the immortal soul.

The greatest challenge to belief in the existence of the immortal soul is *physicalism*, the idea that everything is physical and can be fully accounted for by the empirical sciences, especially physics. If physicalism is true, then there is no immortal soul. After all, if everything is physical, then people and their parts are too. Physicalism is often motivated by a commitment to *naturalism*, the idea that the natural world is all there is, and *scientism*, the idea that empirical science is the only legitimate form of knowledge. If naturalism is true, then there are no spiritual beings beyond the natural world—no souls, no angels, and no God—and thus nothing happens because of such beings; instead, everything happens because of the laws of nature and the state of things in the natural universe at any given time. If scientism is true, then the only things that can be known are things that can be established empirically by the scientific method, ruling out any knowledge of spiritual beings like souls, which cannot be studied in such ways. Thus, in order to successfully defend the existence of the immortal soul, Christians must be able to refute physicalism, naturalism, and scientism.

One way to refute naturalism and scientism is to show that they are self-defeating. The claim that science is the only legitimate form of knowledge is not a claim that can be established empirically by the scientific method. What experiment could possibly show that the only way to know anything is by experiments? Moreover, empirical science itself presupposes many claims that cannot be known in such ways. For example, science assumes the uniformity of nature: the idea that the future will resemble the past, and that other parts of the universe are like our own. If things did not continue to happen in the same way they happened in our experiments, or if our experiments were not representative of how things happen elsewhere in the universe, then we could never draw any conclusions from our experiments about how the natural world works in general. But each experiment shows only what happened then and there in that experiment. No experiment could ever show that things will continue to happen in the same way, or that things happen elsewhere in the universe just as they do here. Thus, science itself relies on claims that cannot be scientifically proven.

Naturalism, the claim that the natural world is all there is and that everything happens because of its laws, is equally self-defeating. If that claim is true, then our beliefs are purely natural things too, and we form them because of nature's laws. But then we never form any of our beliefs based on the reasons for thinking they are true; all our beliefs are forced upon us by natural causes. Yet that should surely shake our confidence in the truth of our beliefs. We do not trust beliefs caused in us by hallucinogenic drugs, for example.

Why should we trust beliefs caused in us by nature and its laws? Of course, we appear to form many of our beliefs based on reasons for thinking they are true. But if naturalism is true, that appearance may well be illusory, for it too will be an effect of nature and its laws. Thus, naturalism undermines the certainty of all our beliefs, including anyone's belief in naturalism.

Physicalism, the claim that everything is physical and can be accounted for by physics, is often defended by appeal to advances in science. Many things that were once explained by nonphysical causes are now explained scientifically by physical causes. The motion of the planets, for example, was once attributed to motive intelligences; the attraction of magnets was once attributed to indwelling spirits. But such things are now explained by physical causes, suggesting that perhaps one day everything will be explained by physics. Hence, one way to refute physicalism is to show that some things could not possibly be explained by physics, no matter how advanced. For example, some argue that physics could never explain consciousness, since consciousness is a matter of first-person subjective experience, while physics offers only third-person objective explanations, making for an unbridgeable explanatory gap. Others argue that physics could never explain intentionality, the way in which our thoughts are *about* something, since no lump of matter, considered merely as a lump of matter, can be *about* anything.

Faced with the challenge of physicalism, it is tempting for Christians to go to the opposite extreme and insist that people are purely nonphysical beings. "People do not *have* souls; they *are* souls. They *have* bodies." That is the claim of substance dualism. The main argument for substance dualism appeals to the fact that we seem able to conceive of ourselves existing without a body (having an out-of-body experience, for example), which suggests that it is possible for us to exist without a body. Yet that would not be possible if we were physical beings, and hence we must not be: we are souls, not bodies. But this argument assumes that we can determine what our existence requires by mere thought experiment—conceiving of ourselves this way and that. If we were physical beings, however, we could not determine what our existence requires without empirical investigation into our nature. Hence, the main argument for substance dualism assumes from the outset that we are not physical beings, which is just what it is supposed to prove. It thus begs the question, offering no support for substance dualism.

Substance dualism also faces many other problems, such as the problem of explaining how we could possibly interact with physical things like our bodies if we were purely nonphysical souls ourselves. Such problems are avoided by the more classical approach to the soul taken by Catholic thinkers like St. Thomas Aquinas. Aquinas thinks of the soul as the ultimate source of life in any living thing. Hence, he thinks that plants have souls, since plants are alive, and he thinks that animals and people have souls for the same reason. Aquinas posits the soul in this sense to explain three main things: (1) why living things like dogs differ from nonliving things like corpses; (2) why living things remain one and the same thing over their lifetime in spite of their matter being constantly replaced; and (3) why living things have their unique abilities, which enable them to perform their characteristic activities in a way coordinated for their good as a whole. To deny the existence of the soul in this sense is to deny that there is anything at all that explains these things. It is a further question just what the soul itself is.

Aquinas argues that physical substances are all composed of matter and form—that is, some material stuff and the specific form that makes that stuff what it is, thus enabling it to do what it can do. For example, matter with a canine form is a dog able to reproduce; the very same matter without that form is a corpse unable to do so. Recognizing that a thing's form is what makes it what it is, and enables it to do what it can do, leads Aquinas to identify the soul of living things with their form, since he conceives of the soul as whatever explains those features of living things. Thus, Aquinas' approach to the soul is called *hylomorphism*, from the Greek words for matter (*hyle*) and form (*morphe*). Since Aquinas thinks of people as physical beings—rational, sensing, living, material substances—he thinks they, too, are composed of matter and form, body and soul. A body without a soul is not a person, and a soul without a body is not a person either.

The challenge for Christian hylomorphists like Aquinas is to explain how the human soul can be immortal if it is the form of the human body. After all, a building's form does not survive its demolition. How can our soul survive the destruction of our body? Aquinas' answer is that the human soul is not merely the form of the body, since it also enables us to perform activities that do not involve the body. For example, we are able to think universal thoughts, such as the thought of a dog—not of any particular dog, but of dogs in general. Such thoughts cannot be material, since every material thing is particular, not universal. Every material dog is *this* or *that* dog, not dogs in general. Hence, such thoughts cannot be identified with any part or process of the body (such as the brain); they exist in the soul alone, which must be immaterial as well. The human soul thus enables us to lead a life that extends beyond the life of the body, which it could not do if it were merely the form of the body.

Since it is not merely the form of the body, the human soul need not cease to be when the body is destroyed. In fact, Aquinas argues that it cannot cease to be, since its life cannot be taken from it in the same way. Physical substances cease to be when their matter loses its specific form. A dog becomes a corpse when its matter loses its canine form. But the human soul cannot cease to be in this way, since it is itself a form, not composed of matter and form. Of course, when a dog ceases to be, its soul ceases to be as well. But that is because a dog's soul is merely the form of its body; it does not enable a dog to live a life beyond the life of its body. The human soul is different; it enables us to perform activities independently of the body, which it could not do if it did not exist independently of the body as well: a thing's way of acting is a function of its way of existing. Hence, the human soul must have an existence of its own, independent of the body's existence, which cannot be taken from it by the destruction of the body.

Although Aquinas thinks the human soul can exist without the body, and in fact will do so between our death and resurrection, he insists that this is a highly unnatural and severely debilitated state for the human soul to be in, since most of what the soul enables us to do requires the body as well. Indeed, as the form of the body, the human soul belongs with the body, making up a complete person. Hence, Aquinas says that without believing in the resurrection of the body, it would be very difficult, nay impossible, to maintain the immortality of the soul. For if human souls were immortal but not destined to be reunited with their bodies, they would all have to remain in a highly unnatural and debilitated state forever, which would call into question the wise ordering of creation and the wisdom of its Creator. So, Christians defending the immortality of the soul, especially as Aquinas conceives of it, should be prepared to defend the resurrection of the body as well.

36

Dark Passages of the Bible

Matthew J. Ramage

One of the most common obstacles to belief in our post-Christian era stems from the violence that the Old Testament portrays as being commanded or committed by God. Pope Benedict XVI referred to these disturbing texts as the "dark passages" of the Bible, and he stressed the importance of helping others to interpret them in the full light of Jesus Christ.[1]

The Bible contains numerous passages that pose hurdles for struggling or would-be Christians, from the global devastation wrought by the flood (Gen. 7:23), to the death of Egypt's firstborn (Exod. 12:29), to the words of the Psalmist, who declares blessed those who would take his enemies' children and "dash them against the rock" (Ps. 137:9). However, the Old Testament narrative describing Israel's conquest of the Promised Land typically draws the most critical attention. Along their march toward Canaan, God commanded his people to "devote to destruction" the nations that lay before them and to "show them no mercy" (Deut. 2:34; 7:2; Josh. 6:21). This ancient Near Eastern practice of totalizing *herem* warfare is reflected in other texts where the Israelites are said to have "utterly destroyed" entire cities—exterminating men, women, children, and animals alike (1 Sam. 15:3–9).

---

1. Benedict XVI, *Verbum Domini* 42, apostolic exhortation, Vatican.va. For a pointed statement of this criticism, see Richard Dawkins, *The God Delusion* (Boston: Houghton Mifflin, 2006), 31.

What We Need to Know: Three Approaches

As is often the case in Catholic theology, there is more than one orthodox way to address this particular difficulty. The following three approaches, some ancient and some recent, may even be combined in view of explaining the meaning of those passages where God appears to act against his nature by committing genocide.[2]

1. God may command violence, for we all merit death because of sin.

This interpretation accentuates that God is the author of life and may take it away since he does not owe it to us in the first place. Noting that all humans deserve death due to original sin, St. Thomas Aquinas states, "By the command of God, death can be inflicted on any man, guilty or innocent, without any injustice whatever."[3] Just as God can issue decrees deputizing people to kill others, Aquinas holds that God could even command one to take another's property or have intercourse with someone else's spouse.[4]

If one finds this traditional answer dissatisfying, there is another, less anthropomorphic way to interpret such a divine "command." This involves recognizing that the Scriptures do not seek to present us with verbatim transcripts of divine dictations. Commenting on Abraham's would-be slaughter of Isaac (Gen. 22), St. Thomas notes that "by God's decree many wicked and many innocent people die every day."[5] Everything that happens in our world—including death—is ultimately part of the Lord's salvific

---

2. For a more in-depth dive into some of the points discussed below along with other options for dealing with dark passages, see Eric Seibert, *Disturbing Divine Behavior* (Minneapolis: Fortress Press, 2009), 69–88.

3. Thomas Aquinas, *Summa theologiae*, 1-2.94.5 ad 2, 1-2.100.8 ad 3.

4. Thomas Aquinas, 1-2.94.5 ad 2, 1-2.100.8 ad 3.

5. Aquinas, *Commentary on the Letter of St. Paul to the Hebrews* (Lander, WY: Aquinas Institute for the Study of Sacred Doctrine, 2012), no. 604.

will, "decreed" by the author of life insofar as he allows evil actions to be carried out through secondary (creaturely) causes.[6]

2. God did not positively command the violence through a verbal decree. Rather, he allowed it as an accommodation because it was the best Israel could understand his will at the time.

This approach, with roots in the patristic period and highlighted by Benedict XVI and recent Vatican documents, accents God in his capacity as the perfect teacher.[7] Like a parent or a missionary teaching the faith, the Lord in his divine pedagogy patiently helped the Israelites to understand his will as best as possible at every moment on their path toward Jesus Christ. This approach acknowledges that the Lord initially permitted the Israelites to think that he directly willed violence because that was their societal norm and thus the starting point of their education in divine matters. A divine pedagogy hermeneutic stresses that God, the author of our nature, respects that we only learn the truth gradually and within a concrete cultural context. As Pope Benedict emphasized, the "evolving" process of the Bible's development took place over a long period of time, in which later texts which stood in community with the past also sometimes "tacitly corrected" what came before with newfound knowledge revealed by God. In the present case, the revelation that the Lord

---

6. For a helpful overview of two major ways of thinking about the relationship of divine and creaturely causality and the "morality of God," see Brian Davies, *An Introduction to the Philosophy of Religion* (Oxford: Oxford University Press, 2004), 1–20, 226–230. The above understanding may also help to resolve a thorny New Testament passage in which Peter appears to curse Ananias and Sapphira (Acts 5:11). For commentaries on this point, see Luke Timothy Johnson, *The Acts of the Apostles* (Collegeville, MN: Liturgical, 1992), 88; F.F. Bruce, *The Book of the Acts* (Grand Rapids, MI: Eerdmans, 1988), 106; James D. G. Dunn, *The Acts of the Apostles* (Grand Rapids, MI: Eerdmans, 2016), 64.

7. Pontifical Biblical Commission, *The Inspiration and Truth of Sacred Scripture* (Collegeville, MN: Liturgical, 2014), xiii–xiv, 123–125, 145–158, 163–167; International Theological Commission, *God the Trinity and the Unity of Humanity: Christian Monotheism and Its Opposition to Violence*, 26–27, Vatican.va. The contributions of these documents to our subject are discussed in Matthew Ramage, "How to Read the Bible and Still Be a Christian: The Problem of Divine Violence as Considered in Recent Curial Documents," *Homiletic and Pastoral Review*, July 12, 2015, https://www.hprweb.com/2015/07/how-to-read-the-bible-and-still-be-a-christian/. For a detailed overview of Benedict XVI's approach, see Matthew Ramage, *Dark Passages of the Bible: Engaging Scripture with Benedict XVI and Thomas Aquinas* (Washington, DC: The Catholic University of America Press, 2013).

is love and allows evils for our greater good could come only after Israel had grasped that he is the only, all-powerful God.[8]

As in the case of the first approach, here it is helpful to observe that the ancient Israelites were not yet privy to the distinction whereby we now know that God does not actively will but rather *permits* the abuse of human freedom as part of his salvific plan. After many centuries, eventually God's people were ready to learn the truth concerning how to treat our enemies—namely, that we are to *love* them (Matt. 5:39–44) in imitation of him who is love itself (1 John 4:16). Emphasizing the necessity of interpreting the Old Testament from this Christological vantage point, Benedict XVI taught that "violence is incompatible with the nature of God and the nature of the soul."[9]

3. God did not command the violence—the violence narrated never actually happened and was intended to inspire a later generation to total devotion.

This last approach takes its cue from the Second Vatican Council's emphasis on the need to grasp the "literary form" of a biblical passage in order to ascertain its intended message.[10] Encouraging readers to do just this, the Pontifical Biblical Commission (PBC) writes that the conquest narratives "do not have the characteristics of a historical account."[11] Rather, it continues, the commands prescribing the extermination of the Canaanites were deliberately *anachronistic*—written centuries later at a time when the cities allegedly destroyed (e.g., Jericho, Ai) had no inhabitants in them to conquer.[12] If this is

---

8. See Ramage, *Dark Passages of the Bible*, 185–195 and Benedict XVI, *Jesus of Nazareth: From the Baptism in the Jordan to the Transfiguration* (New York: Doubleday, 2007), xviii–xix.

9. Benedict XVI, "Faith, Reason and the University: Memories and Reflections," September 12, 2006, Vatican.va.

10. See Vatican Council II, *Dei Verbum* 12, *The Word on Fire Vatican II Collection*, ed. Matthew Levering (Park Ridge, IL: Word on Fire Institute, 2021), 28.

11. Pontifical Biblical Commission, *The Inspiration and Truth of Sacred Scripture* (Collegeville, MN: Liturgical, 2014), 127. See also Pontifical Biblical Commission, 124. In this passage, the PBC also applies this principle to Genesis 1–11, the patriarchal narratives, and the stories of the kings down to the Maccabean revolt.

12. Pontifical Biblical Commission, *The Inspiration and Truth of Sacred Scripture*, 146. For an excellent overview of the archaeological evidence behind this claim, see Seibert, *Disturbing Divine Behavior*, 99–104.

correct, then at least some brutal biblical prescriptions are not so problematic after all, because the violence in question never actually happened.[13]

Why would the sacred authors have written these texts to make it appear that they were offering straightforward historical chronicles if in fact they were not? It was a common Old Testament literary practice to use the past as a literary vehicle for speaking to present-day events (e.g., the story of Adam as the story of Israel).[14] What is more, the Old Testament's use of deliberate anachronism was often also paired with *hyperbole*. As we see in texts from other cultures in the period, the extent of violence done was overstated for a variety of reasons (e.g., so as to foster a sense of national identity, justify territorial expansion, or inspire total devotion to God's laws).[15] For its part, the PBC writes that the purpose of the narratives' vindictiveness was exhortative, and "the apparently violent action is to be interpreted as concern to remove evil."[16] In other words, it was designed to summon the Israel of its day to imitate the zeal against evil described in these texts.

Remarkably, this recent interpretive trend in some way represents a return to the old. As the PBC notes, "the best interpreters of the patristic tradition" already read the conquest narrative symbolically, adding that the law of extermination "requires a nonliteral interpretation" and that "we must

---

13. Pontifical Biblical Commission, *The Inspiration and Truth of Sacred Scripture*, 145.

14. See Seibert, *Disturbing Divine Behavior*, 106–110, 173–176. Seibert argues that the conquest narrative in its final form was likely penned during the seventh century in view of supporting the religious reforms of King Josiah, of whom Joshua is deployed as an archetype. On Adam as an image of Israel and Genesis 1–11 as a miniature version of Israel's nation story, see Matthew J. Ramage, *From the Dust of the Earth: Benedict XVI, the Bible, and the Theory of Evolution* (Washington, DC: The Catholic University of America Press, 2022), chap. 6.

15. This rhetorical device of hyperbole in conquest narratives may be found among nations across the ancient Near Eastern world, from Moab to Egypt, Assyria, and among the Hittites. For a helpful overview of the various possible functions of the hyperbolic conquest narrative mentioned above, see Seibert, *Disturbing Divine Behavior*, 131–144. See also Adele Berlin, Marc Zvi Brettler, and Michael Fishbane, eds., *The Jewish Study Bible* (New York: Oxford University Press, 2004), 382–383, which emphasizes one of these objectives: "The law of the ban is an anachronistic literary formulation. It first arose centuries after the settlement; it was never implemented because there was no population extant against whom it could be implemented. Its polemic is directed at internal issues in 6th century Judah. Often the authors of Deuteronomy use the term 'Canaanite' rhetorically to stigmatize older forms of Israelite religion that they no longer accept."

16. Pontifical Biblical Commission, *The Inspiration and Truth of Sacred Scripture*, 147.

understand the entire event of the conquest as a sort of symbol."[17] Reading these texts in light of the revelation of God's abundant mercy in Christ, we learn that what should be "devoted to destruction" in our lives is not other sinners, but rather *our sinful ways* that prevent us from being true disciples of Jesus.

What We Need to Do: Principles for Application

The above survey is by no means exhaustive, but the principles outlined can readily be applied to any number of passages that are "dark" to us in the sense of appearing to contradict the fullness of revelation in Jesus Christ. Here, then, are some practical takeaways that summarize how any believer may do just this:

1. *Soberly recognize the problem.* Passages depicting divinely ordained violence against men, women, and children abound in Scripture and indeed stand in tension with the fullness of revelation in Jesus Christ.
2. *Employ both ancient and modern sources in the study of Scripture.* Taking inspiration from the practice of monumental figures like Benedict XVI, have recourse to the wisdom of the entire tradition to tackle thorny problems, recognizing that all truth—no matter its source or epoch—is of the Holy Spirit.
3. *Approach the entire Old Testament in light of the divine pedagogy.* Contextualize troubling Old Testament passages within their gradual

---

17. Pontifical Biblical Commission, *The Inspiration and Truth of Sacred Scripture*, 146–147. From the perspective of such greats as St. Gregory of Nyssa, then, the command to "destroy" or "drown" our enemies and their "firstborn" should be seen as an exhortation to put to death everything in our lives that is not of God. Gregory of Nyssa, *The Life of Moses* (New York: Paulist, 1978), 75, 84. The Psalmist's desire to kill the children of his Babylonian enemies (Ps. 137:9) should likewise be interpreted—along with Origen, St. Benedict, and other patristic figures—as an exhortation to bash our enemies' "children" (temptations and nascent sins) against the "rock" of Jesus Christ. See Origen, *Against Celsus*, vol. 4 of *The Ante-Nicene Fathers: Translations of the Writings of the Fathers down to A.D. 325*, ed. Rev. Alexander Roberts and James Donaldson (Grand Rapids, MI: Eerdmans, 1989), 7.22; Benedict, *The Rule*, prologue, in *Benedict Collection*, ed. Brandon Vogt (Park Ridge, IL: Word on Fire Classics, 2018), 7.

progression toward Jesus Christ, who is love incarnate and the definitive interpretive key to all of Scripture.

4. *Seek out the essential teaching of dark passages within their original context.* Seeking to ascertain the "literary form" of the text, ask yourself what the original human author's underlying intention was in penning the passage—as well as why the Church included it in the canon of Scripture.

5. *Pray with Scripture and apply it to your life.* When faced with troublesome texts, follow the venerable practice of *lectio divina* and ask how it applies to your life today. Chances are, God is there waiting to reveal something that you need to "devote to destruction." By prayerfully engaging disturbing portions of Scripture in this way, we may even come to see the meaning of C.S. Lewis' saying that "the value of the Old Testament may be dependent on what seems its imperfection."[18]

---

18. C.S. Lewis, *Reflections on the Psalms* (London: Harvest, 1964), 114. For a treatment of this point in relation to Psalm 139, see Matthew Ramage, "In Praise of 'Perfect Hatred': How to Read the Old Testament's Cursing Psalms," *Evangelization & Culture* 5 (Fall 2020): 72–79. For a practical walkthrough of *lectio's* five steps, see Benedict XVI, *Verbum Domini* 86–87, post-synodal apostolic exhortation, Vatican.va.

37

Resurrection and the Future

David Baird

Few people would deny that Jesus of Nazareth died; but that he came to life again is the central, essential claim of creedal Christianity. The Resurrection is, at the same time, the fundamental expression of Christian hope, and no mere metaphor, but an event held to have actually happened. Indeed, either this man's real death and return to life are historical facts on par with the voyages of Christopher Columbus and the Battle of Gettysburg, or the Christian religion is merely an unhappy farce.

But did the Resurrection really happen? A significant amount of energy has been expended over the years arguing that it did, much of it to good purpose.[1] But Christianity is rightly called a faith, at least in part, because we cannot conclusively demonstrate that it did. To be sure, Christians trust this evidence to be forthcoming—specifically, when the resurrected and ascended Christ returns on the clouds in glory—but in the meantime, there is a real sense in which everyone, believer and nonbeliever alike, must simply wait and see.

So, where does this leave the Christian apologist for the Resurrection? Can we only sit quietly like attendees at the theater, and wait to see what happens when the curtain goes up on the world stage of history? We must wait, certainly, but we need not simply wait: there are valuable things to

---

1. See, for example, the "minimal facts" approach employed by Gary R. Habermas and Michael R. Licona, *The Case for the Resurrection of Jesus* (Grand Rapids, MI: Kregel, 2004); and a general reevaluation of the plausibility of miraculous events in Craig S. Keener, *Miracles: The Credibility of the New Testament Accounts* (Grand Rapids, MI: Baker Academic, 2011).

consider now. Rather than expending all our energies arguing *that* the Resurrection happened, though, a perennially fresh apologetic approach will also devote significant energies to expanding upon *what it means if it did.*

The approach that follows is similar to the strategy of renowned British publishers and street evangelists Frank Sheed and Maisie Ward, who describe the essential work of the Christian apologist as helping one's hearers "see what the doctrines are: not to see that they are true nor to see that they are desirable, but to see *them*: and because they *are* true and good, the doctrines will set about their own effort to capture the man, for God who made them true and good endowed man with faculties whose object is truth and goodness."[2] In other words, if the Resurrection did happen, the doctrine will have an irresistible appeal to lovers of the truth, granting they understand what it means.

So, what does the Resurrection *mean*? And, in particular, how might this meaning be best, and most intriguingly, conveyed to our contemporaries who do not yet perceive its significance? For apologetic purposes today, an especially pertinent aspect of Jesus' bodily return from death is the simple yet profound implication that his body must therefore have been something good. The fact that Jesus of Nazareth returns to life, not as a purely spiritual entity like a ghost, but as a fully physical human being, expresses in a powerful way the fundamental Christian conviction that human bodies and the physical world of which they are a part have been invested by Christ with a superlative and lasting dignity. Such a resounding *yes* to the goodness of the created world offers a perhaps unexpected point of connection, not only with those persons who have lost sight of the beauty and value of their bodies, but also with that significant part of the global population today almost religiously preoccupied with humanity's impact upon our natural surroundings—climate change, sustainability, the ethical use of our planet's finite material resources, etc.

While, undoubtedly, contemporary ecosensitivities can readily tip over into various kinds of secular idolatry—for example, cults of the body or the

---

2. Frank Sheed and Masie Ward, *Catholic Evidence Training Outlines* (Ann Arbor, MI: Catholic Evidence Guild, 1992), 15.

environment—at their best, these attitudes enjoy a large overlap with Christian convictions. The Resurrection speaks to the permanent pertinence and value of physical creation, strengthening and elevating humanity's aboriginal commission to care for and cultivate the creaturely world (see Gen. 1:26–28). Although it is true that Christian hope also looks forward to a radically renewed heavens and earth at Christ's Second Coming, at the same time, the expectation that he will return *physically* and inaugurate *the bodily resurrections of the rest of humanity* suggests that however dramatic the transformation may be at the end of time, there will also be real, substantial continuity between this world and the next. Accordingly, rather than pooh-poohing imperfect ecoactivist agendas, Christians are arguably in a position to affirm, clarify, and make them more effective by imbuing them with an even more radical sense of conviction, power born of supernatural love, and confidence that the relevance of these efforts is not limited to the present age but extends into eternity. Indeed, a Christian might go so far as to say that all work that cultivates, educates, conserves, renews, reforms, and improves upon the genuine good of creation aligns with and actively contributes to Christ's mission in the world.

The Resurrection also offers corrections to potential errors in this area. For dogmatic ecoadvocates who would go so far as to treat this-worldly endeavors as ends in themselves, the Resurrection reminds us that in Jesus Christ the truly valuable goods of creation have been integrated into the ultimately valuable Good, God's own self, whose thoughts and ways involve things higher than merely earthly considerations (see Isa. 55:8–9). Similarly, for those who would prioritize the prerogatives of the nonhuman physical world over the legitimate needs of human beings, the resurrected humanity of Christ establishes that the supreme dignity of the created order is realized precisely in, with, and through man. To summarize, the Resurrection offers a powerful and nuanced affirmation of the intrinsic value of the creaturely world, whereby the physical stuff of our planet is regarded neither as what is most important nor as ultimately separable from what is.

The same principle also challenges those persons who would dismiss, neglect, or aggressively abuse the human body or natural world and thereby contribute, directly or indirectly, to their wastage, damage, or destruction. Christians have too often been among those guilty of such attitudes, whether by overreacting to secular ideologies or by misguided understandings of the insignificance of the created world. However, the destructive habits that result from such beliefs involve direct rebuffs, not only of humanity's natural responsibilities, but also of the invitation, in Christ, to participate in God's supernatural love for and restoration of the world. Far from underplaying the importance of the physical stuff of creation, then, by incorporating it into the eternal life of the Creator, our resurrected and ascended Lord bestows upon it just about the highest endorsement conceivable.

So, how might the Christian apologist today speak about the Resurrection in a way that spontaneously sounds like something worth considering? Backed by the belief that there is a force at work in the world (i.e., the Resurrection) stronger than the most horrible thing human beings can do (i.e., crucifying God-become-man), a Christian can enthusiastically encourage the caretaking efforts of our neighbors and speak with confidence about the eventual triumph of creative love over the most benighted ignorance, fear, and violence of humanity's self-destructive shortsightedness. No matter how broken, exploited, or abused we find our bodies and our world, there is healing, hope, and, one day, complete restoration. This is the promise the Resurrection makes out of the past concerning our shared future, a promise about a regenerative power whose effects we do not have to wait to see but can begin to put into action even now. Our bodies and our world are good—the Resurrection tells us so—and they are *so good*, in fact, that God not only made them and redeemed them, but continues, everlastingly, to seek out, heal, and draw them ever deeper into his own fathomless love. This is what the Resurrection means, at least in part, and if we start here helping our family, friends, and fellow citizens gain some insight into the sense of the doctrine, we might trust it then to set about its own effort finishing the task.

38

Ecumenical Apologetics

Archbishop Donald Bolen

The encouragement in 1 Peter 3:15 to always be ready to give an account of the hope that is within us took a very different turn when Western Christianity suffered deep divisions in the Reformation and post-Reformation periods. A few years ago, I had the privilege of being a part of the international Methodist–Roman Catholic dialogue at a time when we were working on a document on ecclesiology, eventually published in 2006 as *The Grace Given You in Christ: Catholics and Methodists Reflect Further on the Church.*[1]

The dialogue group was cochaired by two extraordinary leaders, the Methodist scholar and liturgist Geoffrey Wainwright and Australian Catholic bishop Michael Putney. They had been engaged in ecumenical relations for decades, were close friends, and fostered within the commission a spirit of deep honesty, faithfulness to our respective traditions, candid conversation, and rigorous pursuit of the unity Christ wills. Several participants had been on the dialogue commission for a long time, which created a context where we were well prepared to tackle particularly challenging topics.

In order to address what we could say of each other ecclesiologically in the present context, our topic also led us to investigate what we had said about each other in the past, and in particular, what we said about each other at the time when Methodists were becoming a distinct Christian community, separating from the Church of England. Early Methodists adopted the

---

1. *The Grace Given You in Christ* (henceforth GGYIC), Pontifical Council for Promoting Christian Unity, 2006, http://www.christianunity.va/content/unitacristiani/en/dialoghi/sezione-occidentale/consiglio-metodista-mondiale/dialogo/documenti-di-dialogo/en12.html.

anti-Catholicism of the Protestantism of the day, viewing the Catholic understanding of tradition as a threat to the authority of Scripture, and at times describing the pope as the Antichrist.[2] Catholics for their part viewed Methodists as part of a Reformation movement that was an unmitigated disaster, undermining the Church's unity and apostolicity. English Catholic bishop Richard Challoner, in his *Caveat against the Methodists* (1760), wrote, "The Methodists are not the People of God: they are not true Gospel Christians: nor is their new raised Society the true Church of Christ, or any Part of it."[3] And those were not the worst things that were said of each other.

It was a rough experience! Through painstaking dialogue, common prayer, and growing friendships within the dialogue commission, we had come to a place of great respect for each other, so it was painful to read all of this—but not altogether surprising. In the post-Reformation period, apologetics were frequently framed in a polemical way, looking to highlight the problems and shortcomings of the other, at times exaggerating them, without much effort to understand. There were exceptions—moments where some respect was shown to each other—but the overall judgement of each upon the other tended to be negative if not hostile.

The Ecclesiological Foundation for an Ecumenical Apologetics

With the Second Vatican Council, the Catholic Church launched into the ecumenical movement and articulated a solid ecclesiological framework from which to pursue relations with other Christian communities. The Council's Dogmatic Constitution on the Church, *Lumen Gentium*, laid the foundations for the Church's principles for ecumenical engagement by noting that the Church willed by Christ "subsists in the Catholic Church" but that "many elements of sanctification and of truth are found outside of its visible struc-

---

2. GGYIC 20–25.
3. Quoted in GGYIC 23; see 26–27.

ture."[4] Conciliar and postconciliar documents have identified some of these ecclesial elements found outside the Catholic Church, in a degree which varies from one Christian community to another: baptism; the written word of God; the life of grace; faith, hope and charity; other interior gifts of the Holy Spirit and sources of spiritual life; other sacred actions; devotion to the Mother of God; the riches of liturgy, spirituality and doctrine proper to each communion.[5]

The helpful language of ecclesial elements present in other Christian communities was intrinsic to the Council's framing of the relationship between the Catholic Church and other Christian communities as one of real but incomplete communion.[6] In his encyclical *Ut Unum Sint*, Pope John Paul II detailed more explicitly how ecclesial elements found and recognized in each other "constitute the objective basis of the communion, albeit imperfect," which exists between other Christian communities and the Catholic Church. "To the extent that these elements are found in other Christian Communities, the one Church of Christ is effectively present in them."[7] Most notably, by virtue of baptism, members of other Christian communities are to be regarded as brothers and sisters in the Lord[8] who are members of Christ's body, called to discipleship and to Christian witness.

The Council's principles for ecumenical engagement acknowledged that Catholics were also responsible for divisions, and acknowledged the scandal of division; recognized that other Christian communities could help to lead people to salvation; and suggested that we could learn from each other, positing that "whatever is truly Christian" in the other "can always bring a deeper realization of the mystery of Christ and the Church."[9] Catholics were

---

4. Vatican Council II, *Lumen Gentium* 8, *The Word on Fire Vatican II Collection*, ed. Matthew Levering (Park Ridge, IL: Word on Fire Institute, 2021), 53.

5. Vatican Council II, *Unitatis Redintegratio* 3, 21–22, Vatican.va; the *Directory for the Application of Principles and Norms on Ecumenism* (Ecumenical Directory), 63, 76b; *Lumen Gentium* 15.

6. *Unitatis Redintegratio* 3.

7. John Paul II, *Ut Unum Sint* 11, encyclical letter, Vatican.va.

8. *Ut Unum Sint* 13; see *Unitatis Redintegratio* 3.

9. *Unitatis Redintegratio* 4.

encouraged to avoid unfair or exaggerated expressions, judgments, and actions about the other.[10]

Most importantly, the council called for dialogue among Christian communities,[11] and that dialogue has shaped the ecumenical landscape over the past fifty-five years. In bilateral and multilateral dialogues, Christian churches have mapped out to a significant degree what elements of faith they hold in common, always seeking to expand that common ground through rigorous exchange. This has allowed participating churches to identify what we can responsibly and appropriately do together in terms of common prayer, witness, and mission. Furthermore, the Catholic Church—along with the World Council of Churches, through its "Lund Principle"—has stressed that we should act together except where deep differences require us to act separately.[12]

The dialogues have brought a great deal of clarity, which has enabled the Catholic Church to take up the invitation of the Council to "bear witness to our common hope."[13] The Catholic Church's principles for ecumenical engagement therefore set the stage for Catholics to work with ecumenical partners in the task of apologetics.

A Field to Be Developed

In an increasingly secular and pluralistic society where Christian faith is challenged and undermined in so many ways and where so many people struggle with doubt, it is vital that we work together with other Christian communities to give a joint account of the hope that is within us, proclaiming the Gospel out of what we have come to know that we hold in common. Of

---

10. *Unitatis Redintegratio* 4.

11. *Unitatis Redintegratio* 4, 9, 11.

12. The Lund Principle was formulated at a meeting of the Faith and Order Commission of the World Council of Churches in 1952. It is echoed in the *Directory for the Application of Principles and Norms on Ecumenism*, 162, which notes that Christians "will want to do everything together that is allowed by their faith." The Lund Principle was explicitly endorsed by Pope Francis in his meeting with members of the Pontifical Council for Promoting Christian Unity on November 10, 2016 ("Address of His Holiness Pope Francis to Participants in the Plenary Assembly of the Pontifical Council for Promoting Christian Unity," November 10, 2016, Vatican.va).

13. *Unitatis Redintegratio* 12.

course, the extent to which that is possible varies from one Christian community to another. But the fact that the ecumenical landscape can be complex and challenging is not an adequate reason to shy away from the task.

While the phrase "ecumenical apologetics" is not widely used, Christians have, in many local contexts, begun to take up the challenge. Where pastors of different churches gather together to reflect on the Word to shape their preaching, where church leaders speak together to address social issues and witness to Christian faith in contexts which are at times hostile to it, when theologians dedicated to the work of apologetics enter into dialogue with their counterparts in other churches working on the same task, an ecumenical approach to apologetics is taking root.

A few years ago, the national Anglican–Roman Catholic dialogue in Canada decided to undertake a project in this field. We chose a series of questions that people, especially young people, were asking, such as: What good is the church? Why believe? Why belong? Will it be okay? Are science and faith in opposition? Why is the world the way it is? In each instance, one of the dialogue members took the lead in preparing a draft, trying to engage with the arguments challenging faith in the present culture, and then bringing the working document back to the whole group. We wanted our responses to these questions not only to be cogent and convincing, but also to be completely acceptable from both Anglican and Catholic perspectives. Challenges arose in places we didn't necessarily expect them, but we worked through them, and the result was an engaging collection of videos launched by our churches under the title "Did You Ever Wonder?" (churchesindialogue.ca). It is a collection that specifically seeks to give an account of the hope that is within us, together and jointly.

Engaging in apologetics in dialogue with ecumenical partners is a rich field open before us. When we stand together before Christ in speaking to a skeptical or doubting world, there is a greater opportunity to gain a hearing and to have our message be heard. To do so well requires not only knowing the audience we are addressing, but knowing and engaging with ecumenical partners and learning from each other along the way. Whenever we do so, we can trust that we will be accompanied by the Risen Lord, as were the disciples as they walked along the road to Emmaus.

ATHEISM AND CULTURE

39

The Mirror of Evil

Eleonore Stump

For reflective people, contemplation of human suffering tends to raise the problem of evil. If there is an omnipotent, omniscient, perfectly good God, how can it be that the world is full of evil? But there is another way to think about evil.

Consider just the examples of human evil in any morning's news. This evil is a mirror for us. It shows us our world; it also shows us ourselves. We ourselves—you and I, that is—are members of the species which does such things, and we live in a world where the wrecked victims of this human evil float on the surface of all history, animate suffering flotsam and jetsam. The author of Ecclesiastes says, "I observed all the oppression that goes on under the sun: the tears of the oppressed with none to comfort them; and the power of their oppressors—with none to comfort them. Then, I accounted those who died long since more fortunate than those who are still living"[1] (Eccles. 4:1–2).

Some people glance into the mirror of evil and quickly look away. They work hard, they worry about their children, they help their friends and neighbors, and they look forward to Christmas dinner. I don't want to disparage them in any way. Tolkien's hobbits are people like this. There is health and strength in their ability to forget the evil they have seen. Their good cheer makes them robust.

---

1. I am quoting from the new Jewish Publications Society translation. With the exception of quotations from Jeremiah 3 and Psalm 34, all quotations from the Hebrew Bible will be from this translation.

But not everybody has a hobbit's temperament. Some people look into the mirror of evil and can't shut out the sight. You sit in your warm house with dinner on the table and your children around you, and you know that not far from you the homeless huddle around grates seeking warmth, children go hungry, and every other manner of suffering can be found. Is it human, is it decent, to enjoy your own good fortune and forget their misery?

Ecclesiastes recognizes the goodness of hobbits. The author says, over and over again, "Eat your bread in gladness, and drink your wine in joy; . . . enjoy happiness with a woman you love all the fleeting days of life that have been granted to you under the sun" (Eccles. 9:7, 9). But the ability to eat, drink, and be merry in this way looks like a gift of God, a sort of blessed irrationality. For himself, Ecclesiastes says, "I loathed life. For I was distressed by all that goes on under the sun, because everything is futile and pursuit of wind" (Eccles. 2:17).

So, some people react with loathing to what they can't help seeing in the mirror of evil—loathing of the world, loathing of themselves. The misery induced by the mirror of evil is vividly described by Philip Hallie in his book on Le Chambon, the village later famous for the efforts of its people at rescuing Jews during the Nazi occupation of France.[2] Hallie was working on a project on the Nazis, and his focus was the medical experiments carried out on Jewish children in the death camps. "Across all these studies," Hallie says, "the pattern of the strong crushing the weak kept repeating itself and repeating itself, so that when I was not bitterly angry, I was bored at the repetition of the patterns of persecution. . . . My study of evil incarnate had become a prison whose bars were my bitterness toward the violent, and whose walls were my horrified indifference to slow murder. Between the bars and the walls I revolved like a madman. . . . Over the years I had dug myself into Hell."[3] Hallie shares with the author of Ecclesiastes an inability to look away from the loathsome horrors in the mirror of evil. The torment of this reaction to evil is evident.

---

2. See Philip Hallie, *Lest Innocent Blood Be Shed* (Philadelphia: Harper & Row, 1979).
3. Hallie, 2.

But how does Hallie know—how do we know—that the torture of Jewish children by Nazi doctors is evil? By reason, we might be inclined to answer. But that answer is not right. We build our reasoned ethical theories on strong intuitions about individual cases which exemplify wrongdoing. If we found that our ethical theory countenanced those Nazi experiments on children, we'd throw away the theory as something evil itself. But what exactly are these intuitions? What cognitive faculty produces them?

At this stage in our understanding of our own minds and brains, we don't know enough to identify the cognitive faculty that recognizes evil intuitively. But it would be a mistake to infer that there is no such faculty. That we have little idea *what* faculty is responsible for those intuitions doesn't mean that there is no such faculty. We don't understand much about the faculty which produces moral intuitions in us, but we all regularly rely on it anyway.

It also seems clear that this cognitive faculty can discern differences in kind and degree. A young Muslim mother in Bosnia was repeatedly raped in front of her husband and father, with her baby screaming on the floor beside her. When her tormentors were finally tired of her, she begged permission to nurse the child. In response, one of the rapists swiftly decapitated the baby and threw the head in the mother's lap. This evil is different, and we feel it immediately. The taste of real wickedness is sharply different from the taste of garden-variety moral evil; and we discern it directly, with pain.

What is perhaps less easy to see is that this faculty also discerns goodness. And when the discerned goodness takes us by surprise, we are sometimes moved to tears by it. Hallie describes his first acquaintance with the acts of the Chambonnais in this way:

> I came across a short article about a little village in the mountains of southern France. . . . I was reading the pages with an attempt at objectivity . . . trying to sort out the forms and elements of cruelty and of resistance to it. . . . About halfway down the third page of the account of this village, I was annoyed by a strange sensation on my cheeks. The story was so simple and

so factual that I had found it easy to concentrate upon *it*, not upon my own feelings. And so, still following the story, and thinking about how neatly some of it fit into the old patterns of persecution, I reached up to my cheek to wipe away a bit of dust, and I felt tears upon my fingertips. Not one or two drops; my whole cheek was wet.[4]

Those tears, Hallie says, were "an expression of moral praise";[5] and that seems right. With regard to goodness, too, I think we readily recognize differences in kind and degree. We don't have a single word for the contrary of wickedness, so "true goodness" will have to do. True goodness tastes as different from ordinary instances of goodness as wickedness does from ordinary wrongdoing; and we discern true goodness, sometimes, with tears. The stories of the Chambonnais rescuing Jews even on peril of their own imprisonment and death went through him like a spear, Hallie says.[6] Perhaps if he had been less filled with the vision of the mirror of evil, he would have wept less over Le Chambon.

Some people glimpse true goodness by seeing it reflected in other people, as Hallie did. Others approach it more indirectly through beauty, the beauty of nature or mathematics or music. But I have come to believe that ultimately all true goodness of the heartbreaking kind is God's. And I think that it can be found first and most readily in the traces of God left in the Bible.

There would be something feeble about attempting to describe in a few lines the moving goodness of God which the biblical stories show us; and the attempt itself isn't the sort of procedure the biblical narratives encourage. Insofar as the Bible presents or embodies any method for comprehending the goodness of God, it can be summed up in the Psalmist's invitation to individual listeners and readers: Taste and see that the Lord is good (Ps. 34:8).

The Psalmist's mixed metaphor seems right. Whether we find it in the Chambonnais or in the mélange of narrative, prayer, poetry, chronicle, and

---

4. Hallie, 3.
5. Hallie, 4.
6. Hallie, 3.

epistle that constitutes the Bible, the taste of true goodness calls to us, wakes us up, opens our hearts. If we respond with surprise, with tears, with gratitude, with determination not to lose the taste, with commitment not to betray it, that tasting leads eventually to seeing, to some sight of or insight into God.

Hallie left his college office and his family and went seeking the villagers of Le Chambon. He concluded his study of the Chambonnais this way:

> We are living in a time, perhaps like every other time, when there are many who, in the words of the prophet Amos, "turn judgment to wormwood." Many are not content to live with the simplicities of the prophet of the ethical plumbline, Amos, when he says in the fifth chapter of his Book: "Seek good, and not evil, that ye may live: and so the Lord, the God of Hosts, shall be with you." . . . We are afraid to be "taken in," afraid to be credulous, and we are not afraid of the darkness of unbelief about important matters. . . . But perplexity is a luxury in which I cannot indulge. . . . For me, as for my family, there is the same *kind* of urgency as far as making ethical judgments about Le Chambon is concerned as there was for the Chambonnais when they were making their ethical judgments upon the laws of Vichy and the Nazis. . . . For me [this] awareness [of goodness] is my awareness of God.[7]

So in an odd sort of way the mirror of evil can also lead us to God. A loathing focus on the evils of our world and ourselves prepares us to be the more startled by the taste of true goodness when we find it and the more determined to follow that taste till we see where it leads. And where it leads is to the truest goodness of all—not to the boss of the universe whose word is moral law or to sovereignty which must not be dishonored, but to the sort of goodness of which the Chambonnais' goodness is only an aftertaste. The mirror of evil becomes translucent, and we can see through it to the goodness of God.

---

7. Hallie, 291–293.

There are some people, then, and I count myself among them, for whom focus on evil constitutes a way to God. For people like this, Ecclesiastes is not depressing but deeply comforting.

I think the Psalmist was speaking for people who take this long way round to peace and cheer when he says, "I have taught myself to be contented like a weaned child with its mother; like a weaned child am I in my mind" (Ps. 131:2). How can a child who is being weaned understand the evil of the weaning? What he wants is right there; there is nothing bad about his having it—it costs his mother nothing to satisfy him; the pain of doing without it is sharp and urgent. And so for a while the child will be overwhelmed by the evil of his situation. But sooner or later in his thrashing he will also see his mother, and that makes all the difference. His desire for what she will not give him is still urgent, and the pain of the deprivation remains sharp. But in seeing her, he feels her love of him. He senses her goodness, and he comes to trust her. As Isaiah puts it, he sucks consolation to the full in another way (Isa. 66:11). That is how he can be both weaned and also resting peacefully by her side.

Although, as Ecclesiastes is fond of saying, we often cannot understand the details of the reason why God does what he does in the world, when we see through the mirror of evil and taste the goodness of the Lord, we do understand the general reason. Like a woman in childbirth, then, as Paul says, we feel our pains of the moment, but they are encircled by an understanding of God's goodness that brings peace and joy.

And so the mirror of evil can bring us around to the hobbit's way of seeing things at the end. "Go," says Ecclesiastes, "eat your bread in gladness and drink your wine in joy; for your action was long ago approved by God" (Eccles. 9:7). If the evils of the earth are in the hands of a good God, then you may be at peace with yourself and your world.

If a truly good God rules the world, then even the most loathsome evils and the most horrendous suffering are in the hands of a God who is truly good. All these things have a season, as Ecclesiastes says, and all of them work together for good for those who love God—for those who are finding their way to the love of God too, we might add. Nothing in this thought makes evil less evil. Suffering remains painful; violence and greed are still execrable. We still have an obligation to lessen the misery of others, and our own troubles retain their power to torment us. But it makes a great difference to suppose that the sufferers of evil, maybe ourselves included, are in the arms of a good God.

Nothing in this view, of course, is incompatible with a robust program of social action. "Send your bread forth upon the waters; for after many days you will find it," Ecclesiastes says; "Distribute portions to seven or even to eight, for you cannot know what misfortune may occur on earth" (Eccles. 11:1–2). If you are moved by goodness, then you will want to ally yourself with it, to diminish evils in the world, to alleviate suffering. Those who love God will hate evil, the Psalmist says (Ps. 97:10). There is no love of God, 1 John says, in those without compassion for the world's needy (1 John 3:17). A good part of true religion, James says, is just visiting "the fatherless and the widows in their affliction" (James 1:27).

So here is the conclusion of the matter. For Hallie, for the author of Ecclesiastes, for me, too, the ghastly vision in the mirror of evil becomes a means to finding the goodness of God, and with it peace and joy. I don't know any better way to sum it up than Habakkuk's.

Habukkuk has the Ecclesiastes temperament. He begins his book this way: "How long, O Lord, shall I cry out and You not listen, shall I shout to You, 'Violence!' and You not save? Why do You make me see iniquity, why do You look upon wrong? Raiding and violence are before me, Strife continues and contention goes on. That is why decision fails and justice never emerges" (Hab. 1:1–4).

But he ends his book this way. He presents the agricultural equivalent of nuclear holocaust: the worst sufferings imaginable to him, the greatest disaster for himself and his people. And he says this: "Though the fig tree does not bud, and no yield is on the vine, though the olive crop has failed, and the fields produce no grain, though sheep have vanished from the fold, and no cattle are in the pen, yet will I rejoice in the Lord, exult in the God who delivers me. My Lord God is my strength" (Hab. 3:17–19).[8]

8. This essay is a shortened and revised version of Eleonore Stump, "The Mirror of Evil," in *God and the Philosophers: The Reconciliation of Faith and Reason*, ed. Thomas Morris (Oxford: Oxford University Press, 1994), 235–247. Copyright © 1994 by Oxford University Press, Inc. Reproduced with permission of the Licensor through PLSclear.

40

The Argument from Divine Hiddenness
Fr. Gregory Pine, OP

It was not for his own glory alone, but for their salvation, that he was doing all things. For if it had not been his will that they should hear and be saved, he would have remained silent and would not have spoken in parables. But now in this very manner he stirs them up, even by speaking under a veil. "For God does not will the death of the sinner but that he should turn to him and live."[1]
—St. John Chrysostom

The agnostic has said in his heart, "If God exists, then why not *prove* it?"

So much rides on the existence of God—from the coherence of life on earth to the possibility of life in heaven. Given the stakes, it stands to reason that God would be motivated to remove doubt in the hearts of those he has created. And yet, he seems in no rush to provide indisputable proof.

The agnostic moves from musing to accusing: "Here," he claims, "is further proof that God does *not* exist. As if the problem of evil weren't enough, add to it the fact of God's enormous silence."

This objection is called the argument from divine hiddenness. Travis Dumsday summarizes it neatly:

> On standard theisms, God supposedly loves us, and so desires our ultimate well-being. But that ultimate well-being necessarily involves having a posi-

---

1. John Chrysostom, *The Gospel of Matthew*, Homily 45:1–2, quoted in *Ancient Christian Commentary on Scripture: Matthew 1–13*, ed. Manlio Simonetti (Downers Grove, IL: InterVarsity, 2001), 272.

tive relationship with God, and in order to have such a relationship one must first believe that God exists. So if God really existed and really loved us, He would make sure that all of us believed in Him. Yet the world is full of rational persons who blamelessly fail to believe in God. Consequently, one must give up some aspect of standard theism, and the aspect it is most sensible to drop is the very idea that God exists.[2]

The argument is powerful, especially in a disenchanted and traumatized age. For many, God's absence seems far more palpable than his presence. The daily experience of the inquirer is like that of one playing hide-and-seek without the conviction that there is someone to be found. And, in the circumstances, it is not uncommon that the game gives way to despair.

Seen from the vantage of Christian revelation, though, there is purpose in the mystery. God does not torture or tantalize. The key lies in the recognition that wherever we find him in communication with man, he is saving— saving from sin, saving from death. In fact, what the agnostic takes to be an argument against the existence of God actually manifests the deep wisdom with which God makes himself known. For there is a profound correspondence between the manner of his revelation and the mystery of our salvation.

God's revelation is intended for us: for human persons with all our metaphysical lack and limitation. Rather than somehow filling our minds with an intuitive awareness of his existence, God seeks entrance to the sanctuary of each human heart in a way best suited to our condition. He enlightens and emboldens us along the way such that we attain to our end in due course.

Throughout salvation history, we see this at every level of his dealings with man. He gives a law to outline the boundaries of communion. He institutes the sacraments to provision us with embodied grace. He establishes a Church wherein his sacred humanity perdures. Mystical transports of an extraordinary sort may make the occasional appearance, but the daily fare is often as ordinary as are bread and wine. Like a good teacher who uses image

---

2. Travis Dumsday, "A Thomistic Response to the Problem of Divine Hiddenness," *American Catholic Philosophical Quarterly* 87, no. 3 (2013): 365–377.

and metaphor to communicate perennial truths, God leads by simple indications to wonderful realizations. And all throughout, we find that he conceals to reveal and reveals to save.

This movement is concretized in the Incarnation. In the fullness of time, he hides himself in human flesh "to seek and to save the lost" (Luke 19:10). In all that he does and suffers—from the Annunciation to the Ascension—lies concealed the salvation he seeks to communicate. When he is conceived of a virgin, he is saving. When he goes to the mountain to pray, he is saving. When he teaches in parables, he is saving.

The parables, especially, help to focus this question of divine hiddenness, for here the Lord is involved in a peculiar paradox—at once revealing and concealing: "For those outside, everything comes in parables; in order that 'they may indeed look, but not perceive, and may indeed listen, but not understand; so that they may not turn again and be forgiven'" (Mark 4:11–12). What is the point of manifest obscurity? What is the sense of hidden disclosure?

In his campaign of salvation, Christ will settle for nothing less than the communication of God. But to ensure that this communication be received, he accommodates it to our nature. And though we are made for God, God is far greater than our hearts. The medieval theologians repeated often that, before the radiance of his glory, we are as bats at noonday. It is for this reason that, in revelation, God constrains himself to our limitations—to the compass of our human frailty. As the Fathers of the Church have it, God condescends to us, lest we be undone by the weight of such glory. Pseudo-Dionysius writes, "We cannot be enlightened by the divine rays except they be hidden within the covering of many sacred veils."[3] And so, God not only hides himself in human flesh, but also hides his revelation in human imagery that, thereby, we might be led to him.

The divine hiddenness is not intended to confound but to save. We are pilgrims who come to our perfection step by step in the flow of time. Along

---

3. Pseudo-Dionysius, *De caelesti hierarchia* 1, quoted in Thomas Aquinas, *Summa theologiae* 1.1.9.

the way, we feel acutely the limits of our nature. We possess our lives only moment to moment. We suffer the vagaries of gain and loss. But left to our own devices, our fallen selves rebel against our existential poverty. Rather than set out in pursuit of the mystery, we are constantly tempted to go in for the overly simplistic answer, the ready-made solution, the conceptual idol that promises to save us the effort of watching and waiting, of striving and struggling. And so, God, in order to keep us from settling, pulls us into his divine fullness through a kind of reticence.

In the parables he preached and in the parables he lived, the Lord draws us by both known and unknown. St. Jerome writes, "Jesus mixes what is clear with what is obscure so that through the things we understand, we may be drawn toward the knowledge of the things we do not."[4] In the Gospels, whenever the Lord speaks figuratively or allegorically, he is met with confusion: "Lord, we do not know where you are going. How can we know the way?" "Lord, show us the Father, and we will be satisfied" (John 14:5, 8). To each demand, the Lord answers with deep riddles, which prove more satisfying than the shallow answers we sought at first: "I am the way, and the truth, and the life"; "Whoever has seen me has seen the Father" (John 14:6, 9).

As human beings, we are too weak and wounded to receive his luminous revelation and accept it on its own terms. We need think only of the Lord's contemporaries, whose basic indisposition we share. It's for us then to present ourselves with a humble estimation of our ability to grasp his revelation. For though his ways may seem unnecessarily difficult, they are perfectly suited to our healing, to our growing, to our flourishing. If we are indeed wounded, it will do us no good to be healed quickly and superficially, especially when the disease is shut up within, where it rages fiercely. And so God, in his love, delays the healing by parables, so that, by those same parables, he may heal more deeply.

For the agnostic, then, who finds God's hiddenness to be vexing and his pace to be plodding, a word of encouragement: Take heart. There is still some

---

4. Jerome, *Commentary on Matthew* 2.13.3.

clarity to be had in the contemplation of God's silence, provided only that one looks to the end. For God's goal in his dealings with man is neither transparency nor dispatch. Rather, his end is salvation, a goal better accomplished by parable than by proof.

41

Wokeness and Social Justice
Matthew R. Petrusek

The rise of critical theory and social justice ideologies poses a unique challenge to Catholic apologists. The fundamental task of apologetics is to make persuasive arguments in defense of the faith to those willing to listen. There is thus a dual *epistemic* presupposition embedded in the enterprise: (a) the apologist believes he or she can formulate a truthful argument that (b) is intelligible to the listener. If either presupposition is absent—if the apologist cannot craft a truthful argument or if the listener cannot grasp the argument—then the apologetic project fails. Yet this is precisely the issue with critical theories and the social justice ideologies they generate: they tend to describe reality and issue moral commands while *denying the possibility* of either speaking or comprehending objective truth. Consequently, while Catholicism can find points of contact with critical theories, apologists should approach them with caution—and courage. Winning converts will likely require more than clever syllogisms.

Once secluded in university departments, critical theories now have widespread cultural influence. Yet defining them, especially in relation to "social justice," remains notoriously difficult. They include "critical race theory" (sometimes abbreviated as CRT), "queer theory," "postcolonial theory," "gender theory," various "ethnic/cultural theories," and some versions of "feminist theory," among others. The theories have complex intellectual genealogies, with roots in Marxist philosophy, postmodern deconstructionist philosophy, anti-colonial philosophy, and, even, existential nihilism. They are also substantively diverse and often vehemently disagree with each other (for example, some feminist theories, which advocate for women's flourishing, stand in direct opposition to gender theories that deny the existence of "women" as an ontologically real, biological category).

Notwithstanding their differences, critical theories typically have the following characteristics:

- **Experientially Based Epistemologies:** Critical theories tend to derive their ideas exclusively from the self-reported "lived experiences" of individuals whom the theory deems to be representative of the group. Often, the theory will assert that "rational objectivity" and "epistemic universality" (the belief that all people can, potentially, apprehend and assent to the same truth) are *social constructs* created to marginalize and oppress. This epistemology is evident in the claim "I am speaking *my* truth," or "We are speaking *our* truth." The theories also regularly contend that dissenting members of the identity group—e.g., a person of color who disagrees with tenets of critical race theory—are not "real" or "authentic" representatives because they have adopted "the oppressor's" viewpoint. Moreover, since "experience" cannot be falsified (i.e., there is no objective way to ascertain whether an "experience" is true or not), those outside the identity group have no rational mechanism to challenge critical theories' epistemic content.

- **Group Control of Language and Logic:** Because critical theories tend to eschew rational objectivity and, by extension, a commitment to coherent, universally intelligible language, they often imbue words with whatever meaning the identity group believes will advance its interests. The theories' creation of "in group" language intended for "out group" consumption often results in contradictory claims—for example, "colorblindness is racism," "looting and property destruction are peaceful protest," "all lives matter" is bigotry, or, as "antiracism" activist Ibram X. Kendi has asserted, "The only remedy to racist discrimination

239

is anti-racist discrimination," which is another way of saying that racial discrimination is both unjust and just at the same time.

- **A Tendency to Generate Neologisms:** Relatedly, critical theories frequently invent words and slogans whose meaning is entirely dependent on the will of the identity group, yet whose moral authority must be respected by those outside the group. Examples include "love is love," "nonbinary," "misgendering," "unconscious bias," "mansplaining," "cultural appropriation," "triggering," "believe all women," "white/male privilege," "heteronormativity," "cisnormativity," "deadnaming," "silence is violence," "microaggression," "Latinx," "equity," "safe space," "birthing person," "diversity," "inclusion," "allyship," and "intersectionality," among *many* others. Questioning the meaning, coherence, or selective applicability of these terms can prompt the charge of having a "phobia" or being motivated by "hate."

- **Conflating Disagreement with "Harm" and "Danger":** Again, because critical theories tend to reject rational standards of truth, falsity, and coherence as tools for defending their positions, they often appeal to "safety" to confront competing ideas. This tactic enables them to tag speech with which they disagree as "dangerous," which, in turn, produces an imperative to "be protected" from the speech. This "protection" can include deplatforming (canceling speaking events), shouting down speakers, and/or socially stigmatizing (and potentially seeking to outlaw) the expression of the viewpoint altogether.

- **Activist in Origin and Purpose:** As another consequence of their epistemology, critical theories tend to find their disciplinary justification not in a search for "truth" per se, but rather in the desire to change sociopolitical structures. In this sense, critical theories often see "truth" as instrumental rather than as a good to be pursued in and of itself or, as is the case in Catholic teaching, seeing "the good" and "the true" as mutually implicative (i.e., what is true must be good; what is good must be true). This dimension of critical theories is what prompts them to pursue "social justice."

- **Focused on Power:** Critical theories tend to reduce *all* forms of knowledge to an assessment of "power dimensions" specifically construed as identifying (a) which group is dominant in society and (b) how to oust that group from its sociopolitical perch. In this sense, critical theories are mercantilist in nature: they believe there is a fixed supply of "power" in the world, and if one group has it, that means it has been stolen from another. They also tend to interpret empirically observable inequalities among groups (as *they* define "group") as ipso facto evidence of "oppression." The existence of people who question the causal relationship between "oppression" and "inequality" is, for many critical theorists, itself dispositive evidence that the "system" is oppressive.

- **Offer Catch-22 "Solutions":** Finally, critical theories tend to offer "out group" individuals a lose-lose proposition: either (a) submit to our demands and, in so doing, confess you are an oppressor (or, at least, his abettor), or (b) refuse our demands and, in so doing, reveal that you want to defend an oppressive system—which means you are an oppressor. The two options are redolent of the late medieval practice of "witch testing": if the accused woman cast into the water by the mob submitted and drowned, she was no longer a communal threat and thus could be counted as "on *our* side"; if, however, she struggled and survived, her very resistance *proved* she was "on *their* side"—and needed to be punished.

How can apologists respond to this form of thinking, which now pervades governments, universities, cultural institutions, and even corporations? Here are four suggestions.

First, recognize the acute threat to free speech, and its corollary, religious freedom. Setting aside the content of any specific critical theory tied to any particular conception of social justice, by equating dissent with, at best, "ignorance" and, at worst, "violence," the *methodology* of critical theory authorizes groups to impose their visions of reality and morality on society with no limiting principle. Totalitarian governments have employed, and continue to employ, this methodology to squelch opposing speech and to prohibit the practice of "unapproved" religion.

Second, look for points of commonality. Despite critical theories' grave flaws, they can attract individuals who are sincerely committed to advancing authentic justice in society. Apologists can seek opportunities to explain how the Catholic conception of social justice embraces many (not all) of critical theories' concerns without adopting their moral relativism and authoritarian inclinations.

Third, speak the truth. Encountering someone who has imbibed a critical theory and is on the offensive can be disorienting. It is crucial to remember that, for a committed critical theorist, there is no space between individuals and their "arguments" because *their lived experience is their argument.* It is thus possible that even gentle pushback will spark a passionate, even hostile response. It is also possible that you will be slandered and receive calls for you to be fired or worse. This fear of losing reputation and income is why critical theories have been so cunningly effective in attaining cultural dominance. As difficult as it may be, however, don't give in. Speak the truth with charity, yes, but also with conviction. If the critical theorist opines, "That is your truth, not mine," repeat those words back—with kindness—as a means of opening the possibility for conversation.

Finally, outdo critical theorists in virtue. Critical theories, especially in a civil context, are ultimately not public arguments, but rather, public performances whose goal is to attain sociopolitical power. Christianity beat Rome in no small part because Christian communities were eventually perceived, by a decadent public that once despised them, to be *doing good for the sake of doing good,* all power calculations aside. That revolutionary evangelical approach worked before, and it can work again—but only if we heed the words and example of Pope St. John Paul II: "Be not afraid."

AFTERWORD
Bishop Robert Barron

In a 1983 address to the bishops of Latin America, Pope John Paul II, very much in line with the missionary élan of the Second Vatican Council, called for a New Evangelization—a proclamation of the Gospel that is new in ardor, new in methods, and new in expression.

While this call remains as urgent as ever, I can verify, on the basis of over twenty years of ministry in the field of evangelization, that a vitally needed aspect of the New Evangelization is a New Apologetics—a revivified defense of the Catholic faith. Innumerable studies over the past ten years have confirmed that people frequently cite intellectual reasons when asked what prompted them to leave the Church or lose confidence in it. These concerns remain crucial stumbling blocks to the acceptance of the faith, especially among the young.

I realize that in some circles within the Church, the term "apologetics" is suspect, since it seems to indicate something rationalistic, aggressive, condescending. I hope it is clear that arrogant proselytizing has no place in our pastoral outreach, but I hope it is equally clear that an intelligent, respectful, and culturally sensitive explication of the faith—giving a reason for the hope that is within us, as St. Peter exhorts (1 Pet. 3:15)—is certainly necessary. The term "apologetics" is derived from the Greek *apologia*, which simply means "bringing a word to bear." It implies, therefore, giving a reason, providing a context, putting things in perspective, offering direction. And people today are hungry and thirsty—not just for friendly companions, but for a word from the Church.

What would this New Apologetics look like? First, it would engage *new audiences*. By far the fastest-growing "religious" group in the United States is the "nones"—that is, those who claim no religious affiliation. In 1970, only

3% of the country self-identified as nones. Today, that number has risen to 25%. When we focus on young people, the picture is even more bleak. Almost 40% of those under thirty are nones, and among young people who were raised Catholic, the number rises to 50%. This rapidly growing audience of nonreligious men and women—atheists, agnostics, and former Catholics, especially—should be the target of the New Apologetics.

Secondly, it would take *new approaches* to presenting the faith, which engage not only the mind but the whole person. It would utilize the new media, find "seeds of the Word" in the culture, engage the imagination, joyfully champion what orthodox Catholicism stands *for*, and perhaps most crucially, lead with beauty. Especially in our postmodern cultural context, commencing with the true and the good is often a nonstarter. However, the beautiful often proves a more winsome, less threatening path. And part of the genius of Catholicism is that we have so consistently embraced the beautiful—in song, poetry, architecture, painting, sculpture, and liturgy. All of this provides a powerful matrix for evangelization.

Thirdly, it would take inspiration from *new models*. Catholicism is a smart religion, and another one of its great virtues is that it has a rich and deep theological tradition. Taking Mary as its model, Catholicism "ponders" revelation and seeks to understand it, using all of the intellectual tools available. A New Apologetics would follow great ponderers of the Word such as Augustine, Aquinas, Pascal, Chesterton, Lewis, and many others in order to meet pressing objections to the faith.

Finally, a New Apologetics would confront *new issues*, especially the kinds of questions that young people are spontaneously asking today. These would include queries about God's existence, the Bible, the meaning of life, and especially the relationship between religion and science. For many people today, "scientific" and "rational" are equivalent. And therefore, since religion is obviously not scientific, it must be irrational. Without for a moment denigrating the sciences, new apologists have to show that there are nonscientific and yet eminently reasonable paths that conduce toward knowledge of the real. Literature, drama, philosophy, the fine arts—all close cousins of religion—not only entertain and delight; they also bear truths that are unavailable in any other way. A renewed apologetics ought to cultivate these approaches.

We find a template for this New Apologetics in the story of Christ's conversation with two erstwhile disciples on the road to Emmaus (Luke 24:13–35). Jesus walks with them in easy fellowship, even though they are going the wrong way, and he gently asks what's on their minds. But this invitational approach aroused questions that called for answers. Jesus then taught—with clarity, at length, and in depth. How wonderful that, recalling Jesus' great apologetic intervention, the Emmaus disciples said, "Were not our hearts burning within us while he was talking to us on the road, while he was opening the scriptures to us?"

This collection of essays from many of today's leading Catholic thinkers and evangelists offers, with considerable clarity and panache, a bold first step in the direction of this renewed vision for apologetics. My hope is that it helps to inaugurate a new era of intellectual vigor for the Church, one in which an army of apologists both walk and talk with those on the road, offering—with "gentleness and reverence" (1 Pet. 3:16), but also boldness and intelligence—a reason for their hope. This, I trust, will set wandering hearts on fire.

RECOMMENDED RESOURCES

New Audiences

Chautard, Jean-Baptiste. *Soul of the Apostolate*. Charlotte, NC: TAN Books, 1946.

Beckwith, Francis J. "Catholicism and the Natural Law: A Response to Four Misunderstandings." *Religions* 12.6 (2021), available at https://www.mdpi.com/2077-1444/12/6/379/htm.

———. *Relativism: Feet Firmly Planted in Mid-Air*. Grand Rapids, MI: BakerBooks, 1998.

Bernanos, Georges and Gregory Koukl. *The Diary of a Country Priest*. Philadelphia, PA: Da Capo, 2002.

Budziszewski, J. *What We Can't Not Know: A Guide*. San Francisco, CA: Ignatius Press, 2003.

Bullivant, Stephen. *Nonverts: The Making of Ex-Christian America(ns)*. New York: Oxford University Press, forthcoming.

Burge, Ryan P. *The Nones: Where They Came From, Who They Are, and Where They Are Going*. Minneapolis, MN: Fortress, 2021.

Frankl, Viktor. *Man's Search for Meaning*. Boston, MA: Beacon, 2006.

Hall, Michael. *Intentional Accompaniment: An Apprenticeship for a New Generation of Builders*. Ottawa, ON: Catholic Christian Outreach Canada, 2021.

John Paul II, Pope. *Ut Unum Sint*. Vatican.va.

Nelson, Matt. *Just Whatever: How to Help the Spiritually Indifferent Find Beliefs That Really Matter*. El Cajon, CA: Catholic Answers, 2018.

Percy, Walker. *Lost in the Cosmos: The Last Self-Help Book*. New York: Farrar, Straus, and Giroux, 1983.

Thiessen, Joel and Sarah Wilkins-Laflamme. *None of the Above: Nonreligious

Identity in the US and Canada. New York: New York University Press, 2020.

New Approaches

Boyagoda, Randy. *Original Prin*. Windsor, ON: Biblioasis, 2019.

Douthat, Ross. *The Decadent Society: How We Became a Victim of Our Own Success*. New York: Simon & Schuster, 2020.

Guite, Malcolm. *Faith, Hope and Poetry: Theology and the Poetic Imagination*. New York: Routledge, 2017.

John Paul II, Pope. *Letter to Artists*. April 4, 1999. Vatican.va.

Lewis, C.S. *Surprised by Joy: The Shape of My Early Life*. New York: Harvest, 1955.

Marsden, George. *Religion and American Culture: A Brief History*. Grand Rapids, MI: Eerdmans, 2018.

Ordway, Holly. *Apologetics and the Christian Imagination: An Integrated Approach to Defending the Faith*. Steubenville, OH: Emmaus Road, 2017.

Poe, Marshall T. *A History of Communications: Media and Society from the Evolution of Speech to the Internet*. Cambridge, MA: Cambridge University Press, 2010.

Ratzinger, Joseph and Peter Seewald. *Salt of the Earth: The Church at the End of the Millennium — An Interview with Peter Seewald*. San Francisco, CA: Ignatius Press, 2017.

Robinson, Andrew. *The Story of Writing: Alphabets, Hieroglyphs & Pictograms*. London: Thames & Hudson, 2007.

Siedell, Daniel A. *God in the Gallery: A Christian Embrace of Modern Art*. Grand Rapids, MI: Baker Academic, 2008.

Urquhart, Peter and Paul Heyer. *Communication in History: Stone Age Symbols to Social Media*. New York: Routledge, 2018.

New Models

Ahlquist, Dale. *Common Sense 101: Lessons from G.K. Chesterton*. San Francisco, CA: Ignatius Press, 2006.

Bailie, Gil. *Violence Unveiled: Humanity at the Crossroads*. New York: Crossroad, 1995.

Chadwick, Henry. *Augustine: A Very Short Introduction*. Oxford: Oxford University Press, 2001.

Chesterton, G.K. *Orthodoxy*. Park Ridge, IL: Word on Fire Classics, 2017.

———. *The Everlasting Man*. New York: Image Books, 1955.

Girard, René. *I See Satan Fall Like Lightning*. Maryknoll, NY: Orbis Books, 2001.

Hooper, Walter. *C.S. Lewis: A Companion and Guide*. San Francisco, CA: Harper, 1996.

Kaplan, Grant. *René Girard, Unlikely Apologist: Mimetic Theory and Fundamental Theology*. Notre Dame, IN: University of Notre Dame Press, 2016.

Kreeft, Peter. *Christianity for Modern Pagans: Pascal's Pensées Edited, Outlined, Explained*. San Francisco, CA: Ignatius Press, 1993.

Levering, Matthew. *The Theology of Augustine: An Introductory Guide to His Most Important Works*. Grand Rapids, MI: Baker Academic, 2013.

Lewis, C.S. *Christian Reflections*. Edited by Walter Hooper. Grand Rapids, MI: Eerdmans, 1994.

———. *God in the Dock: Essays on Theology and Ethics*. Edited by Walter Hooper. Grand Rapids, MI: Eerdmans, 1970.

———. *Miracles: A Preliminary Study*. New York: MacMillan, 1947.

MacSwain, Robert and Michael Ward, eds. *The Cambridge Companion to C.S. Lewis*. Cambridge, MA: Cambridge University Press, 2010.

McGrath, Alister E. *The Intellectual World of C.S. Lewis*. Oxford: Wiley-Blackwell, 2014.

Meconi, David Vincent. *The One Christ: St. Augustine's Theology of Deification.* Washington, DC: Catholic University of America Press, 2013.

O'Connor, Flannery. *Flannery O'Connor Collection.* Edited by Matthew Becklo. Park Ridge, IL: Word on Fire Classics, 2019.

Ratzinger, Joseph. *Faith and the Future.* San Francisco, CA: Ignatius Press, 1995.

———. *Introduction to Christianity.* 2nd ed. Translated by J.R. Foster. San Francisco, CA: Ignatius Press, 2004.

———. *The Nature and Mission of Theology: Essays to Orient Theology in Today's Debates.* Translated by Adrian Walker. San Francisco, CA: Ignatius Press, 1995.

———. *Principles of Catholic Theology: Building Stones for a Fundamental Theology.* Translated by Mary Frances McCarthy. San Francisco, CA: Ignatius Press, 1987.

Pascal, Blaise. *Pensées.* Translated by A.J. Krailsheimer. London: Penguin Books, 1966.

New Issues

Science and Faith

Austriaco, Nicanor Pier Giorgio. "Defending Adam After Darwin." *American Catholic Philosophical Quarterly* 92.2 (2018): 337–352.

———. "A Theological Fittingness Argument for the Historicity of the Fall of Homo Sapiens." *Nova et Vetera* 13.3 (2015): 651–667.

Baglow, Christopher. *Creation: A Catholic's Guide to God and the Universe.* Notre Dame, IN: Ave Maria, 2021.

———. *Faith, Science, and Reason: Theology on the Cutting Edge.* Downers Grove, IL: Midwest Theological Forum, 2019.

Barr, S.M. *Modern Physics and Ancient Faith.* Notre Dame, IN: University of Notre Dame Press, 2003.

Bennett, M.R. and P.M.S. Hacker. *Philosophical Foundations of Neuroscience.* 2nd ed. Oxford: Blackwell, 2021.

Borgmann, Albert. *Power Failure: Christianity in the Culture of Technology.* Ada, MI: Brazos, 2003.

Feser, Edward. *Aristotle's Revenge: The Metaphysical Foundations of Physical and Biological Science.* Heusenstamm, DE: Editiones Scholasticae, 2019.

Houck, Daniel W. *Aquinas, Original Sin, and the Challenge of Evolution.* Cambridge: Cambridge University Press, 2020.

Krauss, Lawrence M. and Robert J. Scherrer. "The End of Cosmology?" *Scientific American*, March 2008, 4753.

Lanier, Jaron. *You Are Not a Gadget: A Manifesto.* New York: Vintage, 2011.

Lunine, Jonathan. "Faith and the Expanding Universe of Georges Lemaî-tre." *Church Life Journal,* https://churchlifejournal.nd.edu/articles/faith-and-the-expanding-universe-of-georges-lemaitre/.

Mele, Alfred. *Free: Why Science Hasn't Disproved Free Will.* Oxford: Oxford University Press, 2014.

Ramelow, Anselm. "Can Computers Create?" *Evangelization & Culture* 1 (2019): 39–46.

Ratzinger, Joseph. *'In the Beginning . . . ': A Catholic Understanding of the Story of Creation and the Fall.* Translated by Boniface Ramsey. Grand Rapids, MI: Eerdmans, 1995.

Smith, Wolfgang. *The Quantum Enigma: Finding the Hidden Key.* 3rd ed. New York: Angelico, 2005.

William M.R. Simpson, Robert C. Koons, and James Orr, eds. *Neo-Aristotelian Metaphysics and the Theology of Nature.* London: Routledge, forthcoming.

Psychology and Anthropology

Anderson, Ryan T. *Truth Overruled: The Future of Marriage and Religious Freedom.* Washington, DC: Regnery, 2015.

250

———. *When Harry Became Sally: Responding to the Transgender Moment.* San Francisco, CA: Encounter Books, 2019.

Connors, Stephanie Gray. *Conceived by Science: Thinking Carefully and Compassionately About Infertility and IVF.* Stephanie Gray Connors, 2021.

———. *Love Unleashes Life: Abortion and the Art of Communicating Truth.* Toronto, ON: Life Cycle Books, 2016.

———. *Start with What: 10 Principles for Thinking about Assisted Suicide.* Swindon, UK: Wongeese, 2021.

Haybron, Daniel M. *Happiness: A Very Short Introduction.* Oxford: Oxford University Press, 2013.

Kaczor, Christopher. *The Gospel of Happiness: How Secular Psychology Points to the Wisdom of Christian Practice.* South Bend, IN: St. Augustine's, 2019.

Kheriaty, Aaron with John Cihak. *The Catholic Guide to Depression: How the Saints, the Sacraments, and Psychiatry Can Help You Break Its Grip and Find Happiness.* Manchester, NH: Sophia Institute, 2012.

Kreeft, Peter. *How to Destroy Civilization and Other Ideas from the Cultural Abyss.* San Francisco, CA: Ignatius Press, 2021.

Lee, Patrick and Robert P. George. *Body-Self Dualism in Contemporary Ethics and Politics.* Cambridge: Cambridge University Press, 2008.

Pieper, Josef. *Happiness and Contemplation.* South Bend, IN: St. Augustine's, 1998.

Pinckaers, Servais. *Morality: The Catholic View.* South Bend, IN: St. Augustine's, 2001.

Pluckrose, Helen and James Lindsay. *Cynical Theories: How Activist Scholarship Made Everything about Race, Gender and Identity—and Why this Harms Everybody.* Durham, NC: Pitchstone, 2020.

Trueman, Carl R. *The Rise and Triumph of the Modern Self: Cultural Amnesia, Expressive Individualism, and the Road to Sexual Revolution.* Wheaton, IL: Crossway, 2020.

Theology and Philosophy

Chryssavgis, John and Bruce V. Foltz, eds. *Toward an Ecology of Transfigura-tion: Orthodox Christian Perspectives on Environment, Nature, and Creation.* New York: Fordham University Press, 2013.

Feser, Edward. *Aquinas: A Beginner's Guide.* London: Oneworld, 2009.

Habermas, Gary and Michael Licona. *The Case for the Resurrection of Jesus.* Grand Rapids, MI: Kregel, 2004.

McNabb, Tyler Dalton. *Religious Epistemology.* Cambridge: Cambridge University Press, 2019.

Plantinga, Alvin. *Warranted Christian Belief.* Oxford: Oxford University Press, 2000.

Pontifical Council for Promoting Christian Unity. "The Grace Given You in Christ: Catholics and Methodists Reflect Further on the Church." Report of the Joint Commission for Dialogue Between the Roman Catholic Church and the World Methodist Council (2006). http://www.christianunity.va/content/unitacristiani/en/dialoghi/sezione-occi-dentale/consiglio-metodista-mondiale/dialogo/documenti-di-dialogo/en12.html.

Pope Francis. *Laudato Si'.* Vatican.va.

Shanley, Brian J. "Commentary on q. 13" in *Treatise on the Divine Nature.* Translated by Brian J. Shanley, 324–54. Indianapolis, IN: Hackett, 2006.

Stacey, Gregory. "Towards a Catholic Epistemology." Unpublished Doctoral Thesis, Oxford University, 2019.

Thomas Aquinas. *Summa theologiae* 2-2.15.3, 2-2.53.6, 2-2.153.5.

———. *Summa theologiae* 1.13. In *Treatise on the Divine Nature,* translated by Brian J. Shanley, 124–151. Indianapolis, IN: Hackett, 2006.

Torrell, Jean-Pierre. *Thomas Aquinas: Spiritual Master.* Washington, DC: The Catholic University of America Press, 2003.

Wright, N.T. *The Resurrection of the Son of God*. Minneapolis, MN: Fortress, 2003.

——. *Surprised by Hope: Rethinking Heaven, the Resurrection, and the Mission of the Church*. New York: HarperCollins, 2008.

Atheism and Culture

Dumsday, Travis. "The Problem of Divine Hiddenness." *American Catholic Philosophical Quarterly* 90 (2016): 395–413.

Feser, Edward. *Five Proofs for the Existence of God*. San Francisco, CA: Ignatius Press, 2007.

Lewis, C.S. *Mere Christianity*. New York: HarperCollins, 2001.

Stump, Eleonore. *Wandering in Darkness: Narrative and the Problem of Suffering*. Oxford: Clarendon, 2010. Recommended Resources

CONTRIBUTORS

Dale Ahlquist is President of The Society of Gilbert Keith Chesterton and the author of several books and articles on G.K. Chesterton, including *Knight of the Holy Ghost.*

Jimmy Akin is an internationally known author and speaker. As Senior Apologist at Catholic Answers, he has more than twenty-five years of experience defending and explaining the Faith. He has an extensive background in the Bible, theology, the Church Fathers, philosophy, canon law, and liturgy. His books include *Teaching with Authority, The Drama of Salvation, The Fathers Know Best, A Daily Defense,* and *The Bible Is a Catholic Book.* He is a popular blogger and the host of the top-rated podcast *Jimmy Akin's Mysterious World.* His personal website is *JimmyAkin.com.*

John L. Allen Jr. is the St. Francis de Sales Fellow of Communication and Media at the Word on Fire Institute and the President and Editor of *Crux,* an independent online news site specializing in coverage of the Vatican and the Catholic Church. Allen is also the Senior Vatican Analyst for CNN, the author of eleven books on Catholic affairs, and a popular speaker both in the US and abroad. He lives in Rome with his wife, Elise Ann Allen, who is a Senior Correspondent at *Crux.*

Ryan T. Anderson, PhD, is the President of the Ethics and Public Policy Center, and the Founding Editor of *Public Discourse,* the online journal of the Witherspoon Institute of Princeton, New Jersey.

Bobby Angel is the Cardinal Jean-Marie Lustiger Fellow of Parish Life at the Word on Fire Institute. He's also the author of *Pray, Decide, and Don't Worry* and *Forever: A Catholic Devotional for Your Marriage*. He holds a master's degree in theology from the Augustine Institute and a bachelor's degree in philosophy from St. John Vianney College Seminary. Bobby worked for eight years as a campus minister and theology teacher, and currently lives in Texas with his wife, Jackie, and their four children.

Fr. Nicanor Pier Giorgio Austriaco, OP, PhD, STD, is Professor of Biology and of Theology at Providence College in Providence, Rhode Island, and Professor of Biological Sciences and Professor of Sacred Theology at the University of Santo Tomas in the Philippines. He is also the founding director of ThomisticEvolution.org, which seeks to promote a Catholic approach to understanding evolution in the light of faith.

Christopher T. Baglow, PhD, is the Director of the Science and Religion Initiative of the McGrath Institute for Church Life at the University of Notre Dame, where he also teaches in the theology department. He is the author of the textbook *Faith, Science, & Reason: Theology on the Cutting Edge*, and his work has been featured in *That Man is You, Crux*, and *Church Life Journal*. He is a corecipient of an Expanded Reason Award from the University of Francisco de Vitoria and the Vatican–Joseph Ratzinger Foundation for his work in forming science and religion educators in integrating faith and science at Catholic high schools.

David Paul Baird, PhD, obtained his doctorate in divinity from the University of St. Andrews, and degrees in English, philosophy, and theology from Wheaton College, the University of Oxford, and the University of St. Andrews' Institute for Theology, Imagination, and the Arts. He is Visiting Professor of Theology at Catholic Pacific College, as well as a film critic, published poet, and regular contributor at *SunkenSunrise.com*.

Stephen M. Barr, PhD, is the President of the Society of Catholic Scientists and Professor Emeritus in the Department of Physics and Astronomy of the University of Delaware and former Director of its Bartol Research Institute. He conducts research in theoretical particle physics, especially grand unified theories, theories of CP violation, neutrino oscillations, and particle cosmology. He is a Fellow of the American Physical Society (2011) and the author of *Modern Physics and Ancient Faith*.

Matthew Becklo is a writer, editor, and the Publishing Director for Bishop Robert Barron's Word on Fire Catholic Ministries. His writing is featured at Word on Fire, Strange Notions, and Aleteia, and has also appeared in *Inside the Vatican* magazine and the *Evangelization & Culture* journal, and online at First Things, RealClear Religion, and The Catholic Herald. He has also contributed an essay for *Wisdom and Wonder: How Peter Kreeft Shaped the Next Generation of Catholics*, and edited multiple books, including the Word on Fire Classics volume the *Flannery O'Connor Collection*.

Francis J. Beckwith, PhD, is Professor of Philosophy & Church-State Studies, Affiliate Professor of Political Science, and Associate Director of the Graduate Program in Philosophy at Baylor University. A graduate of Fordham University (PhD, MA in philosophy) and the Washington University School of Law, St. Louis (M.J.S.), he is the author or editor of nearly twenty books including *Never Doubt Thomas: The Catholic Aquinas as Evangelical and Protestant, Defending Life: A Moral and Legal Case Against Abortion*, and *Taking Rites Seriously: Law, Politics, and the Reasonableness of Faith*. He is also winner of the American Academy of Religion's prestigious Book Award for Excellence in the Study of Religion in the category of Constructive-Reflective Studies.

Archbishop Donald Bolen is the Catholic Archbishop of Regina. He was born on the Canadian prairies, studied in Regina, Ottawa, and Oxford, and after ordination, taught in the Religious Studies department at Campion

College at the University of Regina, and engaged in parish ministry. In 2001 he was appointed to work at the Vatican's Pontifical Council for Promoting Christian Unity. In that capacity he had the opportunity to serve the Catholic Church's international dialogues with Anglicans and Methodists. He was named the Bishop of the Diocese of Saskatoon in 2010 and the Archbishop of Regina in 2016. Within the Canadian Conference for Catholic Bishops, he has been active in ecumenical and justice work. He is a Member of the Pontifical Council for Promoting Christian Unity and co-chairs the International Anglican-Roman Catholic Commission for Unity and Mission.

Fr. James Dominic Brent, OP, completed his doctorate in philosophy at Saint Louis University on the epistemic status of Christian beliefs according to St. Thomas Aquinas. He has articles in the Internet Encyclopedia of Philosophy on "Natural Theology," in the *Oxford Handbook of Thomas Aquinas* on "God's Knowledge and Will," and an article on "Thomas Aquinas" in the *Oxford Handbook of the Epistemology of Theology*. Fr. Brent earned his STL from the Pontifical Faculty of the Immaculate Conception, and was ordained a priest in the same year. He taught in the School of Philosophy at The Catholic University of America from 2010 to 2014, and spent the year of 2014–2015 doing full-time itinerant preaching on college campuses across the United States.

Fr. Blake Britton is a priest of the Diocese of Orlando, Florida, holding degrees in both philosophy and theology. He is a published author and frequent guest speaker for conferences, talk shows, radio programs, podcasts, retreats, and lectures. His writings are featured in several national and international publications, including in the Word on Fire Institute's *Evangelization & Culture* journal, the Word on Fire blog, *National Catholic Register*, Ignatius Press, and Ave Maria Press. He is author of the book *Reclaiming Vatican II*. In addition to writing, Fr. Blake has also been featured on EWTN and other media outlets. Finally, he is cohost, with Brandon Vogt, of *The Burrowshire Podcast*, a nationally acclaimed production. Fr. Blake currently serves four parish communities in Lakeland, Florida, and is an Assistant Vocations Director of the Diocese of Orlando.

Stephen Bullivant, PhD, is Professor of Theology and the Sociology of Religion, and Director of the Benedict XVI Centre for Religion and Society. He holds doctorates in theology and sociology. He has published ten books, including *Mass Exodus: Catholic Disaffiliation in Britain and America since Vatican II*; *Why Catholics Leave, What They Miss, and How They Might Return* (with C. Knowles, H. Vaughan-Spruce, and B. Durcan); *The Oxford Dictionary of Atheism* (with L. Lee); and *The Trinity: How Not to Be a Heretic*. He is coeditor of the two-volume *Cambridge History of Atheism* with Michael Ruse, with whom he previously coedited *The Oxford Handbook of Atheism*.

Stephanie Gray Connors is a public speaker who has presented and debated on pro-life topics more than 1,000 times over two decades in ten countries, including speaking on abortion at Google headquarters and debating in Mexico at La Ciudad de las Ideas (CDI), an event similar to TED Talks. She holds a bachelor of arts in political science from the University of British Columbia in Vancouver, and a Certification, with Distinction, in health care ethics from the National Catholic Bioethics Center in Philadelphia. Stephanie has authored pro-life apologetics books on the beginning and end of life, and blogs over at www.loveunleasheslife.com.

Daniel D. De Haan, PhD, is the Frederick Copleston Senior Research Fellow and Lecturer in Philosophy and Theology in the Catholic Tradition at Blackfriars and Campion Hall, University of Oxford. His research draws upon the thought of St. Thomas Aquinas to address contemporary issues in philosophical anthropology, neuroscience, metaphysics, and natural theology. He is a regular speaker for the Thomistic Institute and is the author of *Neces-*

sary Existence and the Doctrine of Being in Avicenna's Metaphysics of the Healing (Brill, 2020).

Richard DeClue, PhD, is the Cardinal Henri de Lubac Fellow of Theology at the Word on Fire Institute. In addition to his undergraduate degree in theology (Belmont Abbey College), he earned three ecclesiastical degrees in theology at the Catholic University of America. He specializes in systematic theology with a particular interest and expertise in the thought of Joseph Ratzinger / Pope Emeritus Benedict XVI. His STL thesis treated Ratzinger's Eucharistic ecclesiology in comparison to the Eastern Orthodox theologian John Zizioulas. His doctoral dissertation expounded and evaluated Ratzinger's theology of divine revelation. Dr. DeClue has published articles in peer-reviewed journals on Ratzinger's theology and taught a college course on the thought of Pope Benedict XVI. He is also interested in the ecclesiology of Henri de Lubac, the debate over nature and grace, and developing a rapprochement between *Communio* (*ressourcement*) theology and Thomism.

John DeRosa is a high school math teacher and host of the *Classical Theism Podcast*. He is also the author of *One Less God Than You: How to Answer the Slogans, Clichés, and Fallacies that Atheists Use to Challenge Your Faith.* He lives in New Jersey with his wife, Christine, and they hope to become adoptive parents.

Edward Feser, PhD, is Professor of Philosophy at Pasadena City College. He has been a Visiting Assistant Professor at Loyola Marymount University in Los Angeles and a Visiting Scholar at the Social Philosophy and Policy Center at Bowling Green State University in Bowling Green, Ohio. Feser is the author of many books and academic articles. His books include *Five Proofs of the Existence of God*, *Aquinas*, and *The Last Superstition: A Refutation of the New Atheism.*

Jennifer Frey, PhD, is Associate Professor of Philosophy at the University of South Carolina and Fellow of the Institute for Human Ecology at the Catholic University of America. She has written numerous academic essays on virtue and human agency, has edited three books, and frequently writes and lectures for nonacademic audiences. She is the host of a literature, philosophy, and theology podcast titled *Sacred and Profane Love.*

Trent Horn serves as a Staff Apologist for Catholic Answers. He is a regular guest on the Catholic Answers Live radio program. He is the host of *The Counsel of Trent* podcast. Trent has earned master's degrees in the fields of theology, philosophy, and bioethics, and has been invited to debate at UC Berkeley, UC Santa Barbara, and Stanford University. He is an Adjunct Professor of Apologetics at Holy Apostles College, has written for *The National Catholic Bioethics Quarterly*, and is the author of nine books, including *Answering Atheism, The Case for Catholicism,* and *Why We're Catholic: Our Reasons for Faith, Hope, and Love.*

Christopher Kaczor, PhD, is Professor of Philosophy at Loyola Marymount University. He graduated from the Honors Program of Boston College and earned a PhD four years later from the University of Notre Dame. A Fulbright Scholar, Dr. Kaczor did postdoctoral work as an Alexander von Humboldt German Chancellor Fellow at the University of Cologne. He was appointed a Corresponding Member of the Pontifical Academy for Life of Vatican City, a Fellow of the Word on Fire Institute, and William E. Simon Visiting Fellow in the James Madison Program at Princeton University. The winner of a Templeton Grant, he has written more than one hundred scholarly articles and book chapters. An award-winning author, his sixteen books include, most recently, *Jordan Peterson, God, and Christianity: The Search for a Meaningful Life.*

Grant Kaplan, PhD, is Professor of Historical and Systematic Theology at Saint Louis University. He writes and researches in mimetic theory and in nineteenth-century German theology. He is the author of the forthcoming *Faith and Reason through Christian History: A Theological Essay,* and editor of the forthcoming *Oxford History of Modern German Theology, Volume 1: 1781–1848.*

Robert C. Koons, PhD, is Professor of Philosophy at the University of Texas at Austin, where he has taught for thirty-four years. He is the author or coauthor of four books, including *Realism Regained* and *The Atlas of Reality: A Comprehensive Guide to Metaphysics,* with Timothy H. Pickavance. He is the coeditor (with George Bealer) of *The Waning of Materialism,* and coeditor (with Nicholas Teh and William Simpson) of *Neo-Aristotelian Perspectives on Contemporary Science.* Koons has authored over fifty peer-reviewed articles in metaphysics, philosophical logic, theology, and philosophy of science. He has been working recently on an Aristotelian interpretation of quantum theory, on defending and articulating Thomism in contemporary terms, and on arguments for classical theism. Koons joined the Catholic Church in 2007. He described his theological journey in *A Lutheran's Case for Roman Catholicism.*

Peter Kreeft, PhD, is Professor of Philosophy at Boston College and the author of almost one hundred books. His many bestsellers cover a vast array of topics in spirituality, theology, and philosophy. They include *Making Sense of Suffering, Because God Is Real, Angels and Demons, Heaven: The Heart's Deepest Longing, Summa of the Summa, Christianity for Modern Pagans,* and *How to Destroy Western Civilization.*

Matthew Levering, PhD, holds the James N. Jr. and Mary D. Perry Chair of Theology at Mundelein Seminary. He is the author or editor of over fifty books, including, most recently, *The Wisdom of the Word: Biblical Answers to Ten Pressing Questions about Catholicism,* coauthored with Michael Dauphinais.

Jonathan I. Lunine, PhD, is David C. Duncan Professor in the Physical Sciences of Cornell University and Chair of the Astronomy Department at Cornell University. He does research in astrophysics, planetary science, and astrobiology. He is a member of the U.S. National Academy of Sciences, and is the recipient of, among other awards, the Jean Dominique Cassini Medal of the European Geosciences Union (2015) and the Basic Sciences Award of the International Academy of Astronautics (2009). Lunine is the author of *Astrobiology: A Multidisciplinary Approach* and *Earth: Evolution of a Habitable World.* He is Vice President of the Society of Catholic Scientists.

Tyler Dalton McNabb, PhD, is Associate Professor of Philosophy at the University of Saint Joseph, Macau. Dr. McNabb is the author of *Religious Epistemology* (CUP), coauthor of *Plantingian Religious Epistemology and World Religions* (Lexington), and coeditor and contributor of *Debating Christian Religious Epistemology: Five Views on the Knowledge of God.* Dr. McNabb has also authored/coauthored over a dozen articles that have been featured in journals such as *Religious Studies, European Journal of Philosophy of Religion, Open Theology, Heythrop Journal,* and *Philosophia Christi.*

Matthew Nelson, DC, is an apologetics consultant and Teaching Fellow of the Word on Fire Institute. He holds a Doctor of Chiropractic (DC) degree from the Canadian Memorial Chiropractic College and is pursuing a master of arts in philosophy from Holy Apostles College and Seminary. He has contributed articles to a variety of publications, including *Evangelization & Culture, Church Life Journal,* and *Catholic Answers Magazine.* He is the author of *Just Whatever: How to Help the Spiritually Indifferent Find Beliefs That Really Matter* and the forthcoming book *At the Far Side of Reason,* and is the editor of *The New Apologetics.* He is a Scholar Associate of the Society of Catholic Scientists.

Turner Nevitt, PhD, is Associate Professor of Philosophy at the University of San Diego. He holds degrees from the University of St. Thomas and Fordham University. He is the translator (with Brian Davies, OP) of *Thomas Aquinas's Quodlibetal Questions.* His work on the metaphysical thought of St. Thomas Aquinas has appeared in such journals as *The Thomist, History of Philosophy Quarterly,* and *American Catholic Philosophical Quarterly.*

Holly Ordway, PhD, is the Cardinal Francis George Fellow of Faith and Culture at the Word on Fire Institute, and Visiting Professor of Apologetics at Houston Baptist University. She holds a PhD in English from the University of Massachusetts Amherst, and is the author of *Tolkien's Modern Reading: Middle-earth Beyond the Middle Ages.*

Andrew Petiprin is the Venerable Fulton J. Sheen Fellow of Popular Culture at the Word on Fire Institute. He holds an MPhil from Oxford University and an MDiv from Yale Divinity School. Andrew is a former Anglican cleric, and the author of the book *Truth Matters: Knowing God and Yourself.* He lives in North Texas with his wife, two children, two cats, and a dog.

Matthew Petrusek, PhD, is Associate Professor of Theological Ethics at Loyola Marymount University and serves as a Word on Fire Institute Fellow. In addition to numerous articles, his books include *Jordan Peterson, God, and Christianity: The Search for a Meaningful Life, Value and Vulnerability: An Interfaith Dialogue on Human Dignity, Evangelization and Politics* (forthcoming), and *Ethics and Advocacy: Bridges and Boundaries* (forthcoming). Petrusek lectures in English and Spanish on ethics, the Catholic intellectual tradition, and the intersection between Christian theology and philosophy. He has a *Mandatum* from the Archdiocese of Los Angeles and lives in the Inland Empire with his wife and three children.

Fr. Gregory Pine, OP, is a Dominican friar of the Province of St. Joseph. He studies presently as a doctoral candidate in dogmatic theology at the University of Fribourg (Switzerland), having worked previously at the Thomistic Institute. He is the coauthor of *Marian Consecration with Aquinas* (TAN Books) and has published articles in *Nova et Vetera*, *The Thomist*, and *Angelicum*. He is a regular contributor to the podcasts *Pints with Aquinas* and *Godsplaining*.

Matthew Ramage, PhD, is Professor of Theology at Benedictine College and Adjunct Professor of Sacred Scripture at Holy Apostles College and Seminary. He is author, contributing author, or translator of over fifteen books, including *Dark Passages of the Bible: Engaging Scripture with Benedict XVI and Thomas Aquinas*; *Jesus, Interpreted: Benedict XVI, Bart Ehrman, and the Historical Truth of the Gospels*; *The Experiment of Faith: Pope Benedict XVI on Living the Theological Virtues in a Secular Age*; and *Christ's Church and World Religions*. His next book, *From the Dust of the Earth: Benedict XVI, the Bible, and the Theory of Evolution*, is forthcoming from the Catholic University of America Press in early 2022. His website is www.matthewramage.com.

Fr. Anselm Ramelow, OP, is Professor of Philosophy and Philosophy Department Chair at the Dominican School of Philosophy and Theology in Berkeley, CA. He holds a PhD in Philosophy from the University of Munich. At Munich, he studied with Robert Spaemann, and wrote a dissertation investigating the concept of "the best of all possible worlds." In 2018, he published the first comprehensive, article-length overview of Robert Spaemann's thought in *Communio*. He regularly teaches courses on modern philosophy and theology, covering Leibniz, Kant, Fichte, Hegel, Schleiermacher, Kierkegaard, Wittgenstein, Gadamer, phenomenology, Heidegger, and the linguistic turn in philosophy and theology.

Michael Stevens is the Art Director for Word on Fire Catholic Ministries. He has helped to lead the design approach for *The Word on Fire Bible* and curated its sacred artwork. He is also a painter, illustrator, and typeface designer.

Eleonore Stump, PhD, is the Robert J. Henle Professor of Philosophy at Saint Louis University. She is also Honorary Professor at Wuhan University, the Logos Institute and School of Divinity at St. Andrews, and York University; and she is a Professorial Fellow at Australian Catholic University. She has published extensively in philosophy of religion, contemporary metaphysics, and medieval philosophy. Her books include *Aquinas* (2003), *Wandering in Darkness: Narrative and the Problem of Suffering* (2010), and *Atonement* (2018). Her book *The Image of God: The Problem of Evil and the Problem of Mourning* will appear in 2022. She has given the Gifford Lectures (Aberdeen, 2003), the Wilde lectures (Oxford, 2006), the Stewart lectures (Princeton, 2009), and the Stanton lectures (Cambridge, 2018). She is past president of the Society of Christian Philosophers, the American Catholic Philosophical Association, and the American Philosophical Association, Central Division; and she is a member of the American Academy of Arts and Sciences. In 2021, she was given the award of Johanna Quandt Young Academy Distinguished Senior Scientist by the Goethe University (Frankfurt, Germany).

Brandon Vogt is the Senior Publishing Director at Word on Fire. He's the author of ten books, including *Return: How to Draw Your Child Back to the Church* and *Why I Am Catholic (And You Should Be Too)*. He's the President of the Central Florida Chesterton Society and lives on a small farm outside Orlando, Florida, with his wife and seven children.

Fr. Michael Ward, PhD, is Senior Research Fellow at Blackfriars Hall, University of Oxford, and Professor of Apologetics at Houston Baptist University. He is the author of *Planet Narnia: The Seven Heavens in the Imagination of C.S. Lewis* and *After Humanity: A Guide to C.S. Lewis's* The Abolition of Man.

Tod Worner, MD, is a husband, father, practicing physician, and Catholic convert. He serves as Managing Editor of *Evangelization & Culture*, the journal of the Word on Fire Institute, and his collected works can be read at www. todworner.com. He is best known for being constantly outsmarted by his two young daughters.